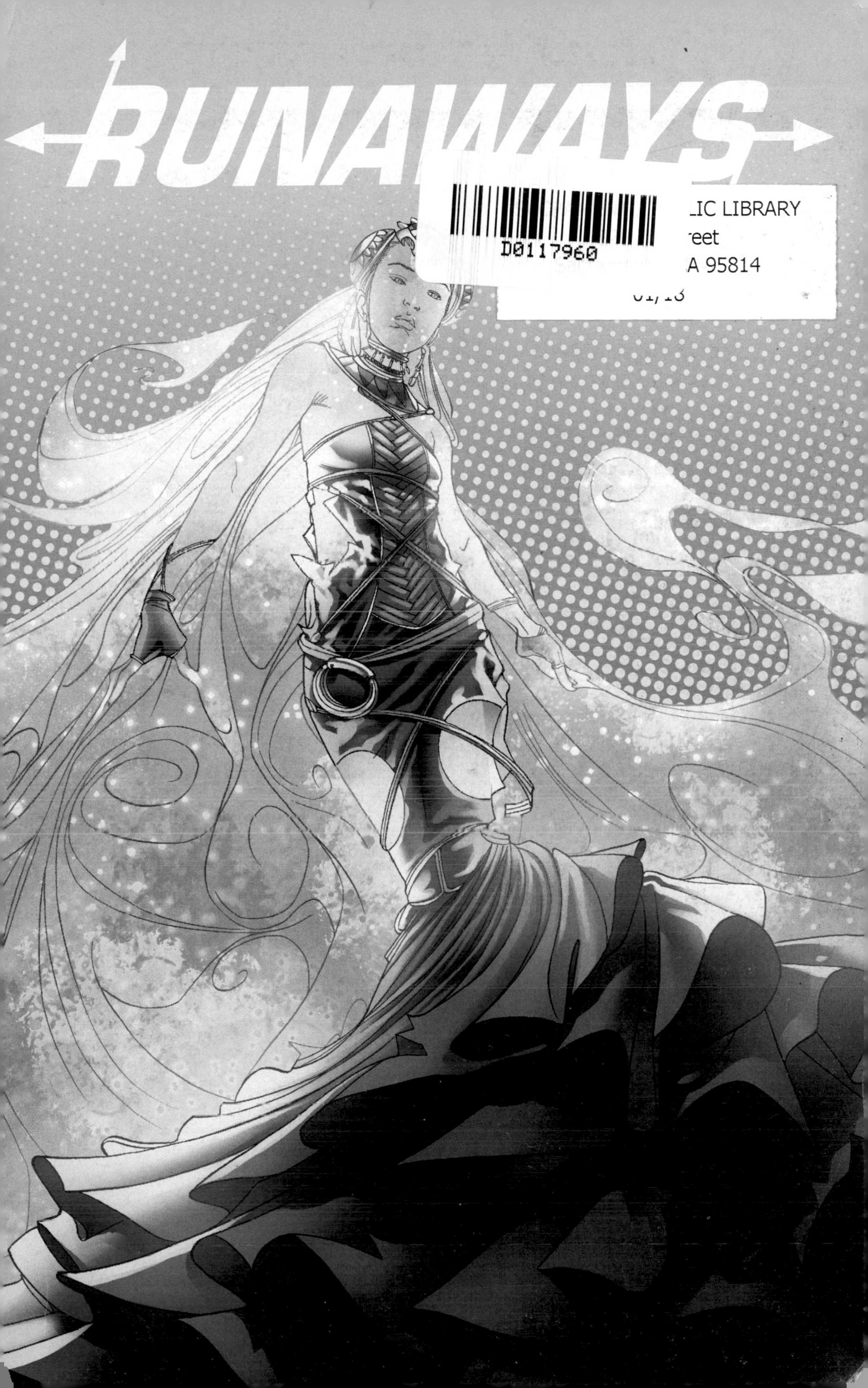
RUNAWAYS

RUNAWAYS

PARENTAL GUIDANCE

WRITER: **BRIAN K. VAUGHAN**

PENCILS: **ADRIAN ALPHONA**

INKS: **CRAIG YEUNG**

COLORS: **CHRISTINA STRAIN**

LETTERS: **VC's RANDY GENTILE**

COVER ART: **MARCOS MARTIN**

ASSISTANT EDITOR: **NATHAN COSBY**

EDITORS: **MACKENZIE CADENHEAD** & **NICK LOWE**

SPECIAL THANKS TO C.B. CEBULSKI

RUNAWAYS CREATED BY
BRIAN K. VAUGHAN & **ADRIAN ALPHONA**

RUNAWAYS VOL. 6: PARENTAL GUIDANCE. Contains material originally published in magazine form as RUNAWAYS #13-18. Second edition. Second printing 2017. ISBN# 978-1-302-90871-3. Published by MARVEL WORLDWIDE, INC., a subsidiary of MARVEL ENTERTAINMENT, LLC. OFFICE OF PUBLICATION: 135 West 50th Street, New York, NY 10020. Copyright © 2017 MARVEL No similarity between any of the names, characters, persons, and/or institutions in this magazine with those of any living or dead person or institution is intended, and any such similarity which may exist is purely coincidental. **Printed in the U.S.A.** DAN BUCKLEY, President, Marvel Entertainment; JOE QUESADA, Chief Creative Officer; TOM BREVOORT, SVP of Publishing; DAVID BOGART, SVP of Business Affairs & Operations, Publishing & Partnership; C.B. CEBULSKI, VP of Brand Management & Development, Asia; DAVID GABRIEL, SVP of Sales & Marketing, Publishing; JEFF YOUNGQUIST, VP of Production & Special Projects; DAN CARR, Executive Director of Publishing Technology; ALEX MORALES, Director of Publishing Operations; SUSAN CRESPI, Production Manager; STAN LEE, Chairman Emeritus. For information regarding advertising in Marvel Comics or on Marvel.com, please contact Jonathan Parkhideh, VP of Digital Media & Marketing Solutions, at jparkhideh@marvel.com. For Marvel subscription inquiries, please call 888-511-5480. **Manufactured between 10/18/2017 and 11/6/2017 by QUAD/GRAPHICS WASECA, WASECA, MN, USA.**

1 0 9 8 7 6 5 4 3 2

COLLECTION EDITOR: JENNIFER GRÜNWALD
ASSISTANT EDITOR: CAITLIN O'CONNELL
ASSOCIATE MANAGING EDITOR: KATERI WOODY
EDITOR, SPECIAL PROJECTS: MARK D. BEAZLEY
VP PRODUCTION & SPECIAL PROJECTS: JEFF YOUNGQUIST
SVP PRINT, SALES & MARKETING: DAVID GABRIEL

EDITOR IN CHIEF: AXEL ALONSO
CHIEF CREATIVE OFFICER: JOE QUESADA
PRESIDENT: DAN BUCKLEY
EXECUTIVE PRODUCER: ALAN FINE

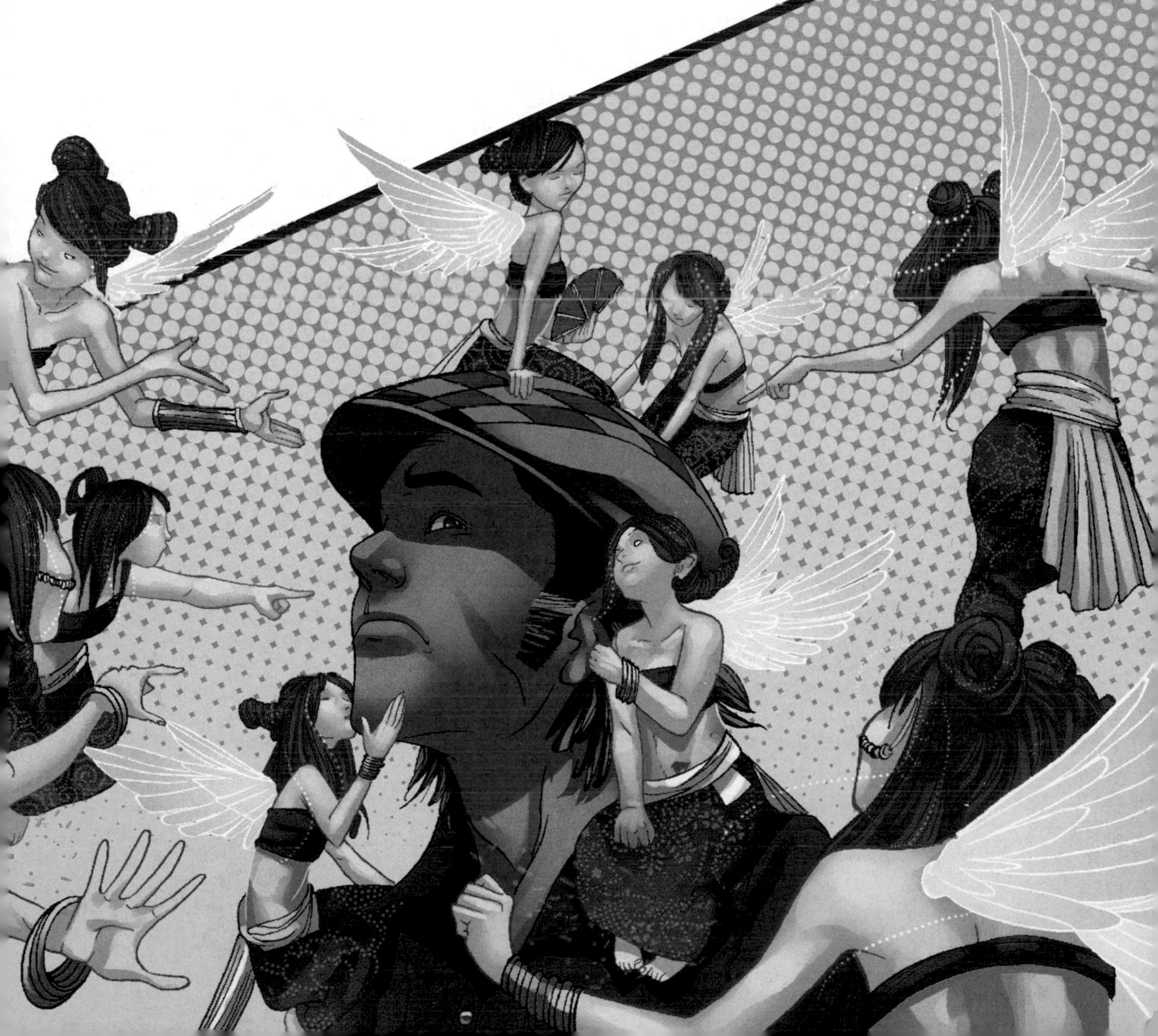

PREVIOUSLY:

AT SOME POINT IN THEIR LIVES, ALL KIDS THINK THAT THEY HAVE THE MOST EVIL PARENTS IN THE WORLD, BUT NICO MINORU AND HER FRIENDS REALLY DID.

DISCOVERING THEY WERE THE CHILDREN OF A GROUP OF SUPER VILLAINS KNOWN AS THE PRIDE, THE LOS ANGELES TEENAGERS STOLE WEAPONS AND RESOURCES FROM THESE CRIMINALS BEFORE RUNNING AWAY FROM HOME AND EVENTUALLY DEFEATING THEIR PARENTS. BUT THAT WAS JUST THE BEGINNING. TOGETHER, THE TEENAGE RUNAWAYS NOW HOPE TO ATONE FOR THEIR PARENTS' CRIMES BY TAKING ON THE NEW THREATS TRYING TO FILL THE PRIDE'S VOID.

THE TEAM'S YOUNGEST MEMBER IS MOLLY HAYES, ONE OF THE WORLD'S LAST LIVING MUTANTS. WHILE MOLLY IS EXTREMELY POWERFUL, THE MORE OF HER SUPERHUMAN STRENGTH SHE USES, THE MORE TIRED SHE BECOMES.

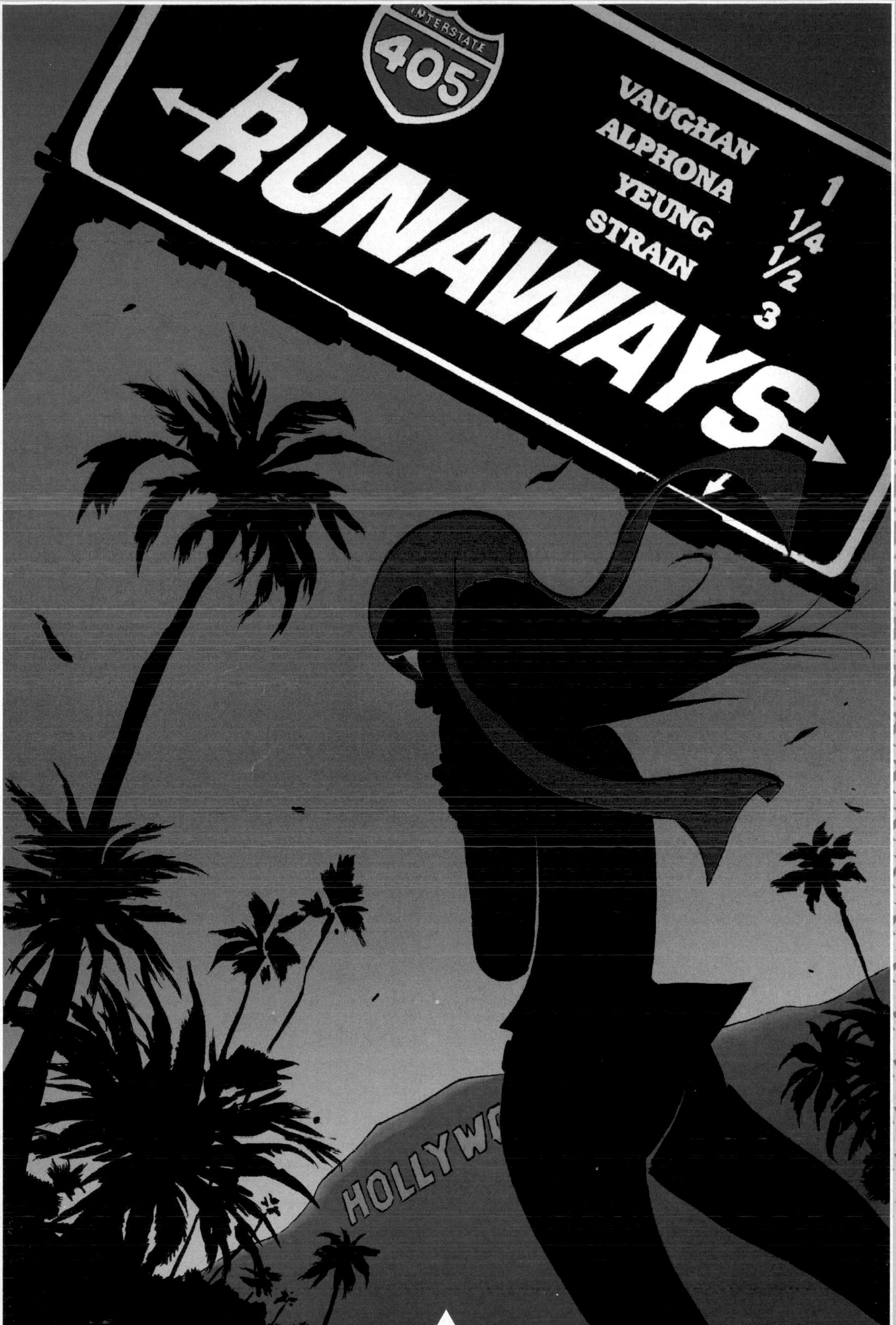
INTERSTATE
405
RUNAWAYS
VAUGHAN 1
ALPHONA 1/4
YEUNG 1/2
STRAIN 3
HOLLYWO

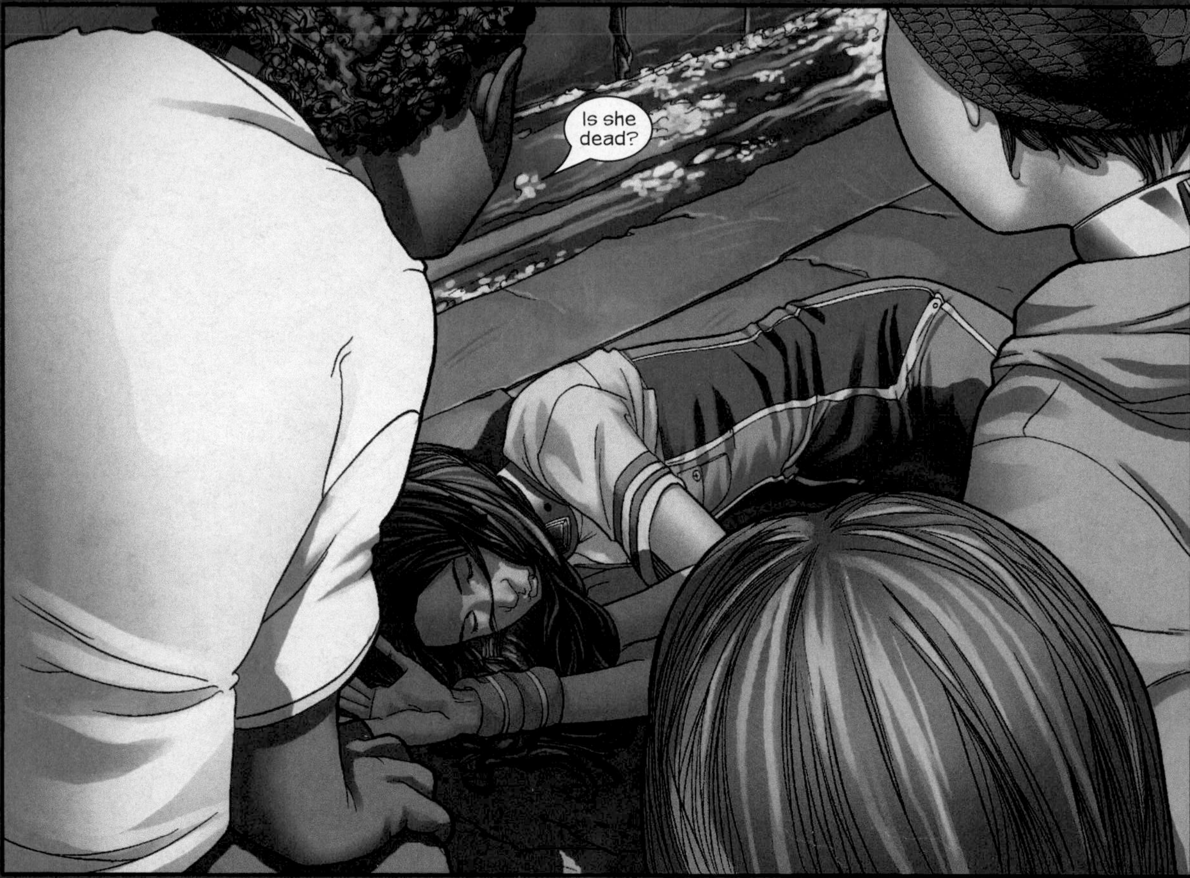
Is she dead?

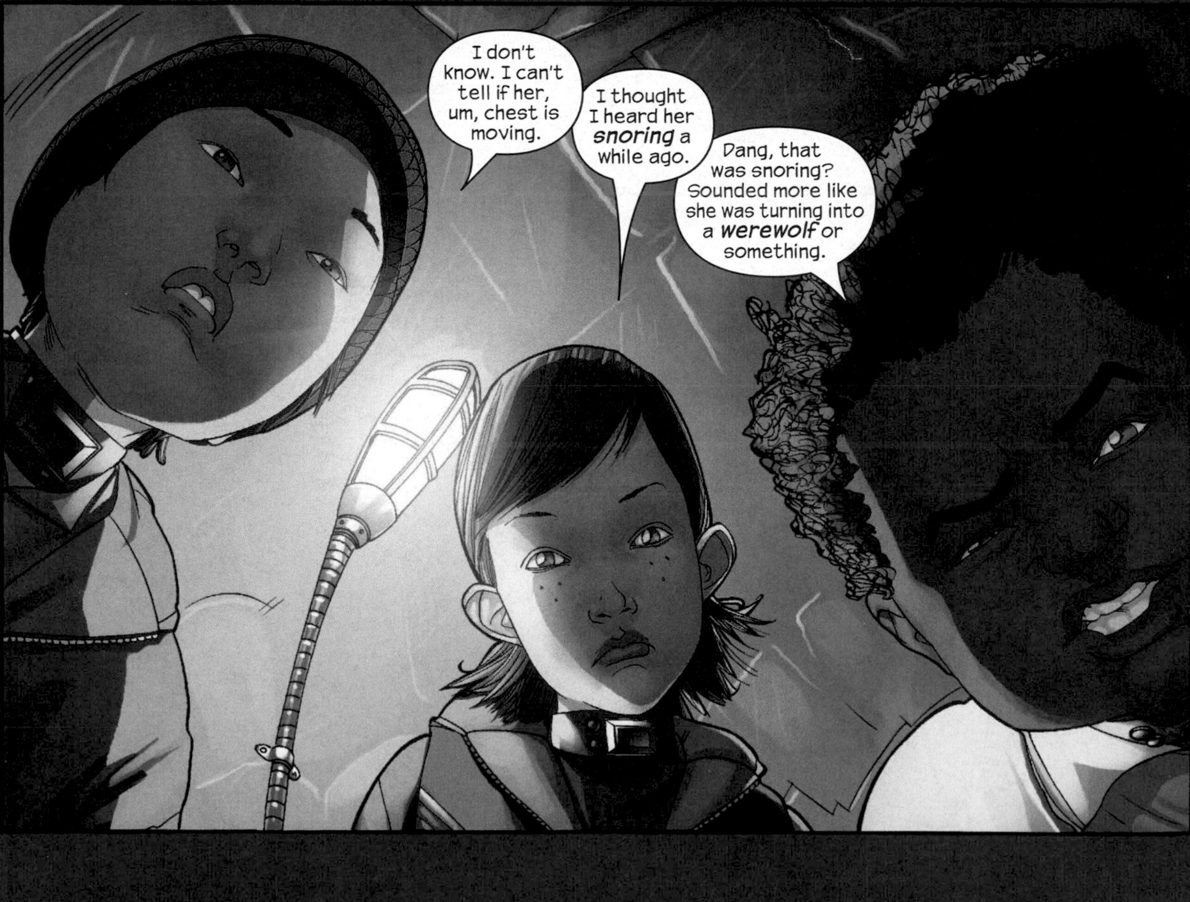
I don't know. I can't tell if her, um, chest is moving.
I thought I heard her *snoring* a while ago.
Dang, that was snoring? Sounded more like she was turning into a *werewolf* or something.

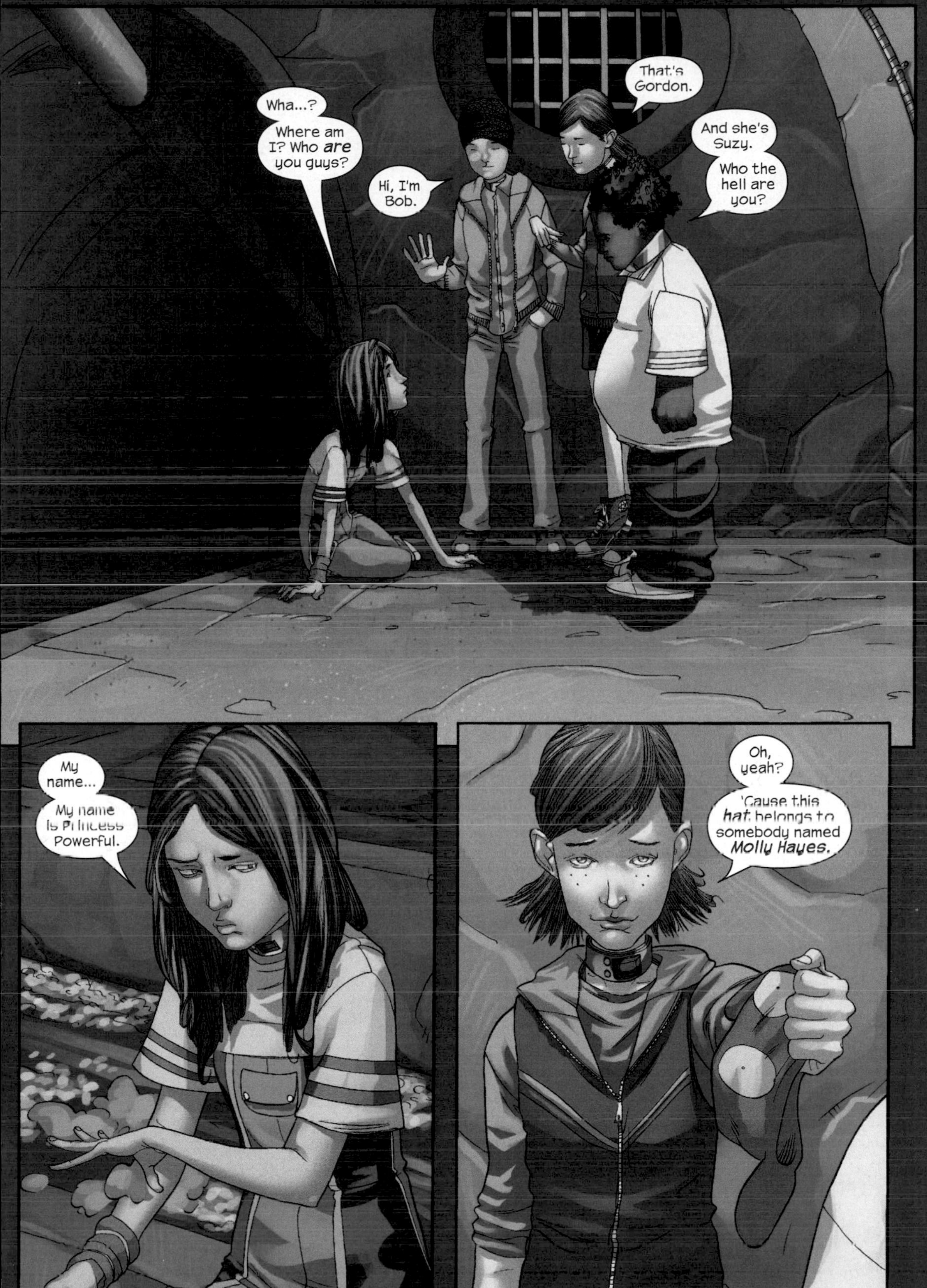

Wha...?
Where am I? Who are you guys?
Hi, I'm Bob.
That's Gordon.
And she's Suzy.
Who the hell are you?
My name...
My name is Princess Powerful.
Oh, yeah?
'Cause this hat belongs to somebody named Molly Hayes.

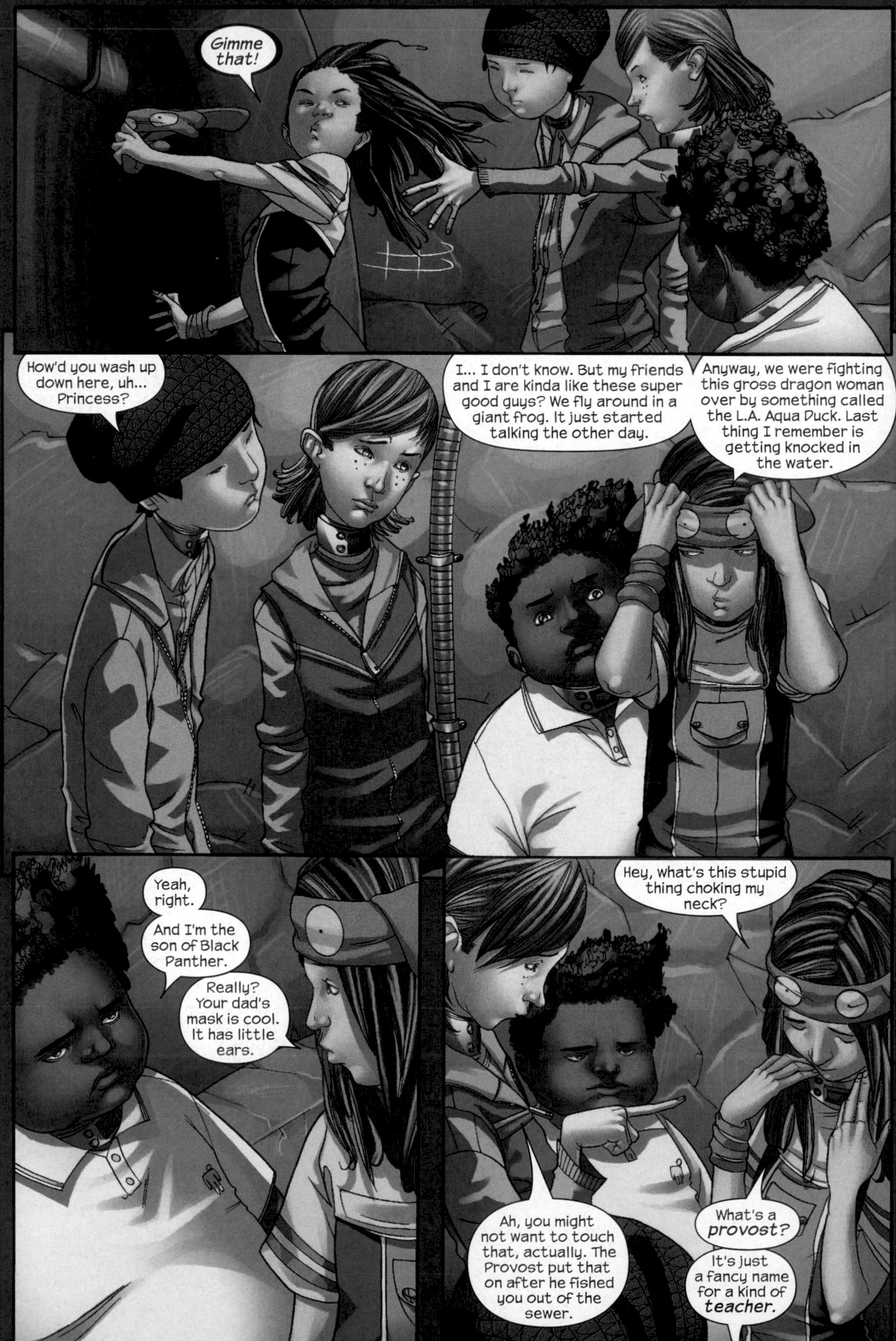
Gimme that!
How'd you wash up down here, uh... Princess?
I... I don't know. But my friends and I are kinda like these super good guys? We fly around in a giant frog. It just started talking the other day.
Anyway, we were fighting this gross dragon woman over by something called the L.A. Aqua Duck. Last thing I remember is getting knocked in the water.
Yeah, right.
And I'm the son of Black Panther.
Really? Your dad's mask is cool. It has little ears.
Hey, what's this stupid thing choking my neck?
Ah, you might not want to touch that, actually. The Provost put that on after he fished you out of the sewer.
What's a *provost?*
It's just a fancy name for a kind of *teacher.*

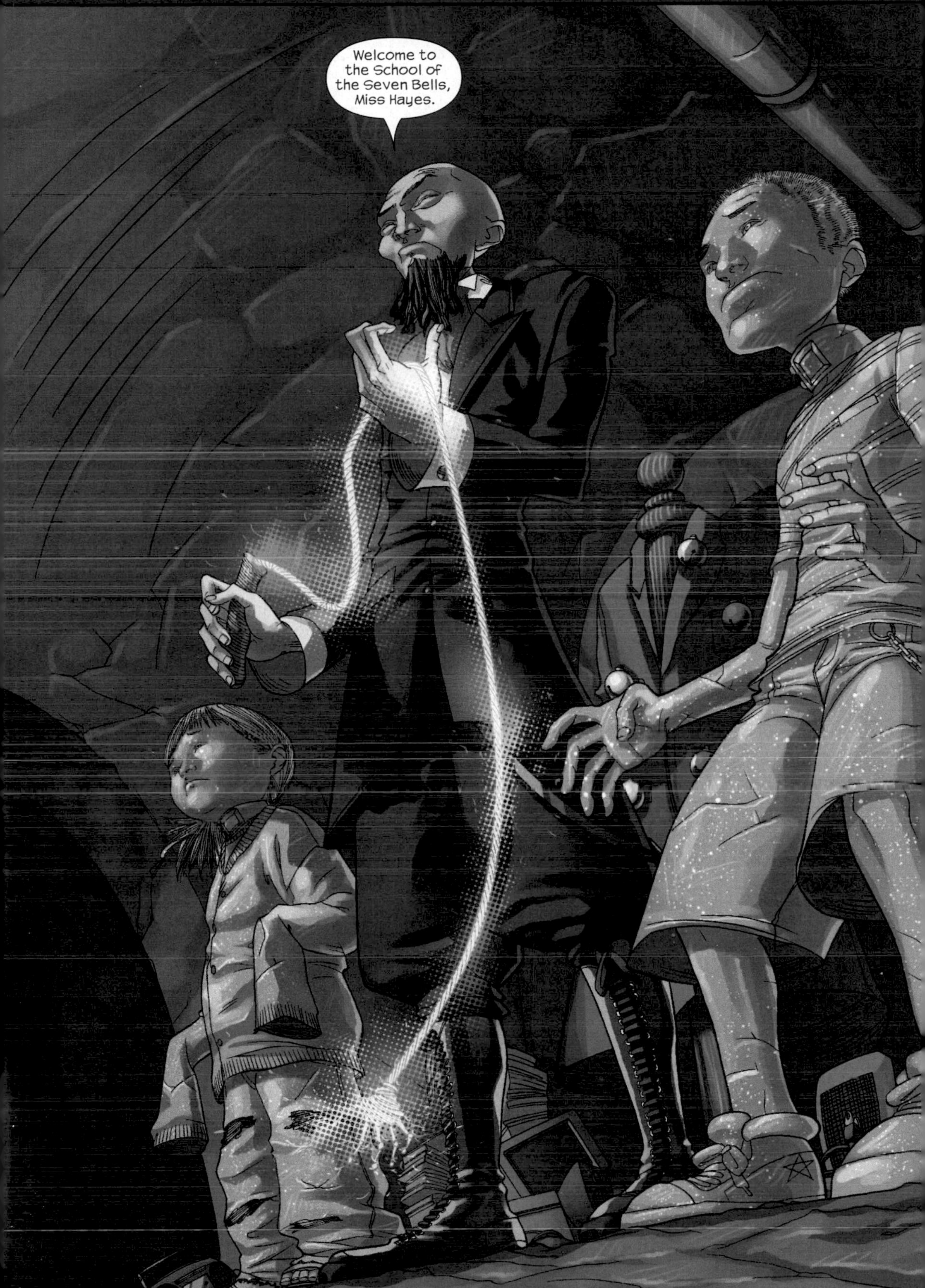
Welcome to the School of the Seven Bells, Miss Hayes.

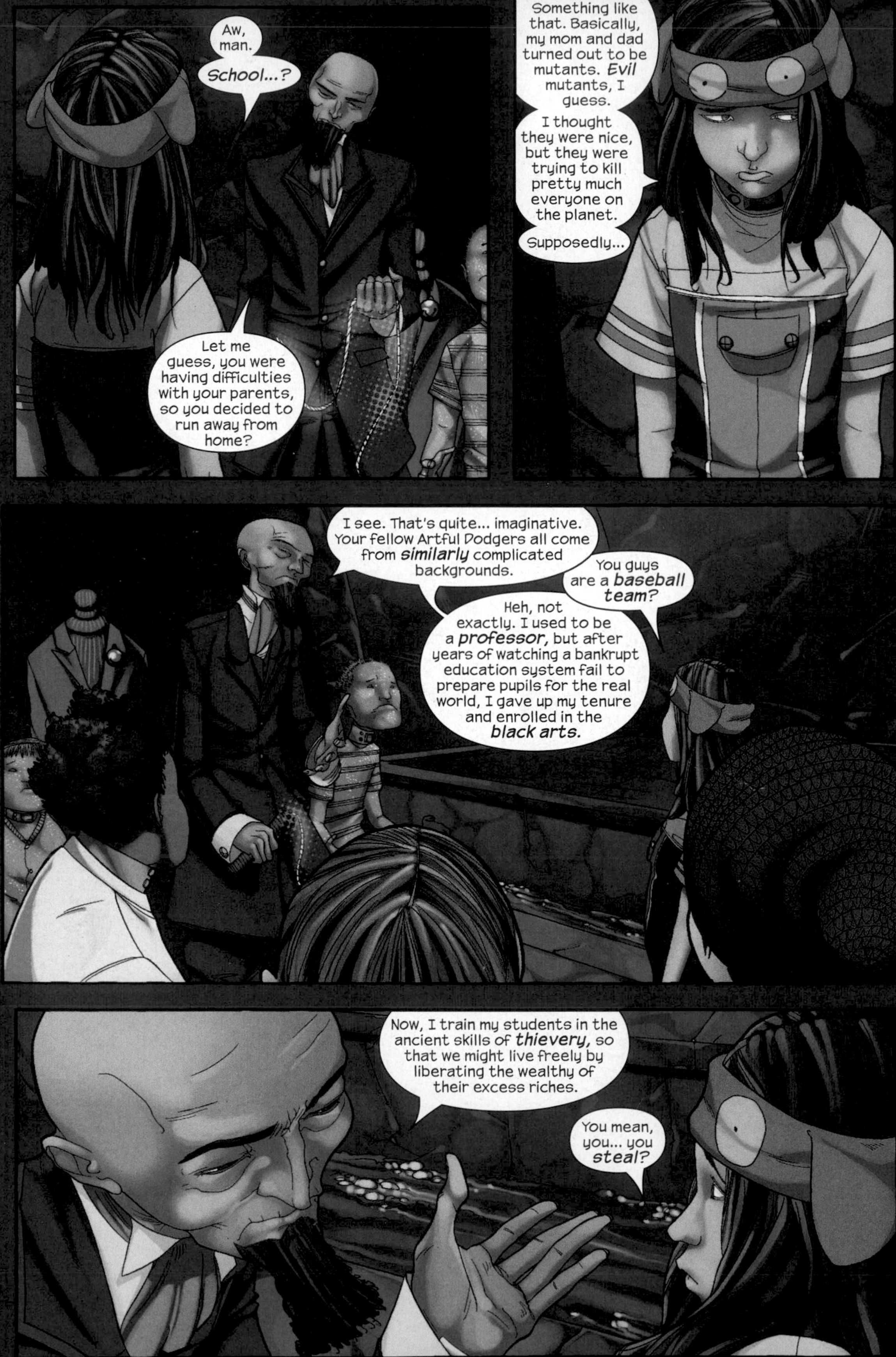
Aw, man.
School...?
Let me guess, you were having difficulties with your parents, so you decided to run away from home?
Something like that. Basically, my mom and dad turned out to be mutants. Evil mutants, I guess.
I thought they were nice, but they were trying to kill pretty much everyone on the planet.
Supposedly...
I see. That's quite... imaginative. Your fellow Artful Dodgers all come from similarly complicated backgrounds.
You guys are a baseball team?
Heh, not exactly. I used to be a professor, but after years of watching a bankrupt education system fail to prepare pupils for the real world, I gave up my tenure and enrolled in the black arts.
Now, I train my students in the ancient skills of thievery, so that we might live freely by liberating the wealthy of their excess riches.
You mean, you... you steal?

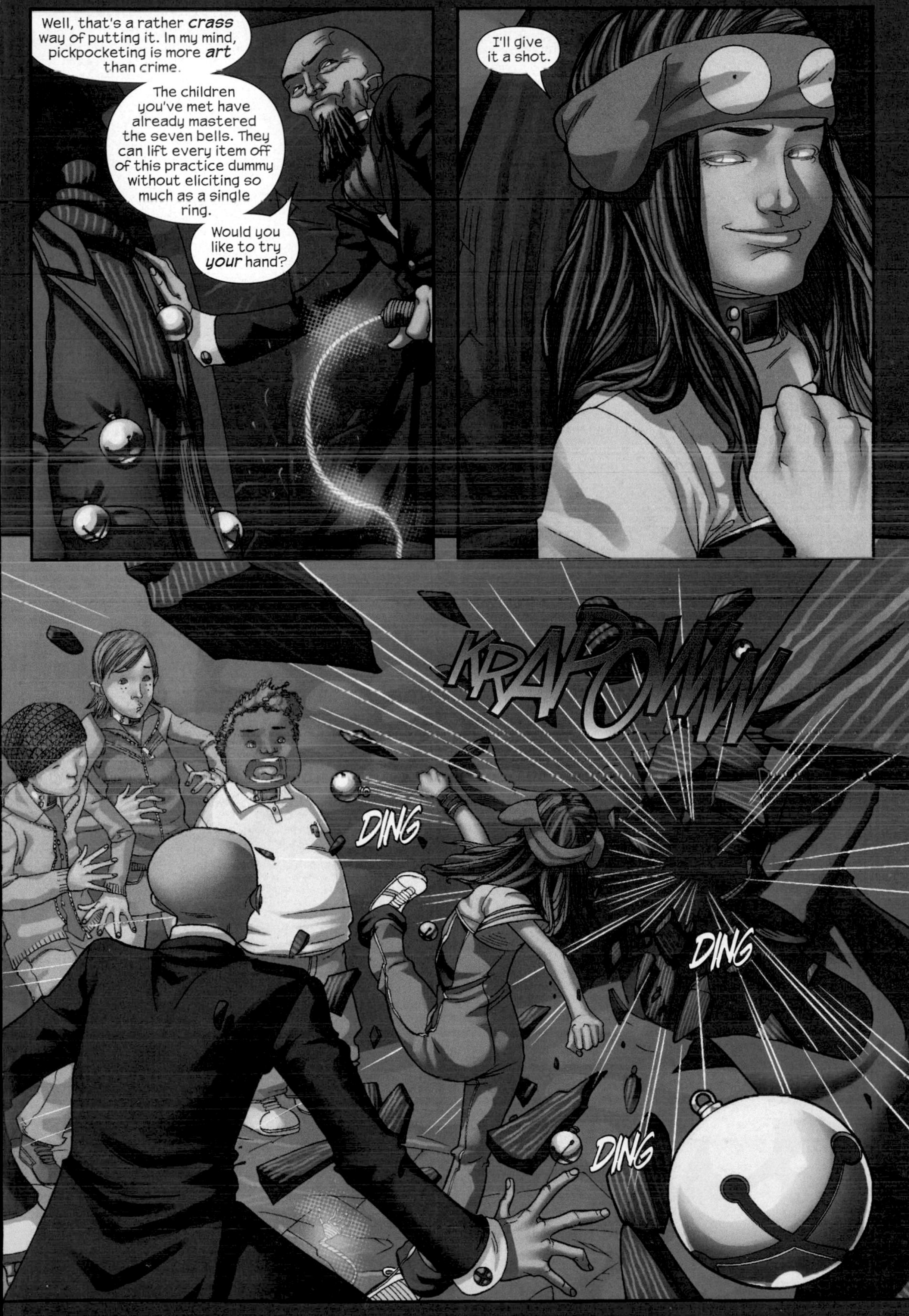

Well, that's a rather crass way of putting it. In my mind, pickpocketing is more art than crime.
The children you've met have already mastered the seven bells. They can lift every item off of this practice dummy without eliciting so much as a single ring.
Would you like to try your hand?
I'll give it a shot.
KRAPOWW
DING
DING
DING

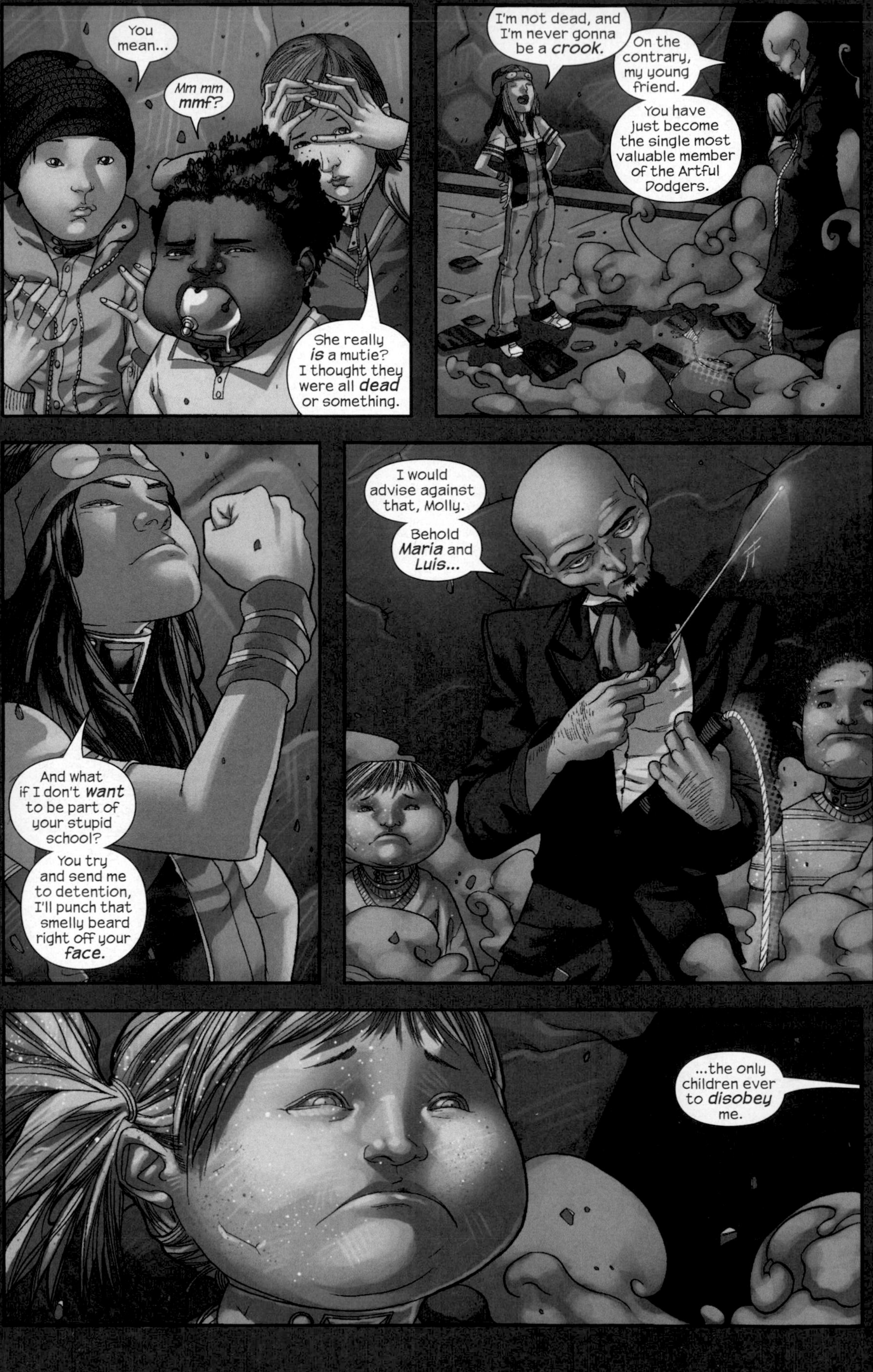
You mean...
Mm mm mmf?
She really is a mutie? I thought they were all dead or something.
I'm not dead, and I'm never gonna be a crook.
On the contrary, my young friend.
You have just become the single most valuable member of the Artful Dodgers.
And what if I don't want to be part of your stupid school?
You try and send me to detention, I'll punch that smelly beard right off your face.
I would advise against that, Molly.
Behold Maria and Luis...
...the only children ever to disobey me.

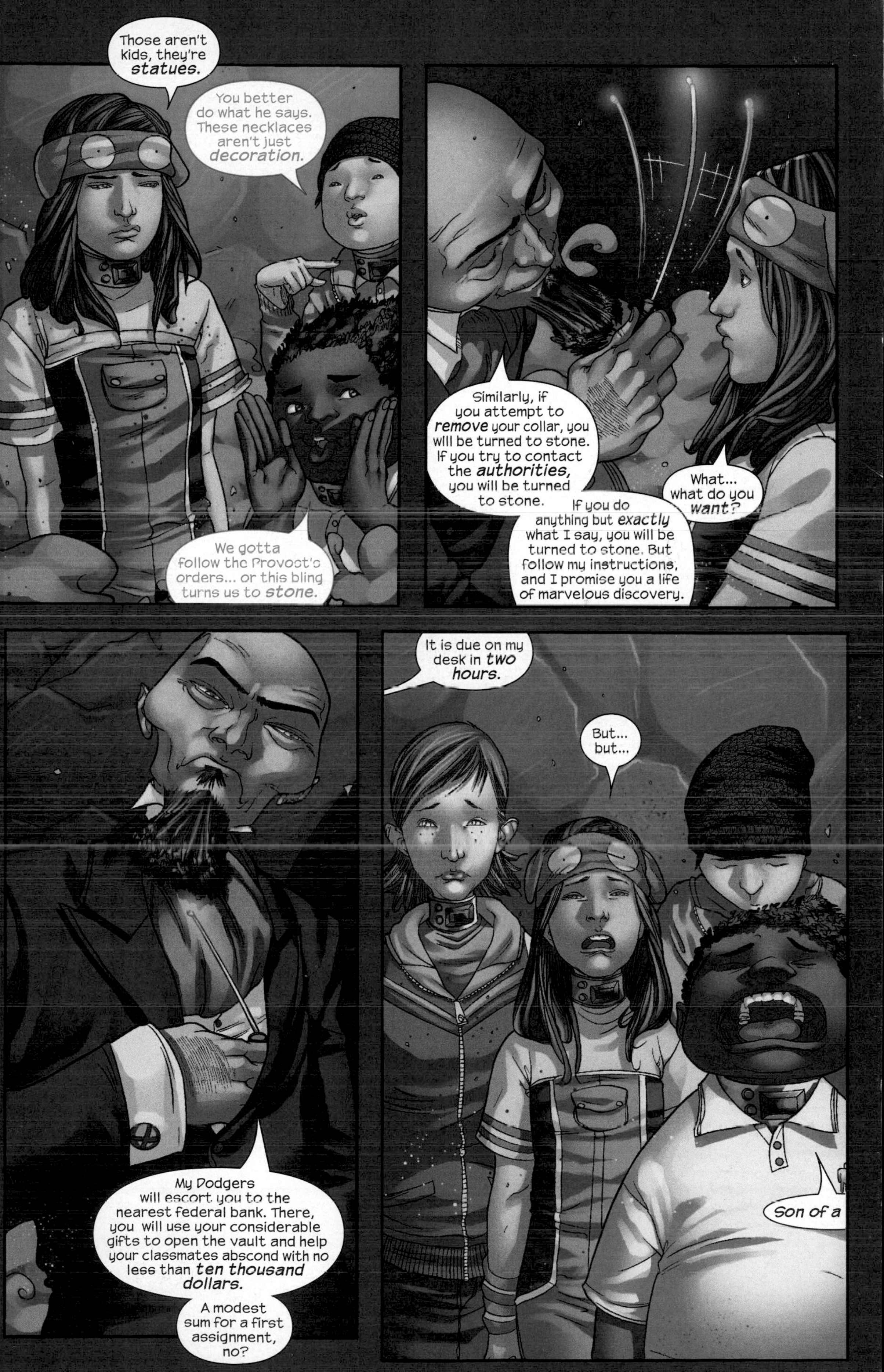
Those aren't kids, they're statues.
You better do what he says. These necklaces aren't just decoration.
We gotta follow the Provost's orders... or this bling turns us to stone.
Similarly, if you attempt to remove your collar, you will be turned to stone. If you try to contact the authorities, you will be turned to stone.
If you do anything but exactly what I say, you will be turned to stone. But follow my instructions, and I promise you a life of marvelous discovery.
What... what do you want?
My Dodgers will escort you to the nearest federal bank. There, you will use your considerable gifts to open the vault and help your classmates abscond with no less than ten thousand dollars.
A modest sum for a first assignment, no?
It is due on my desk in two hours.
But... but...
Son of a

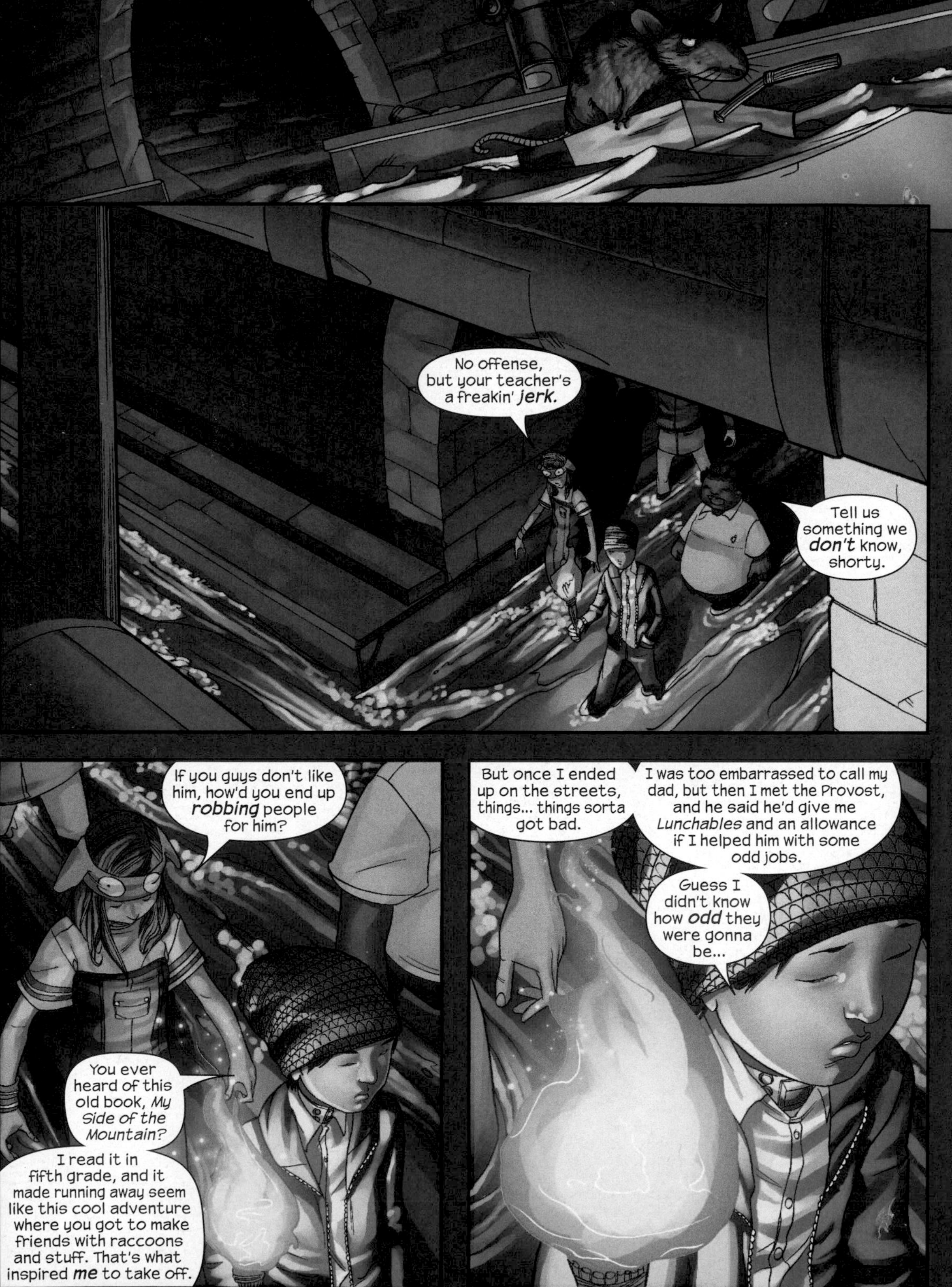
No offense, but your teacher's a freakin' *jerk.*
Tell us something we *don't* know, shorty.
If you guys don't like him, how'd you end up *robbing* people for him?
You ever heard of this old book, *My Side of the Mountain*?
I read it in fifth grade, and it made running away seem like this cool adventure where you got to make friends with raccoons and stuff. That's what inspired *me* to take off.
But once I ended up on the streets, things... things sorta got bad.
I was too embarrassed to call my dad, but then I met the Provost, and he said he'd give me *Lunchables* and an allowance if I helped him with some odd jobs.
Guess I didn't know how *odd* they were gonna be...

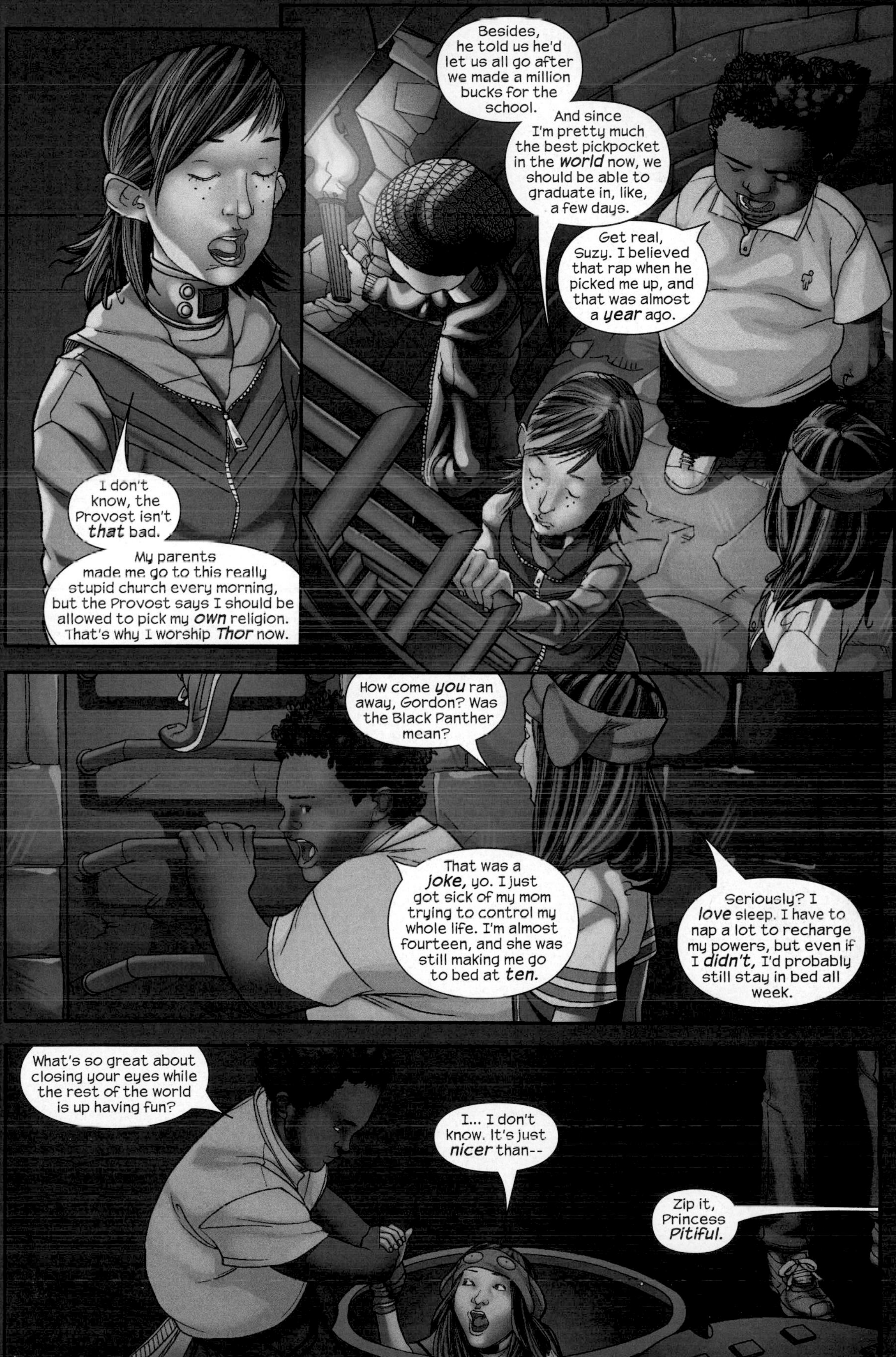
Besides, he told us he'd let us all go after we made a million bucks for the school.
And since I'm pretty much the best pickpocket in the world now, we should be able to graduate in, like, a few days.
Get real, Suzy. I believed that rap when he picked me up, and that was almost a year ago.
I don't know, the Provost isn't that bad.
My parents made me go to this really stupid church every morning, but the Provost says I should be allowed to pick my own religion. That's why I worship Thor now.
How come you ran away, Gordon? Was the Black Panther mean?
That was a joke, yo. I just got sick of my mom trying to control my whole life. I'm almost fourteen, and she was still making me go to bed at ten.
Seriously? I love sleep. I have to nap a lot to recharge my powers, but even if I didn't, I'd probably still stay in bed all week.
What's so great about closing your eyes while the rest of the world is up having fun?
I... I don't know. It's just nicer than--
Zip it, Princess Pitiful.

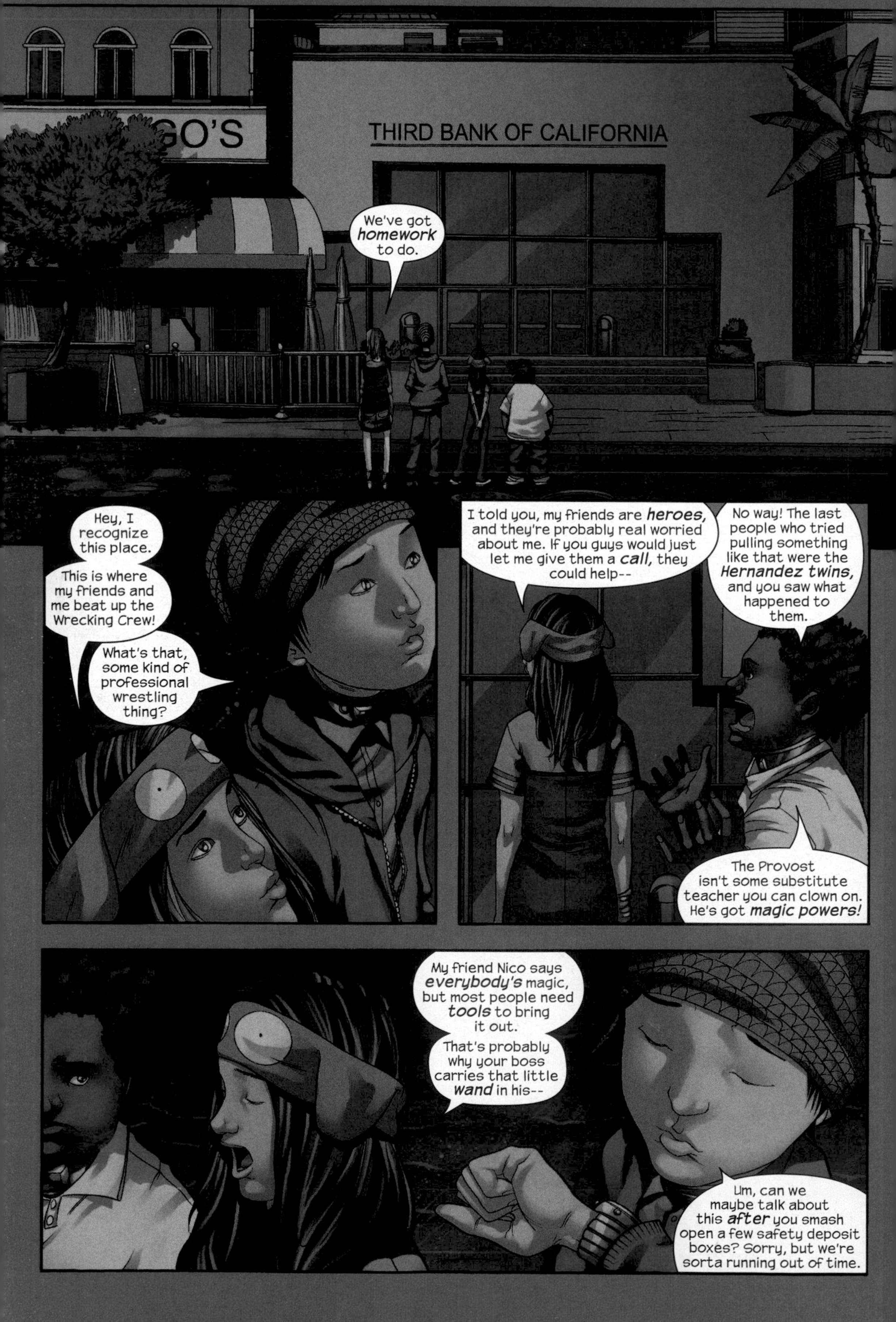
GO'S
THIRD BANK OF CALIFORNIA
We've got homework to do.
Hey, I recognize this place.
This is where my friends and me beat up the Wrecking Crew!
What's that, some kind of professional wrestling thing?
I told you, my friends are heroes, and they're probably real worried about me. If you guys would just let me give them a call, they could help--
No way! The last people who tried pulling something like that were the Hernandez twins, and you saw what happened to them.
The Provost isn't some substitute teacher you can clown on. He's got magic powers!
My friend Nico says everybody's magic, but most people need tools to bring it out.
That's probably why your boss carries that little wand in his--
Um, can we maybe talk about this after you smash open a few safety deposit boxes? Sorry, but we're sorta running out of time.

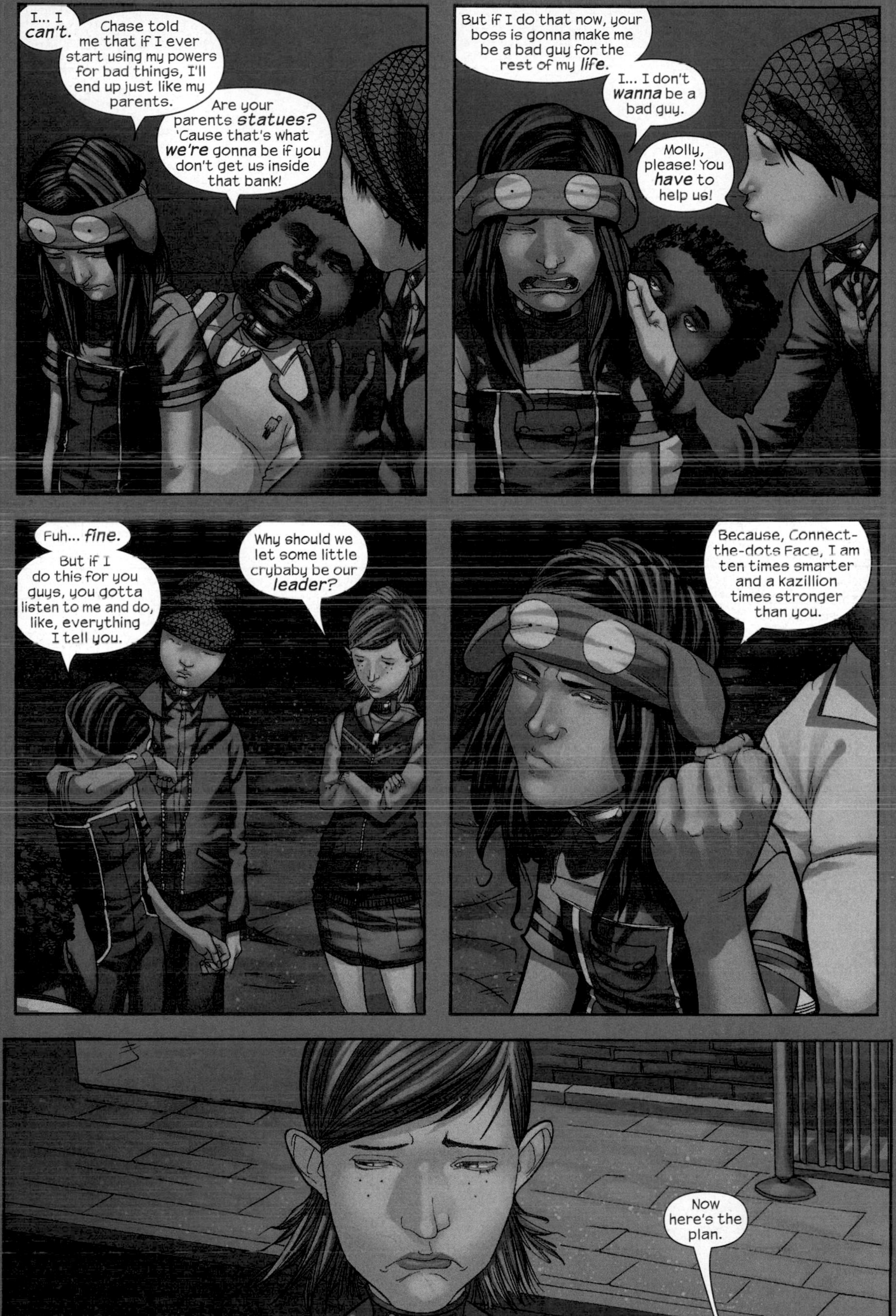

I... I can't.
Chase told me that if I ever start using my powers for bad things, I'll end up just like my parents.
Are your parents statues? 'Cause that's what we're gonna be if you don't get us inside that bank!
But if I do that now, your boss is gonna make me be a bad guy for the rest of my life.
I... I don't wanna be a bad guy.
Molly, please! You have to help us!
Fuh... fine.
But if I do this for you guys, you gotta listen to me and do, like, everything I tell you.
Why should we let some little crybaby be our leader?
Because, Connect-the-dots Face, I am ten times smarter and a kazillion times stronger than you.
Now here's the plan.

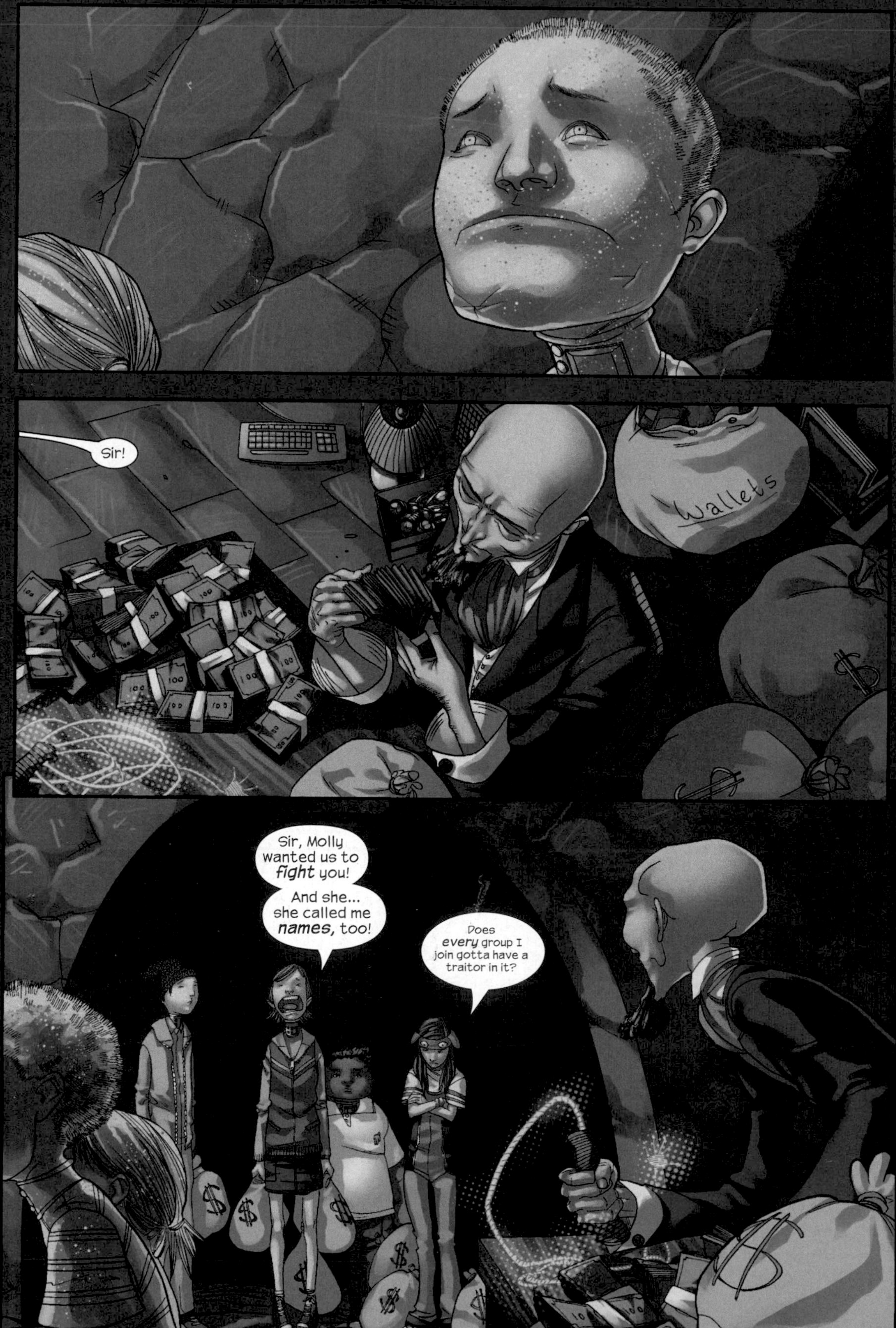
Sir!
Wallets
Sir, Molly wanted us to fight you!
And she... she called me names, too!
Does every group I join gotta have a traitor in it?

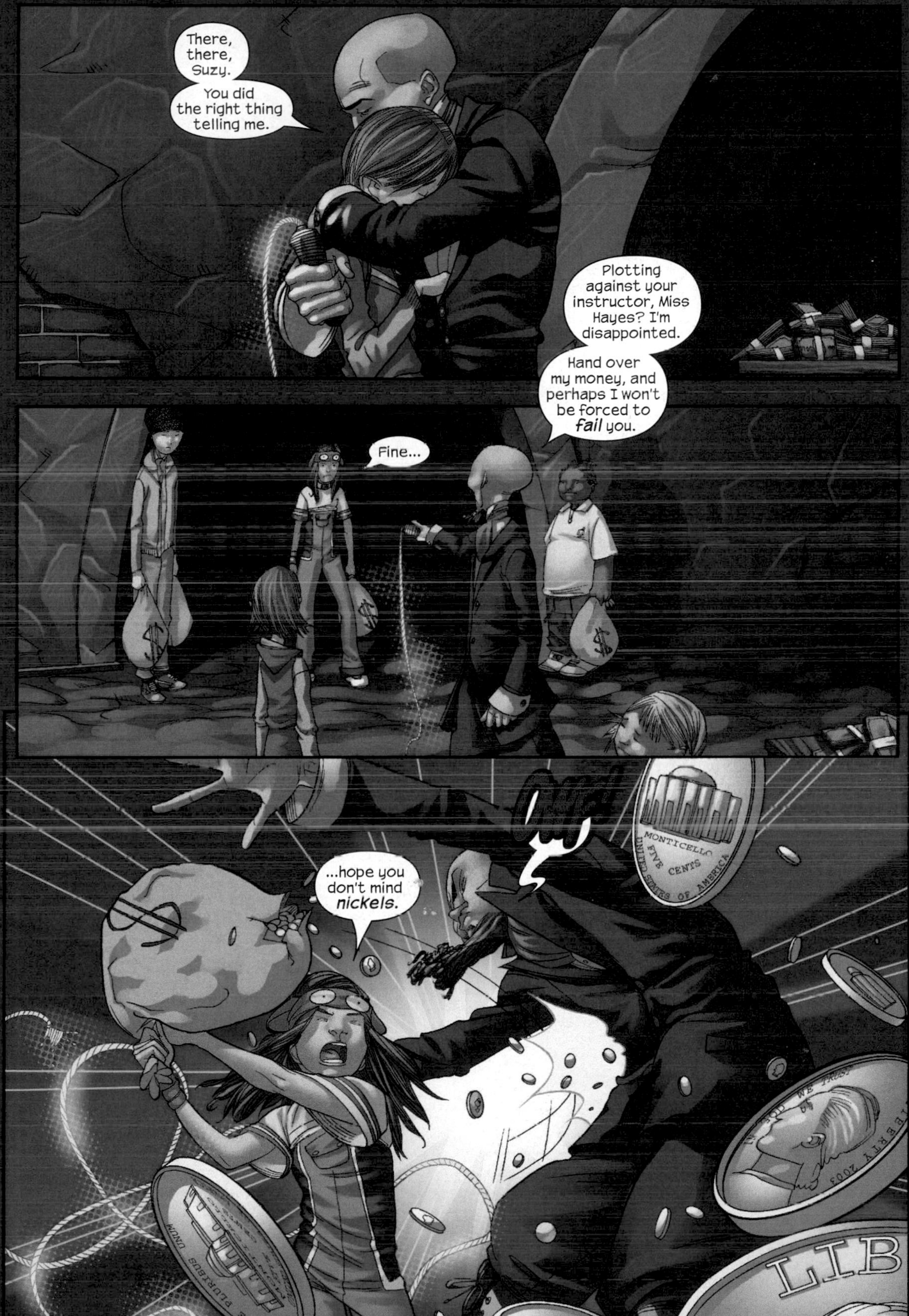
There, there, Suzy.
You did the right thing telling me.
Plotting against your instructor, Miss Hayes? I'm disappointed.
Hand over my money, and perhaps I won't be forced to *fail* you.
Fine...
...hope you don't mind *nickels.*
MONTICELLO
FIVE CENTS
UNITED STATES OF AMERICA
E PLURIBUS UNUM
IN GOD WE TRUST
LIBERTY 2003
LIB

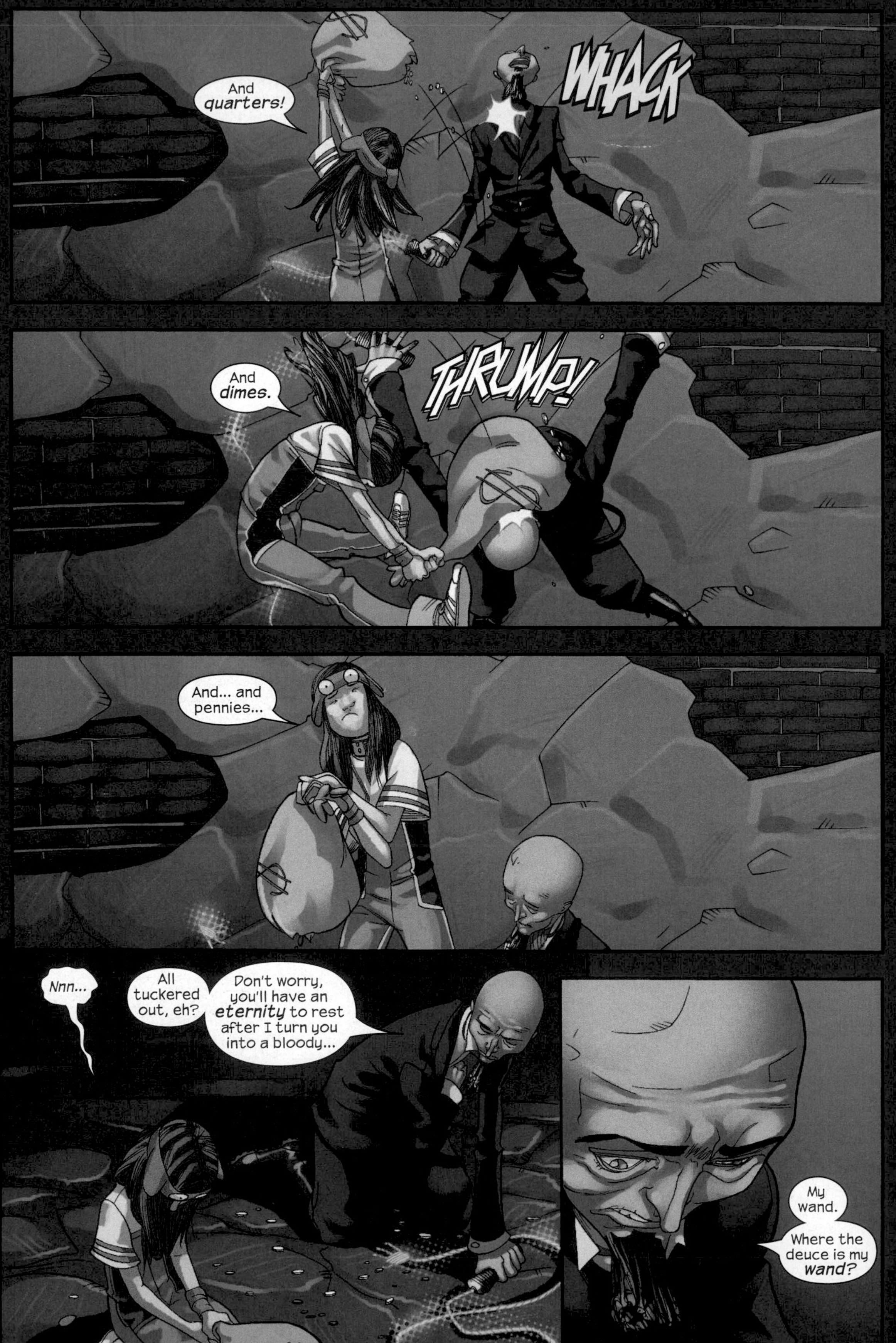
And quarters!
WHACK
And dimes.
THRUMP!
And... and pennies...
Nnn...
All tuckered out, eh?
Don't worry, you'll have an eternity to rest after I turn you into a bloody...
My wand.
Where the deuce is my wand?

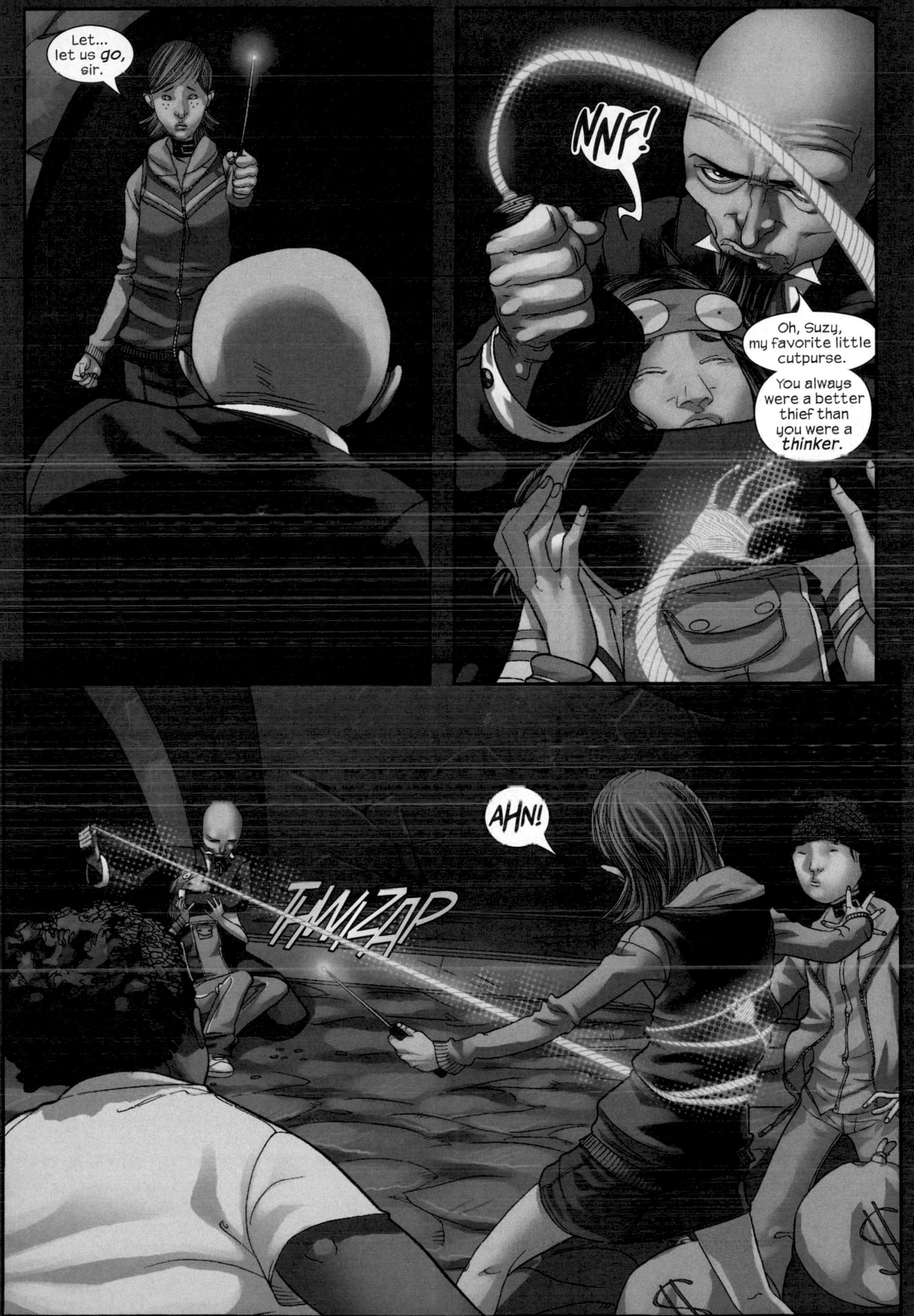
Let... let us go, sir.
NNF!
Oh, Suzy, my favorite little cutpurse.
You always were a better thief than you were a thinker.
AHN!
THWZAP

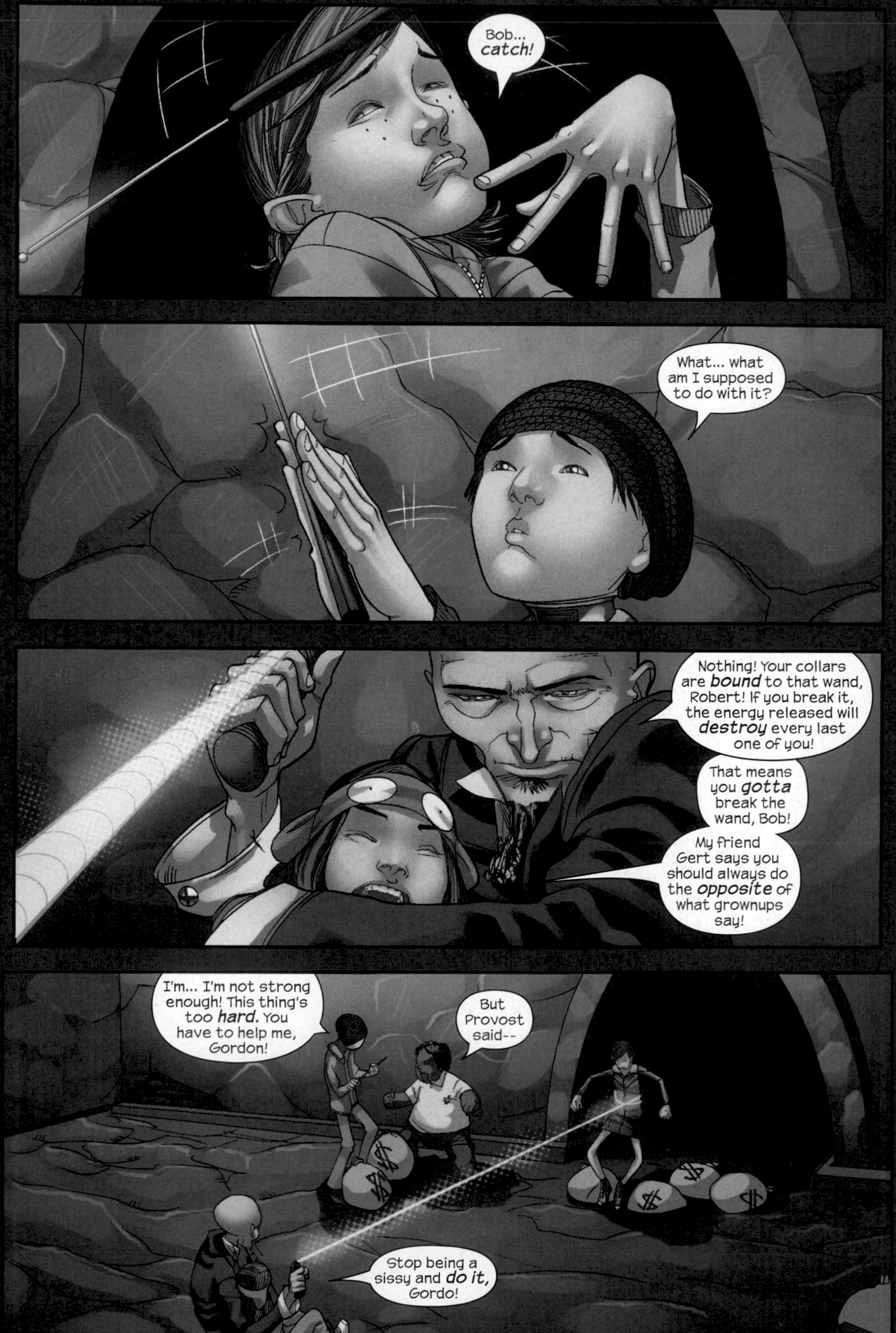
Bob... catch!
What... what am I supposed to do with it?
Nothing! Your collars are bound to that wand, Robert! If you break it, the energy released will destroy every last one of you!
That means you gotta break the wand, Bob!
My friend Gert says you should always do the opposite of what grownups say!
I'm... I'm not strong enough! This thing's too hard. You have to help me, Gordon!
But Provost said--
Stop being a sissy and do it, Gordo!

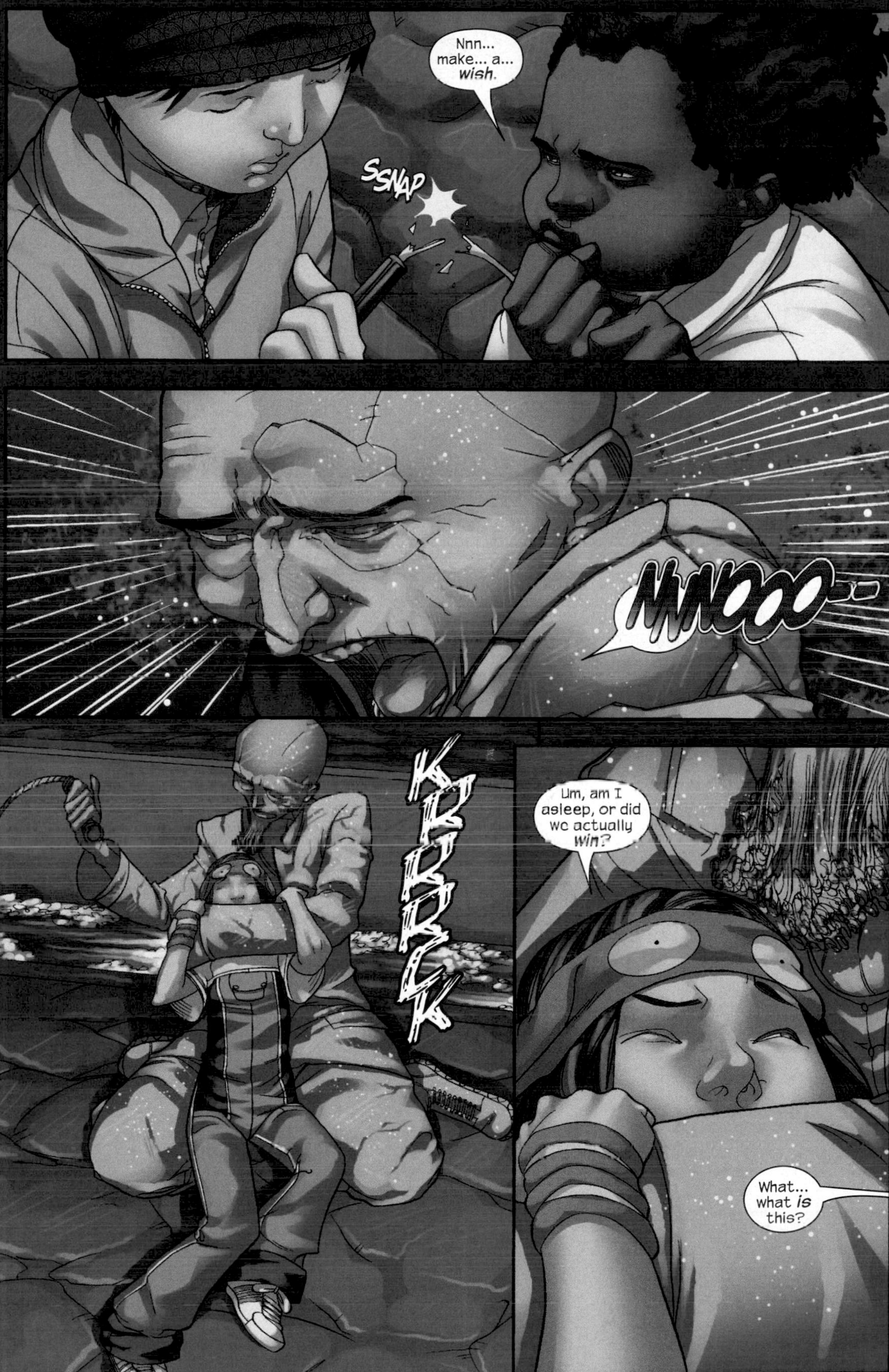
Nnn... make... a... wish.
SSNAP
NNNOOO--
KRRRCK
Um, am I asleep, or did we actually win?
What... what is this?

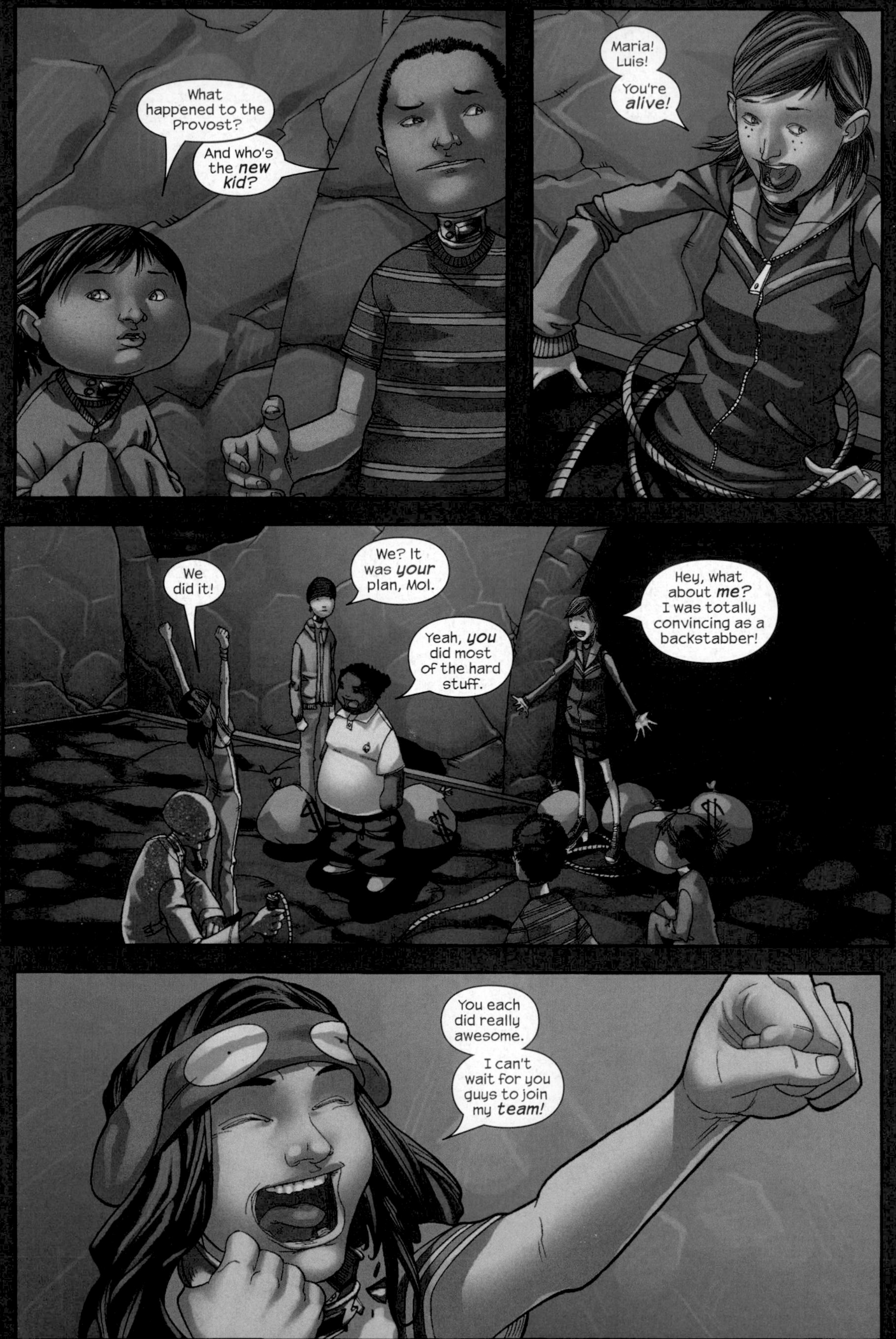
What happened to the Provost?
And who's the *new kid?*
Maria! Luis!
You're *alive!*
We did it!
We? It was *your* plan, Mol.
Yeah, *you* did most of the hard stuff.
Hey, what about *me?* I was totally convincing as a backstabber!
You each did really awesome.
I can't wait for you guys to join my *team!*

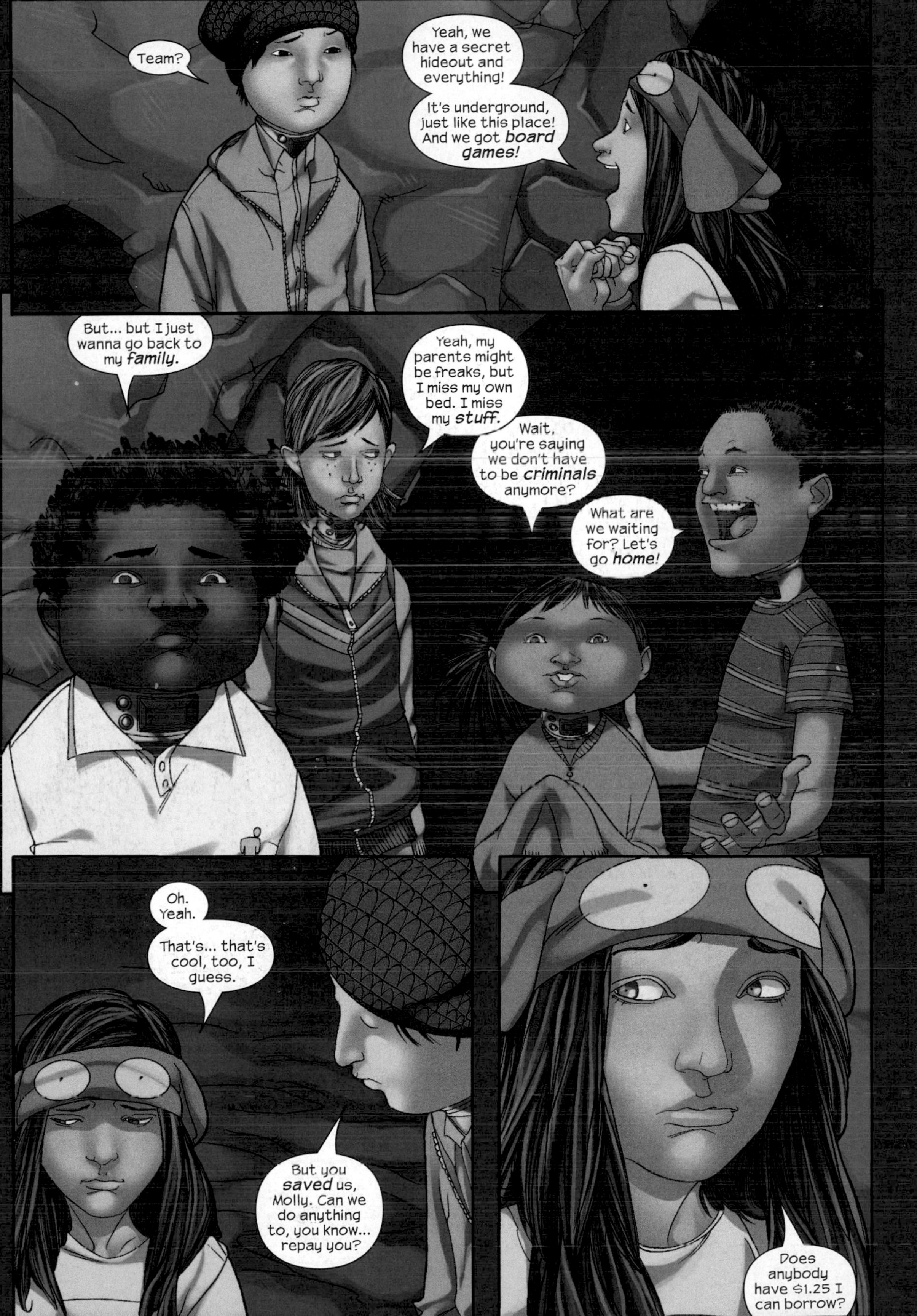
Team?
Yeah, we have a secret hideout and everything!
It's underground, just like this place! And we got *board games!*
But... but I just wanna go back to my *family.*
Yeah, my parents might be freaks, but I miss my own bed. I miss my *stuff.*
Wait, you're saying we don't have to be *criminals* anymore?
What are we waiting for? Let's go *home!*
Oh. Yeah.
That's... that's cool, too, I guess.
But you *saved* us, Molly. Can we do anything to, you know... repay you?
Does anybody have $1.25 I can borrow?

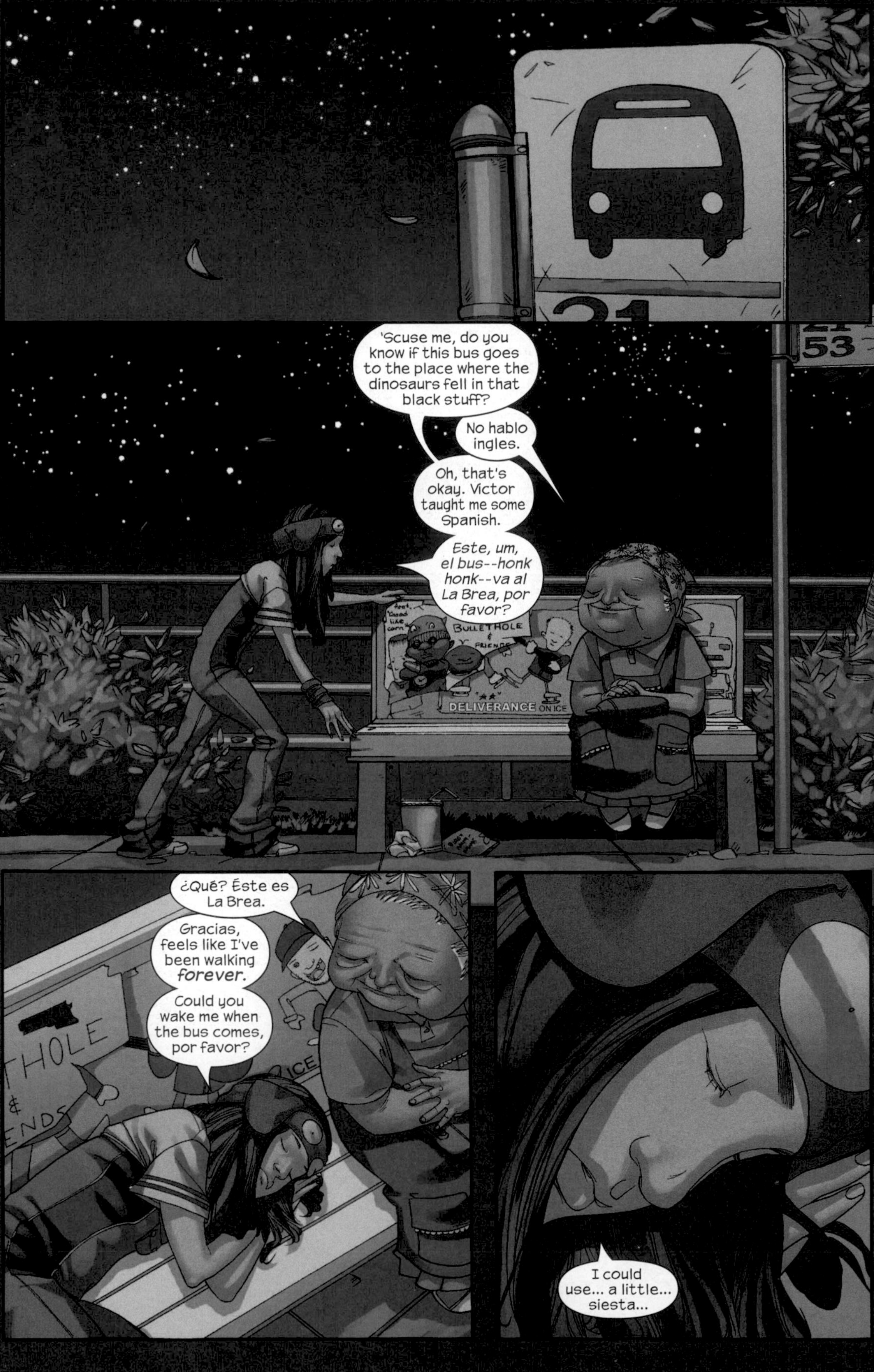
21
53
'Scuse me, do you know if this bus goes to the place where the dinosaurs fell in that black stuff?
No hablo ingles.
Oh, that's okay. Victor taught me some Spanish.
Este, um, el bus--honk honk--va al La Brea, por favor?
BULLETHOLE & FRIENDS
DELIVERANCE ON ICE
¿Qué? Éste es La Brea.
Gracias, feels like I've been walking *forever*.
Could you wake me when the bus comes, por favor?
THOLE
& ENDS
ICE
I could use... a little... siesta...

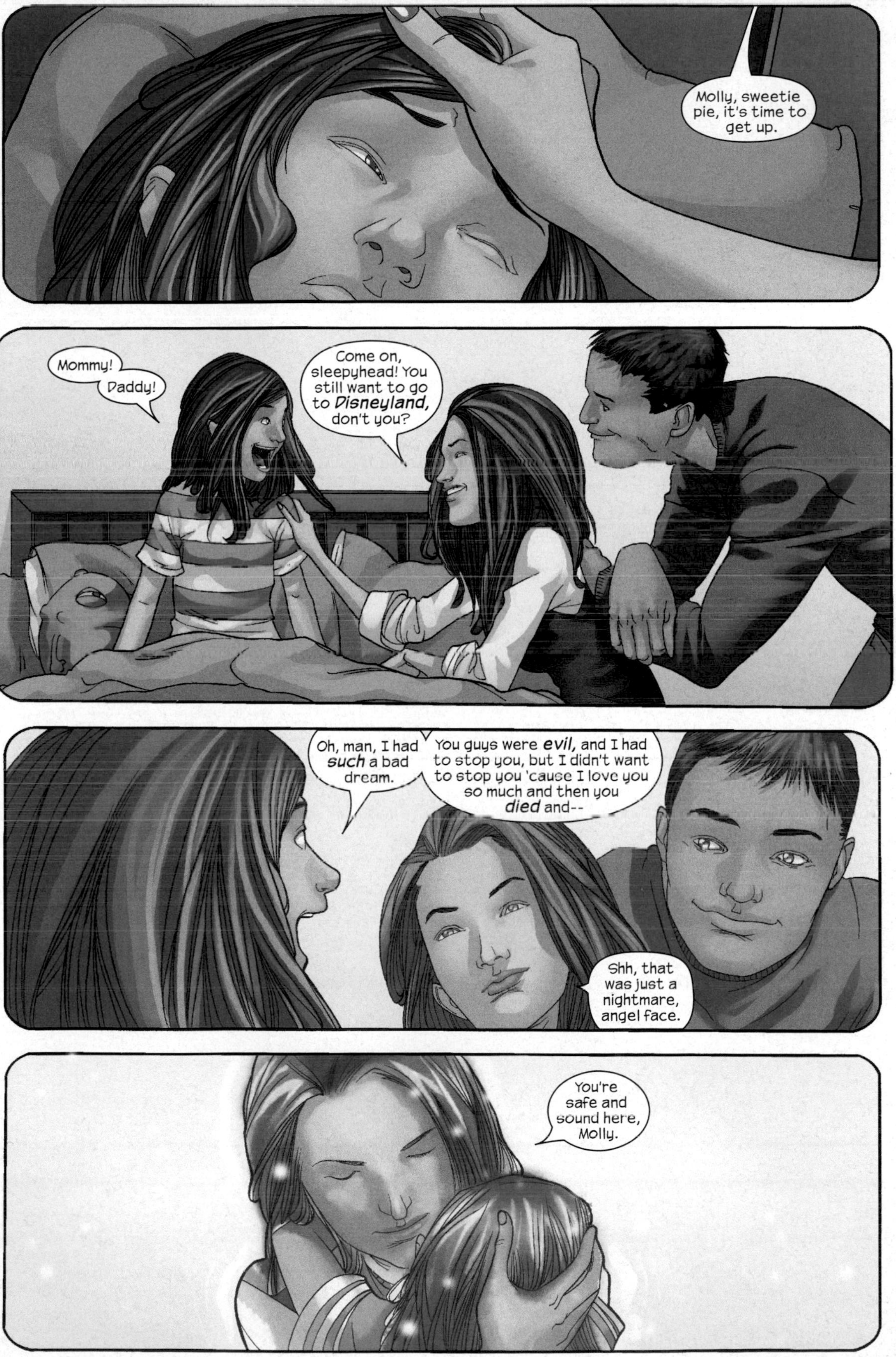
Molly, sweetie pie, it's time to get up.
Mommy!
Daddy!
Come on, sleepyhead! You still want to go to *Disneyland,* don't you?
Oh, man, I had *such* a bad dream.
You guys were *evil,* and I had to stop you, but I didn't want to stop you 'cause I love you so much and then you *died* and--
Shh, that was just a nightmare, angel face.
You're safe and sound here, Molly.

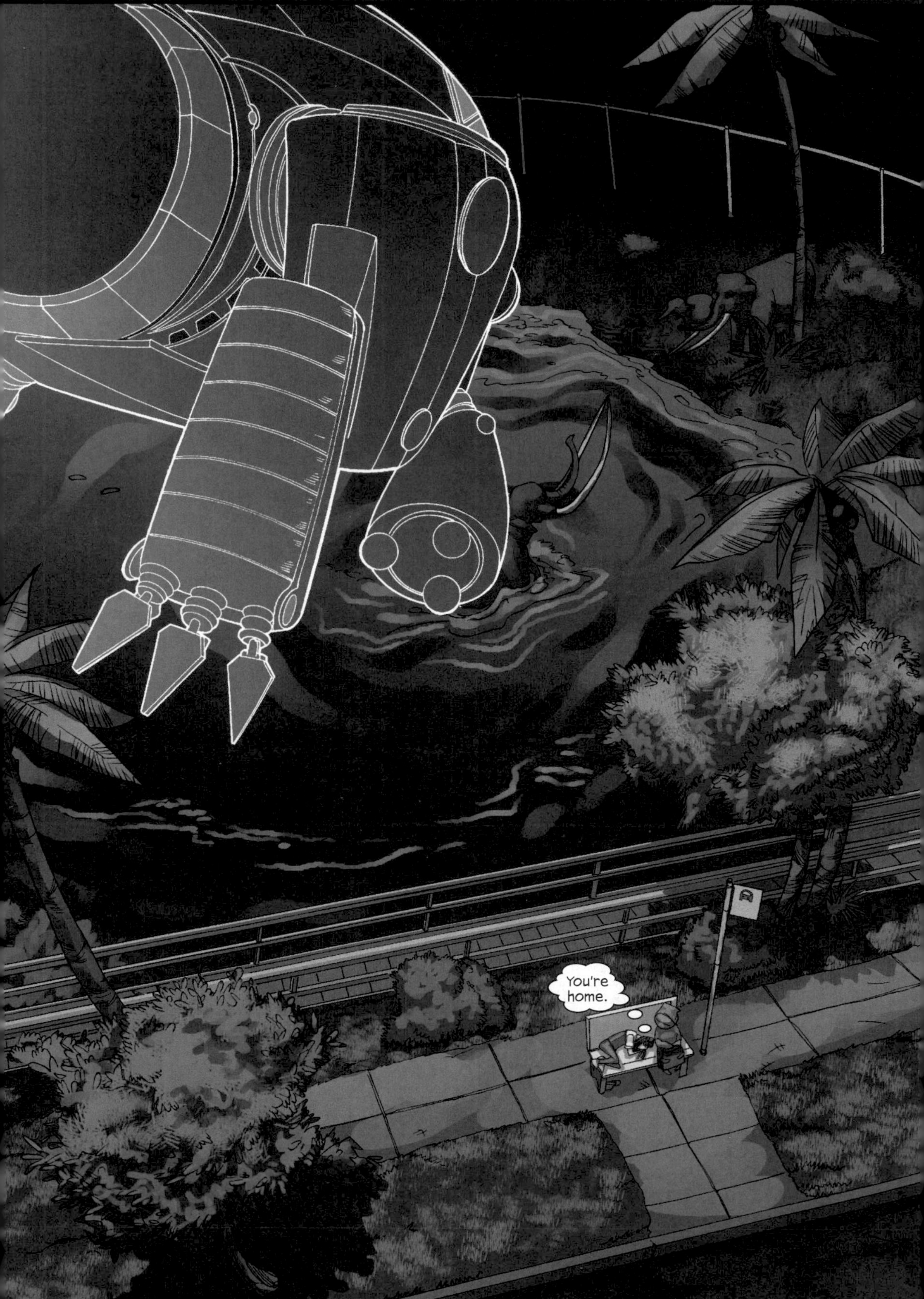
You're home.

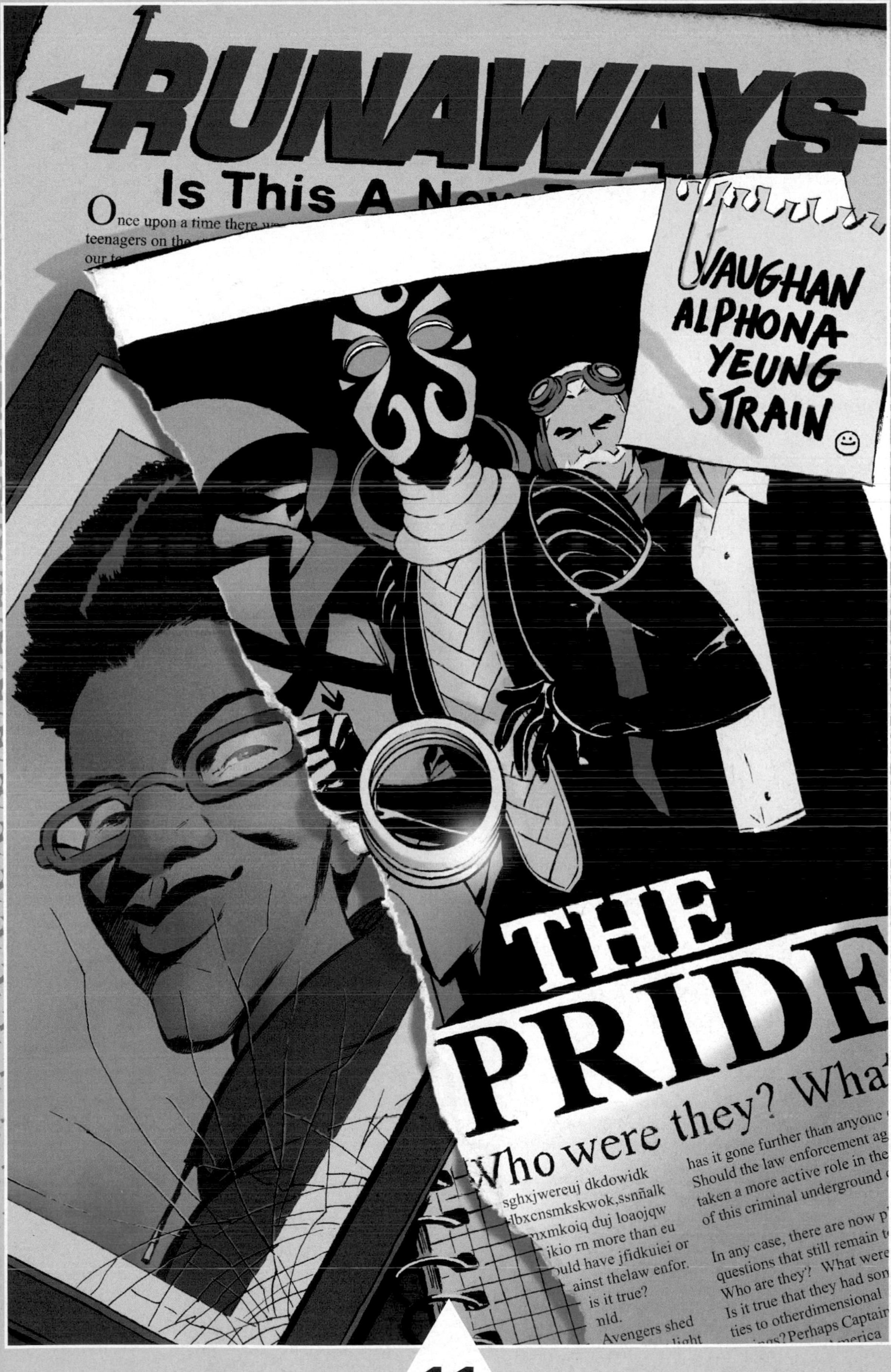
RUNAWAYS
Is This A
Once upon a time there
teenagers on
VAUGHAN
ALPHONA
YEUNG
STRAIN
THE
PRIDE
Who were they?
has it gone further than anyone
Should the law enforcement
taken a more active role in the
of this criminal underground
sghxjwereuj dkdowidk
jikio rn more than eu
ainst thelaw enfor.
is it true?
nld.
Avengers shed
In any case, there are now
questions that still remain
Who are they? What were
Is it true that they had
ties to otherdimensional

Tarnax VII
Yesterday

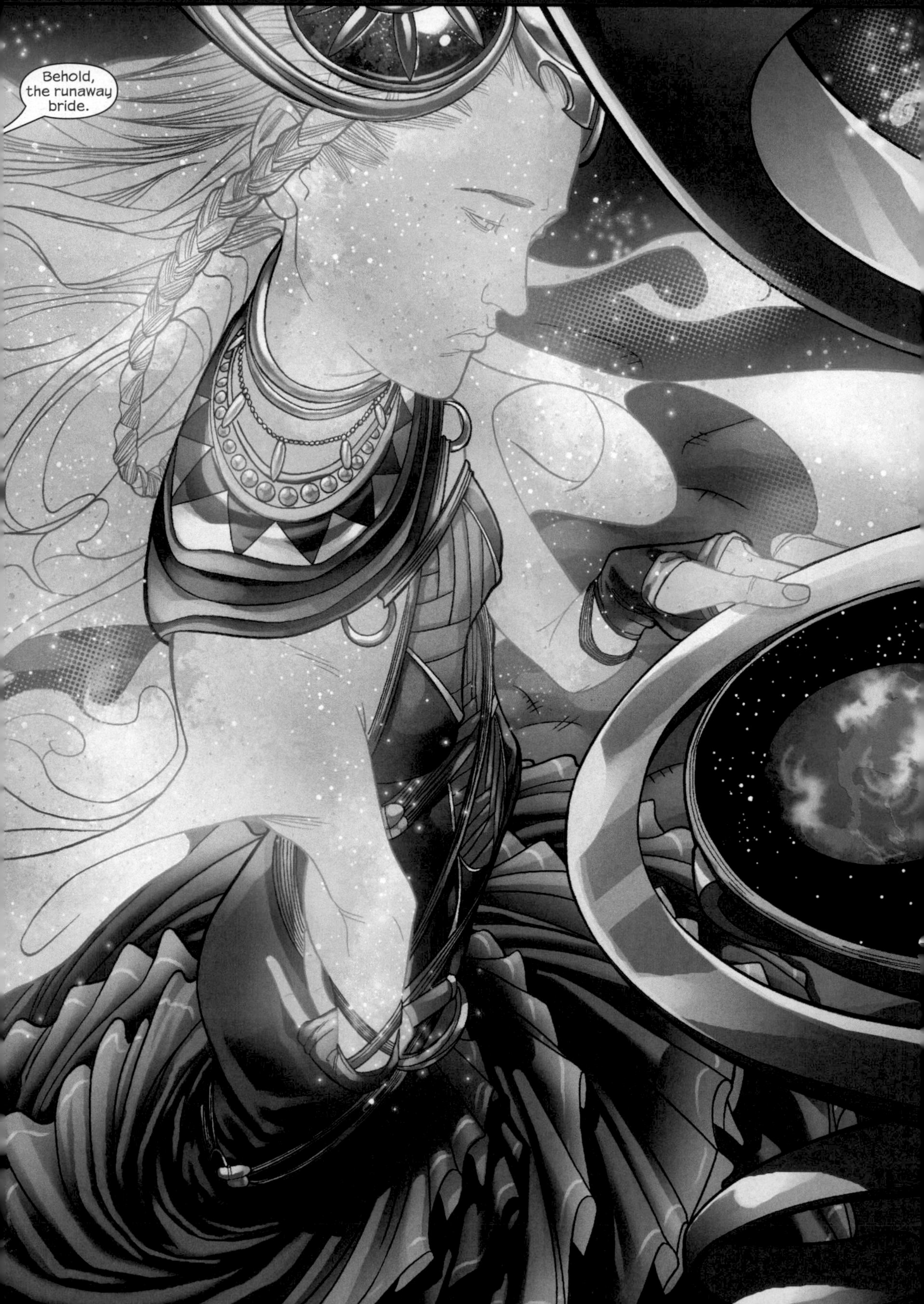
Behold, the runaway bride.

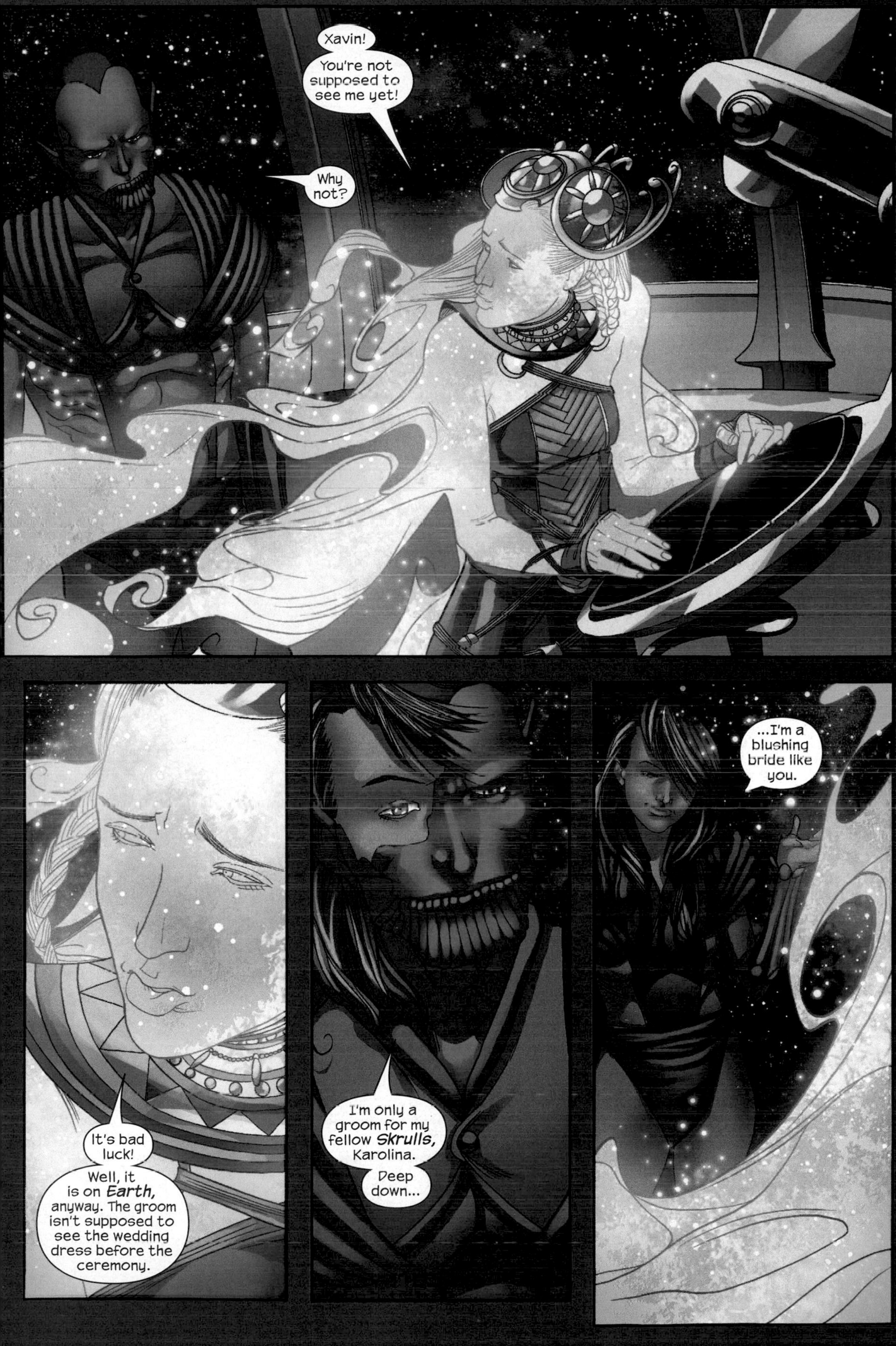
Xavin!
You're not supposed to see me yet!
Why not?
It's bad luck!
Well, it is on *Earth,* anyway. The groom isn't supposed to see the wedding dress before the ceremony.
I'm only a groom for my fellow *Skrulls,* Karolina.
Deep down...
...I'm a blushing bride like you.

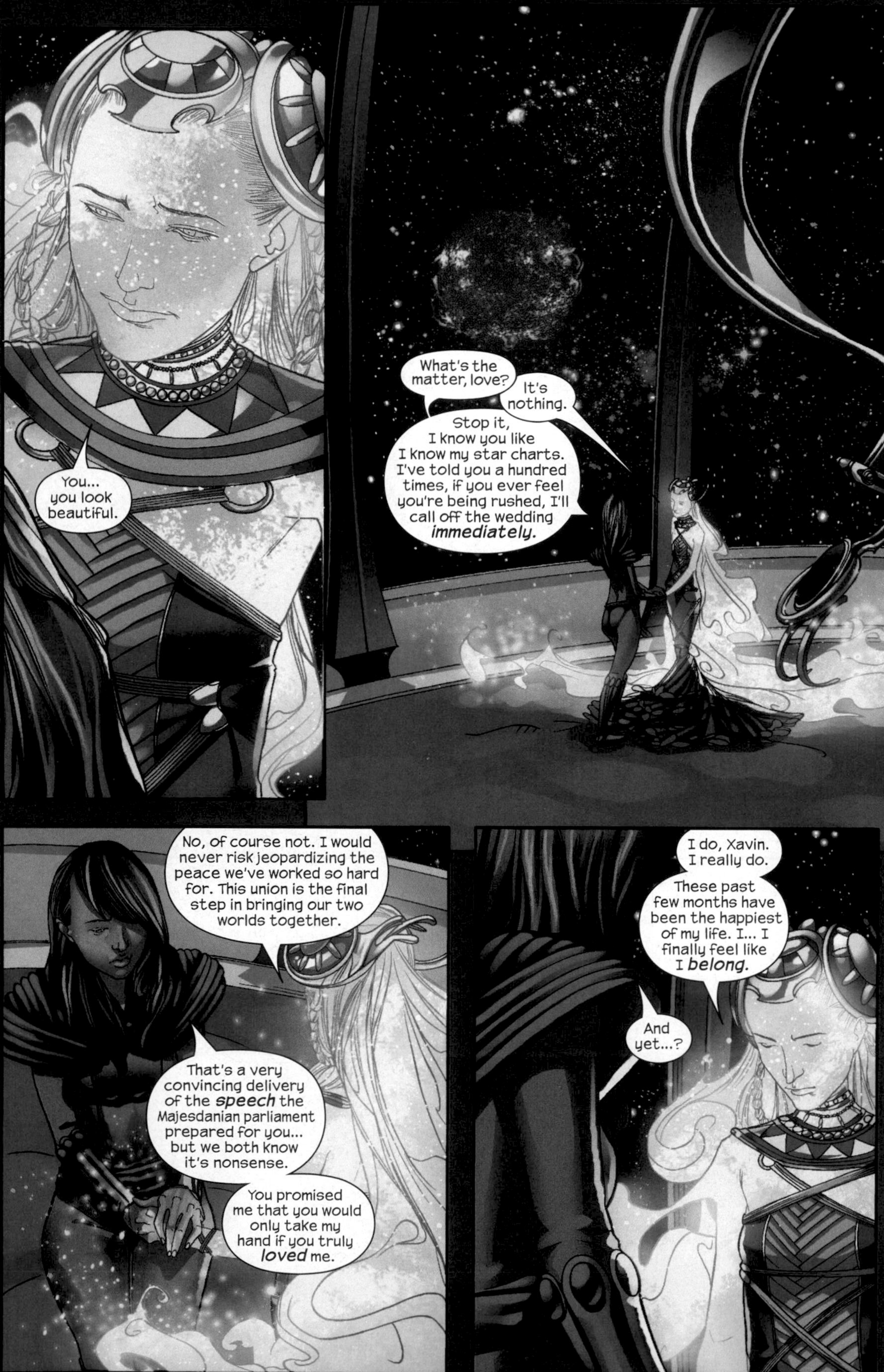
You... you look beautiful.
What's the matter, love?
It's nothing.
Stop it, I know you like I know my star charts. I've told you a hundred times, if you ever feel you're being rushed, I'll call off the wedding *immediately.*
No, of course not. I would never risk jeopardizing the peace we've worked so hard for. This union is the final step in bringing our two worlds together.
That's a very convincing delivery of the *speech* the Majesdanian parliament prepared for you... but we both know it's nonsense.
You promised me that you would only take my hand if you truly *loved* me.
I do, Xavin. I really do.
These past few months have been the happiest of my life. I... I finally feel like I *belong.*
And yet...?

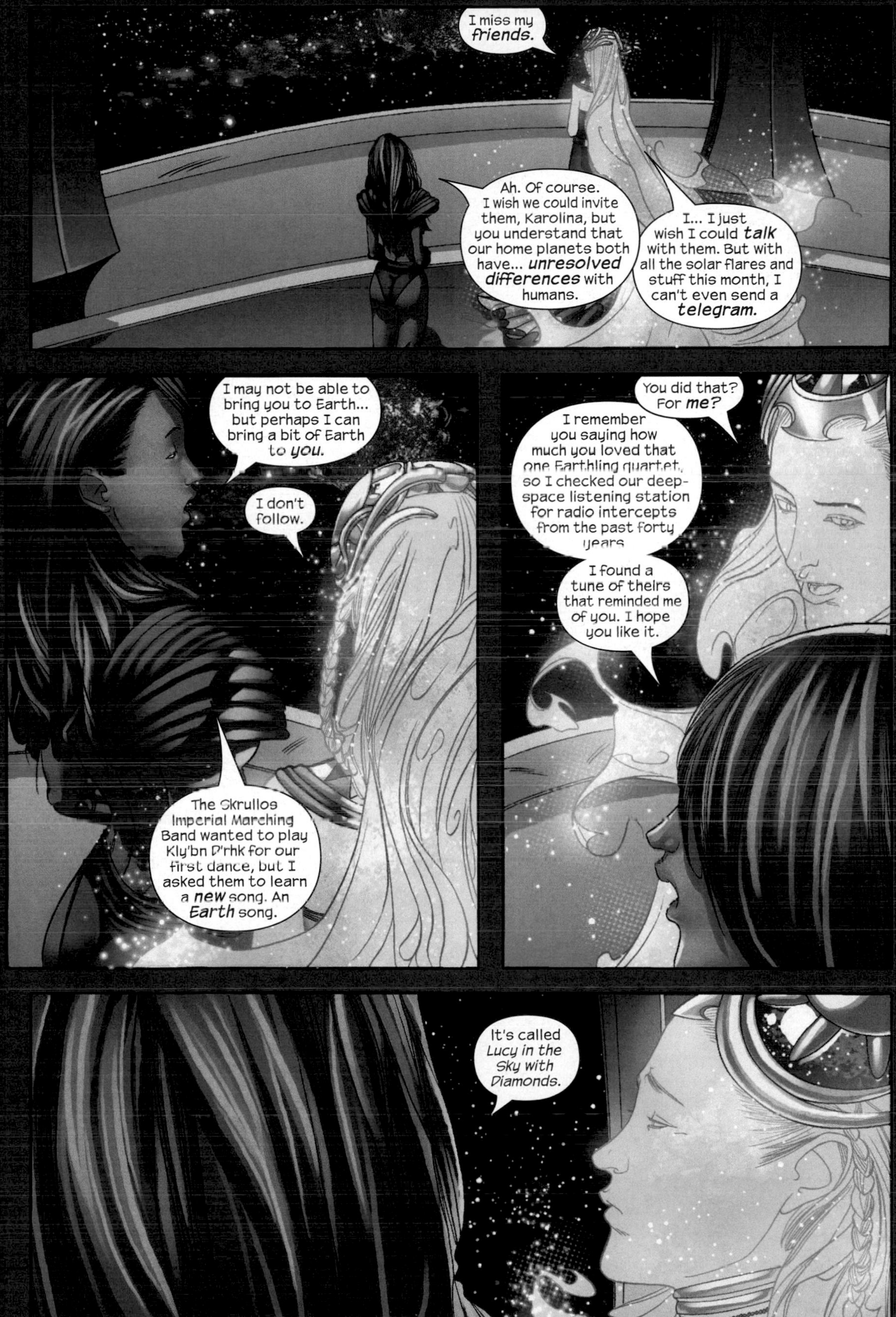
I miss my friends.
Ah. Of course. I wish we could invite them, Karolina, but you understand that our home planets both have... unresolved differences with humans.
I... I just wish I could talk with them. But with all the solar flares and stuff this month, I can't even send a telegram.
I may not be able to bring you to Earth... but perhaps I can bring a bit of Earth to you.
I don't follow.
The Skrullos Imperial Marching Band wanted to play Kly'bn D'rhk for our first dance, but I asked them to learn a new song. An Earth song.
You did that? For me?
I remember you saying how much you loved that one Earthling quartet, so I checked our deep-space listening station for radio intercepts from the past forty years.
I found a tune of theirs that reminded me of you. I hope you like it.
It's called Lucy in the Sky with Diamonds.

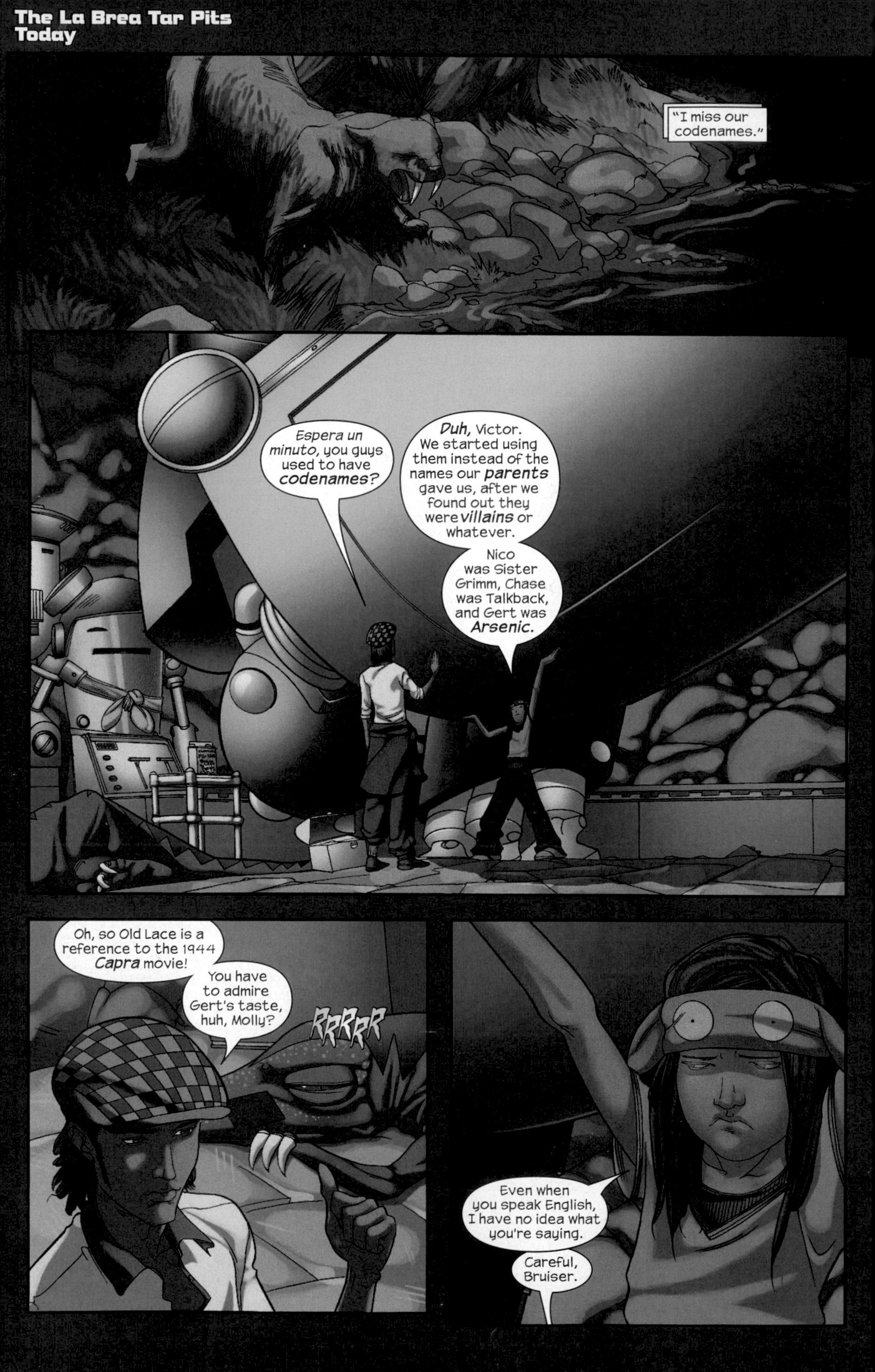
The La Brea Tar Pits
Today
"I miss our codenames."
Espera un minuto, you guys used to have codenames?
Duh, Victor. We started using them instead of the names our parents gave us, after we found out they were villains or whatever.
Nico was Sister Grimm, Chase was Talkback, and Gert was Arsenic.
Oh, so Old Lace is a reference to the 1944 Capra movie!
You have to admire Gert's taste, huh, Molly?
RRRRR
Even when you speak English, I have no idea what you're saying.
Careful, Bruiser.

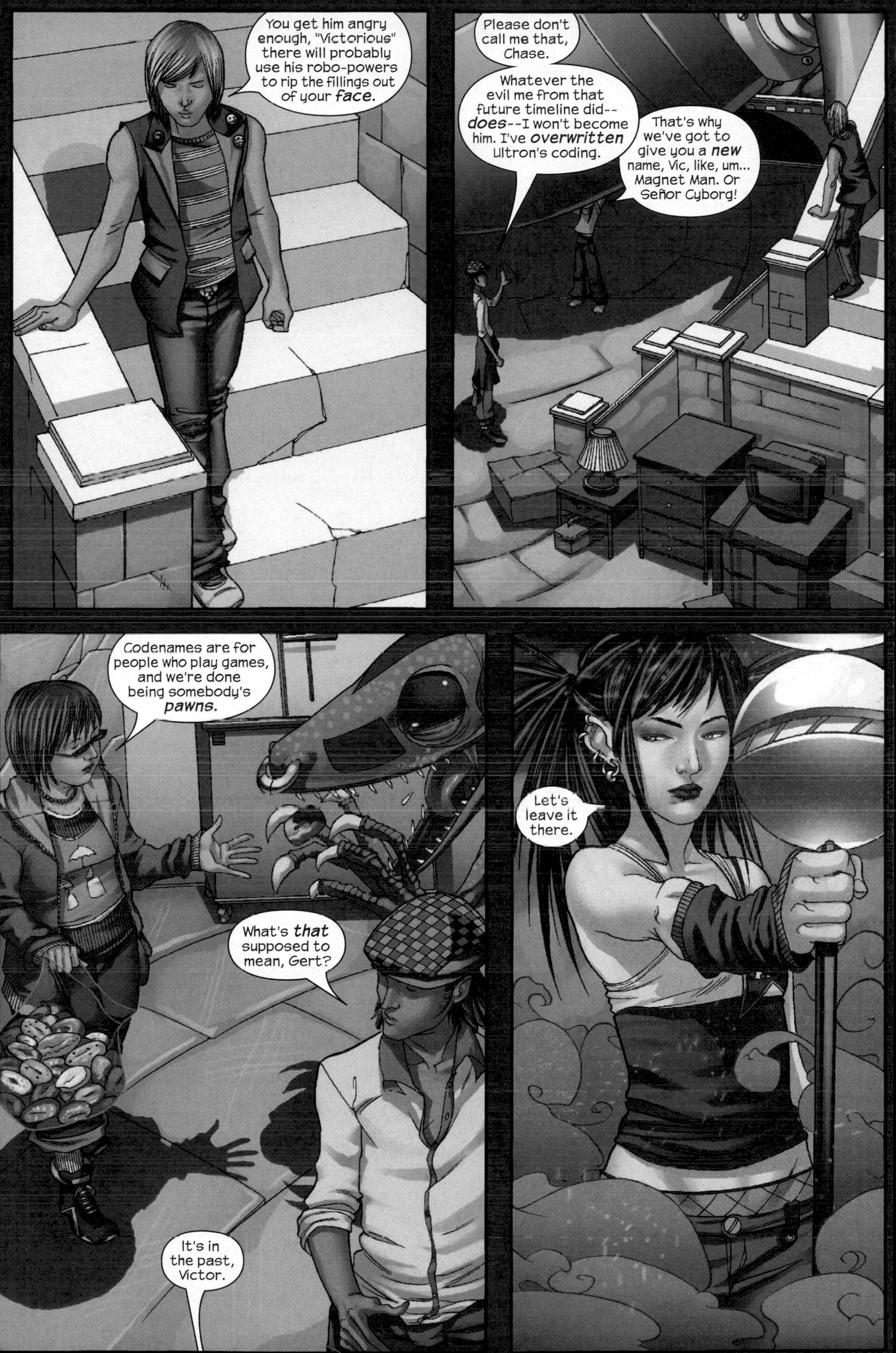
You get him angry enough, "Victorious" there will probably use his robo-powers to rip the fillings out of your *face.*
Please don't call me that, Chase.
Whatever the evil me from that future timeline did-- *does*--I won't become him. I've *overwritten* Ultron's coding.
That's why we've got to give you a *new* name, Vic, like, um... Magnet Man. Or Señor Cyborg!
Codenames are for people who play games, and we're done being somebody's *pawns.*
What's *that* supposed to mean, Gert?
It's in the past, Victor.
Let's leave it there.

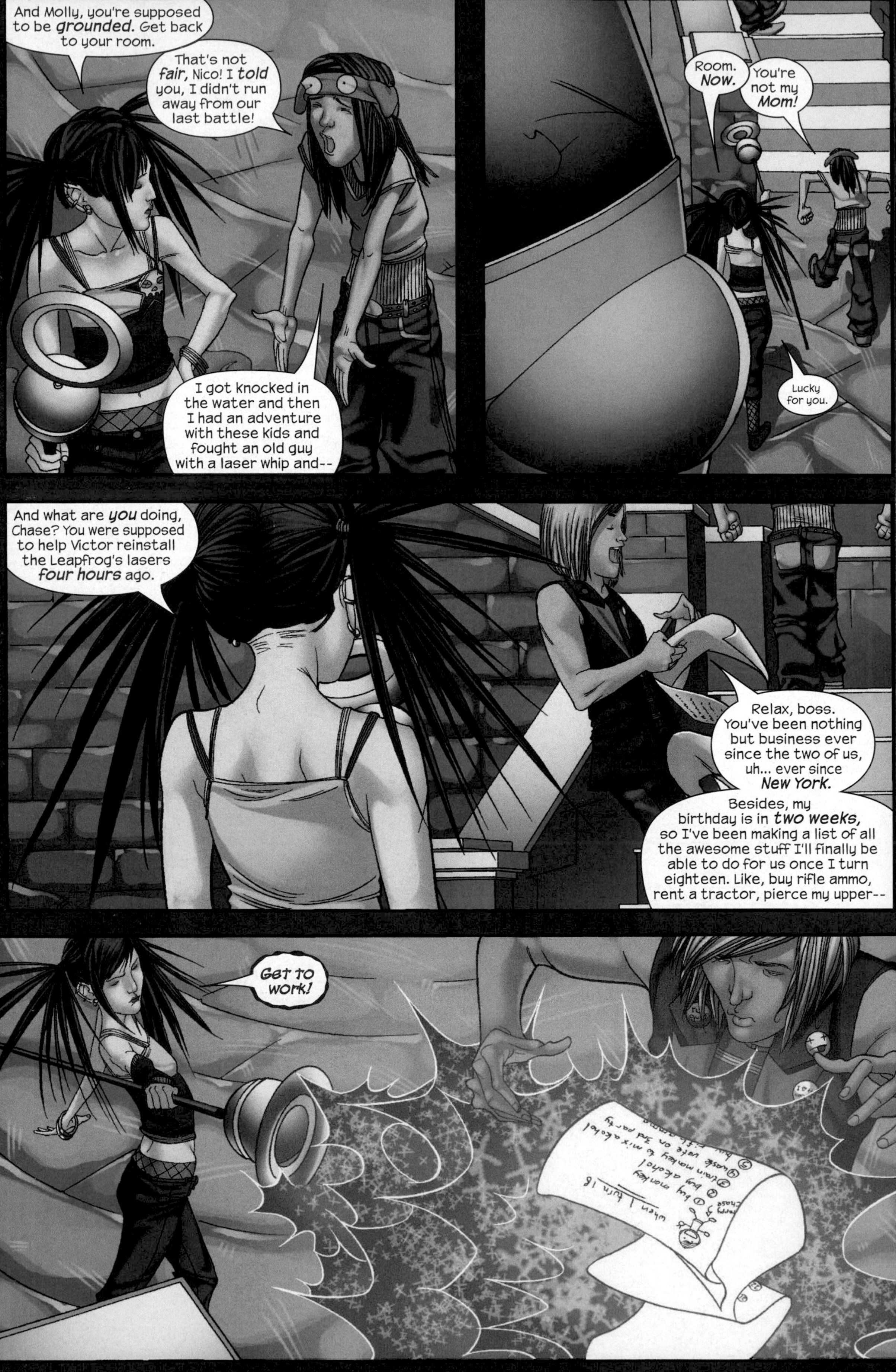
And Molly, you're supposed to be grounded. Get back to your room.
That's not fair, Nico! I told you, I didn't run away from our last battle!
I got knocked in the water and then I had an adventure with these kids and fought an old guy with a laser whip and--
Room. Now.
You're not my Mom!
Lucky for you.
And what are you doing, Chase? You were supposed to help Victor reinstall the Leapfrog's lasers four hours ago.
Relax, boss. You've been nothing but business ever since the two of us, uh... ever since New York.
Besides, my birthday is in two weeks, so I've been making a list of all the awesome stuff I'll finally be able to do for us once I turn eighteen. Like, buy rifle ammo, rent a tractor, pierce my upper--
Get to work!

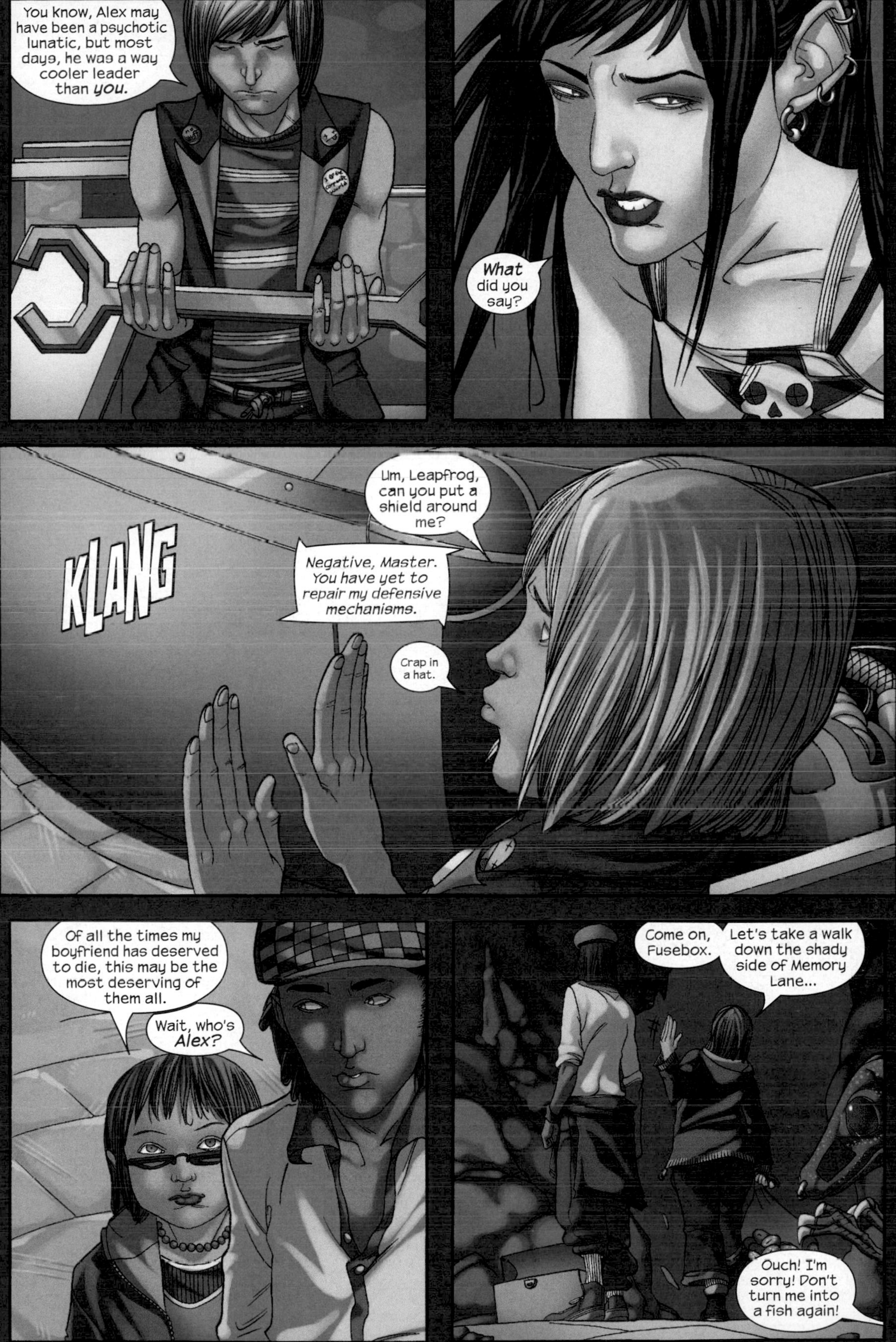
You know, Alex may have been a psychotic lunatic, but most days, he was a way cooler leader than *you.*
What did you say?
KLANG
Um, Leapfrog, can you put a shield around me?
Negative, Master. You have yet to repair my defensive mechanisms.
Crap in a hat.
Of all the times my boyfriend has deserved to die, this may be the most deserving of them all.
Wait, who's *Alex?*
Come on, Fusebox.
Let's take a walk down the shady side of Memory Lane...
Ouch! I'm sorry! Don't turn me into a fish again!

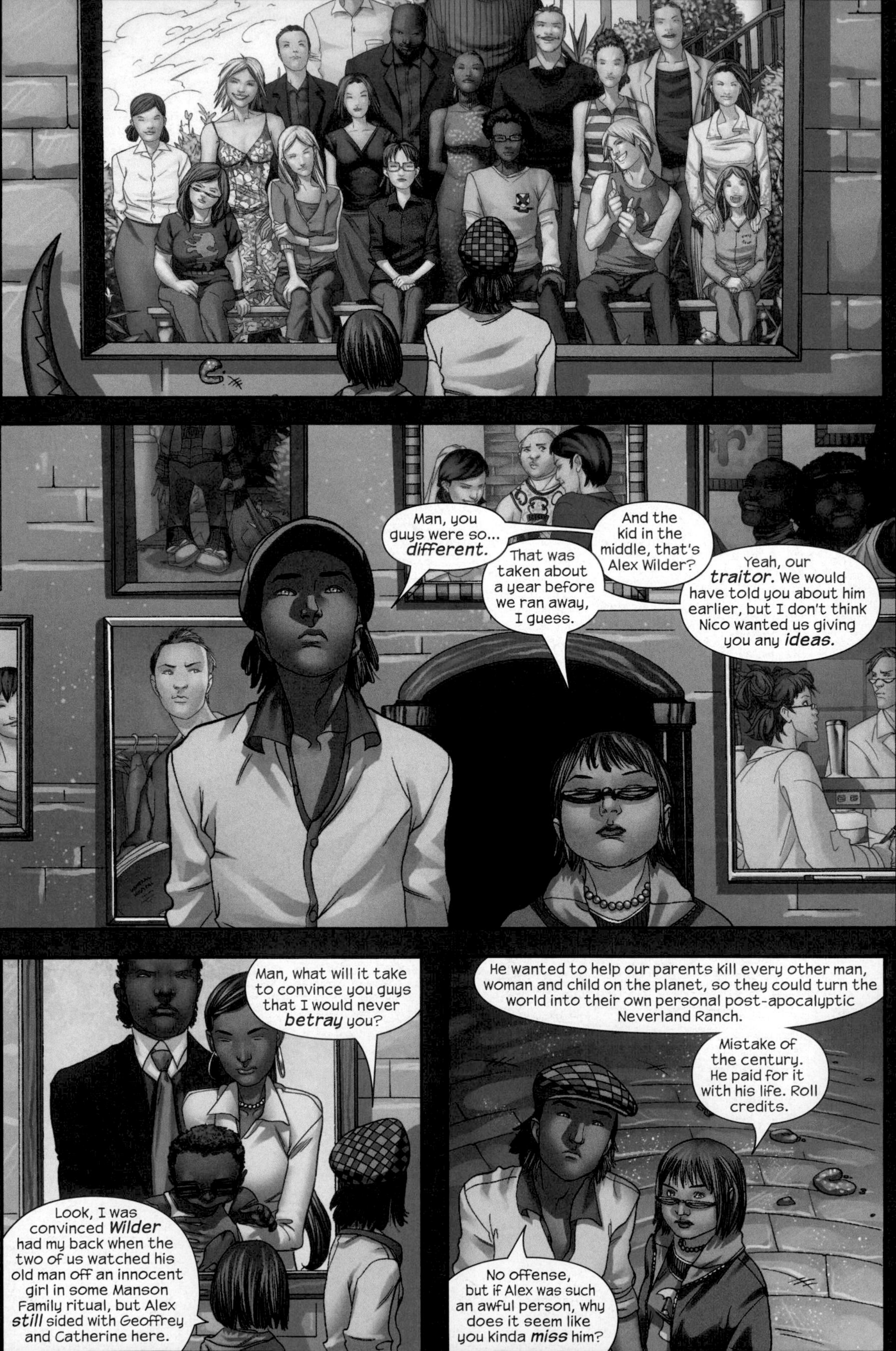
Man, you guys were so... different.
And the kid in the middle, that's Alex Wilder?
That was taken about a year before we ran away, I guess.
Yeah, our traitor. We would have told you about him earlier, but I don't think Nico wanted us giving you any ideas.
Man, what will it take to convince you guys that I would never betray you?
Look, I was convinced Wilder had my back when the two of us watched his old man off an innocent girl in some Manson Family ritual, but Alex still sided with Geoffrey and Catherine here.
He wanted to help our parents kill every other man, woman and child on the planet, so they could turn the world into their own personal post-apocalyptic Neverland Ranch.
Mistake of the century. He paid for it with his life. Roll credits.
No offense, but if Alex was such an awful person, why does it seem like you kinda miss him?

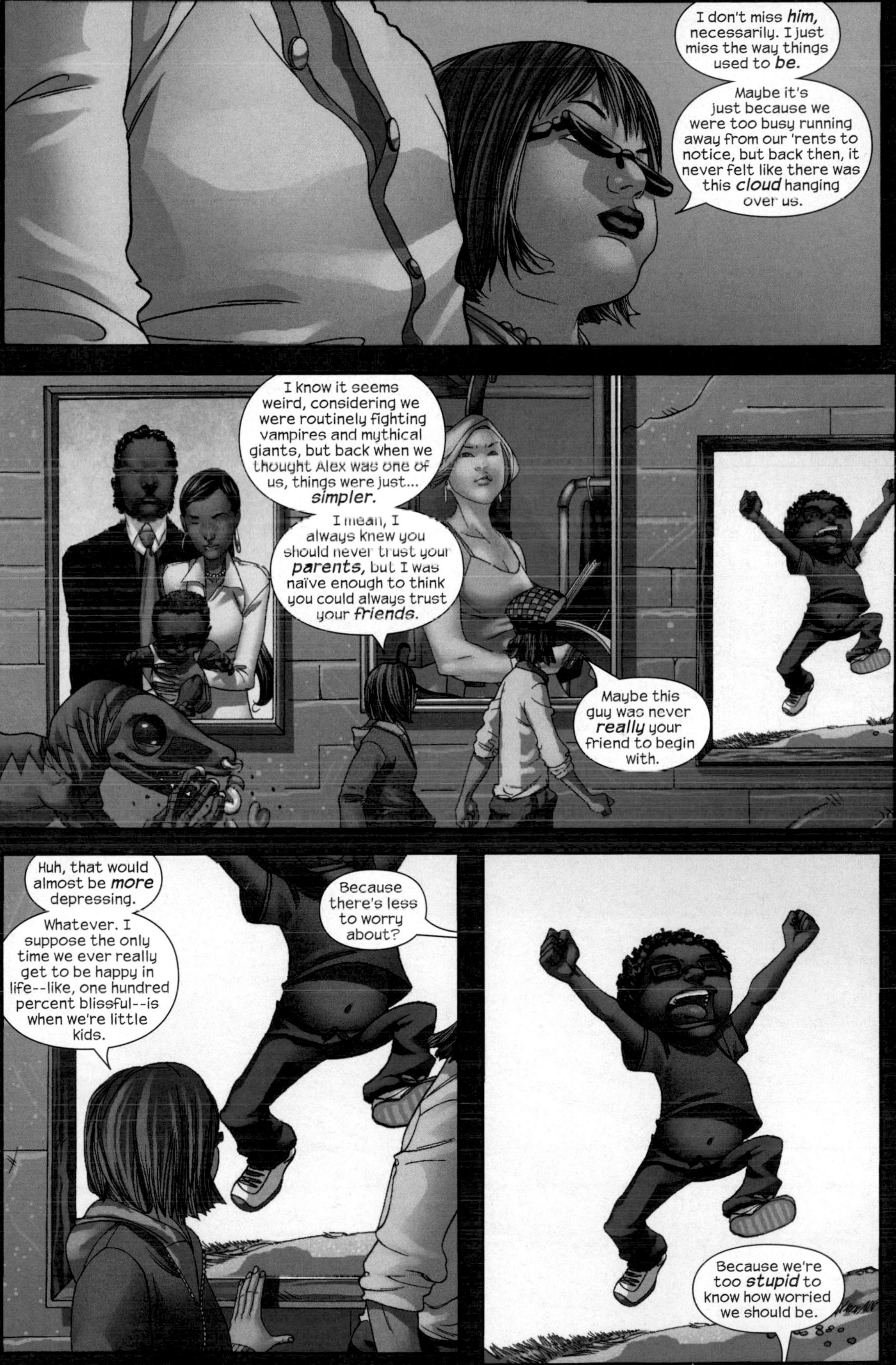

I don't miss *him,* necessarily. I just miss the way things used to *be.*
Maybe it's just because we were too busy running away from our 'rents to notice, but back then, it never felt like there was this *cloud* hanging over us.
I know it seems weird, considering we were routinely fighting vampires and mythical giants, but back when we thought Alex was one of us, things were just... *simpler.*
I mean, I always knew you should never trust your *parents,* but I was naïve enough to think you could always trust your *friends.*
Maybe this guy was never *really* your friend to begin with.
Huh, that would almost be *more* depressing.
Whatever. I suppose the only time we ever really get to be happy in life--like, one hundred percent blissful--is when we're little kids.
Because there's less to worry about?
Because we're too *stupid* to know how worried we should be.

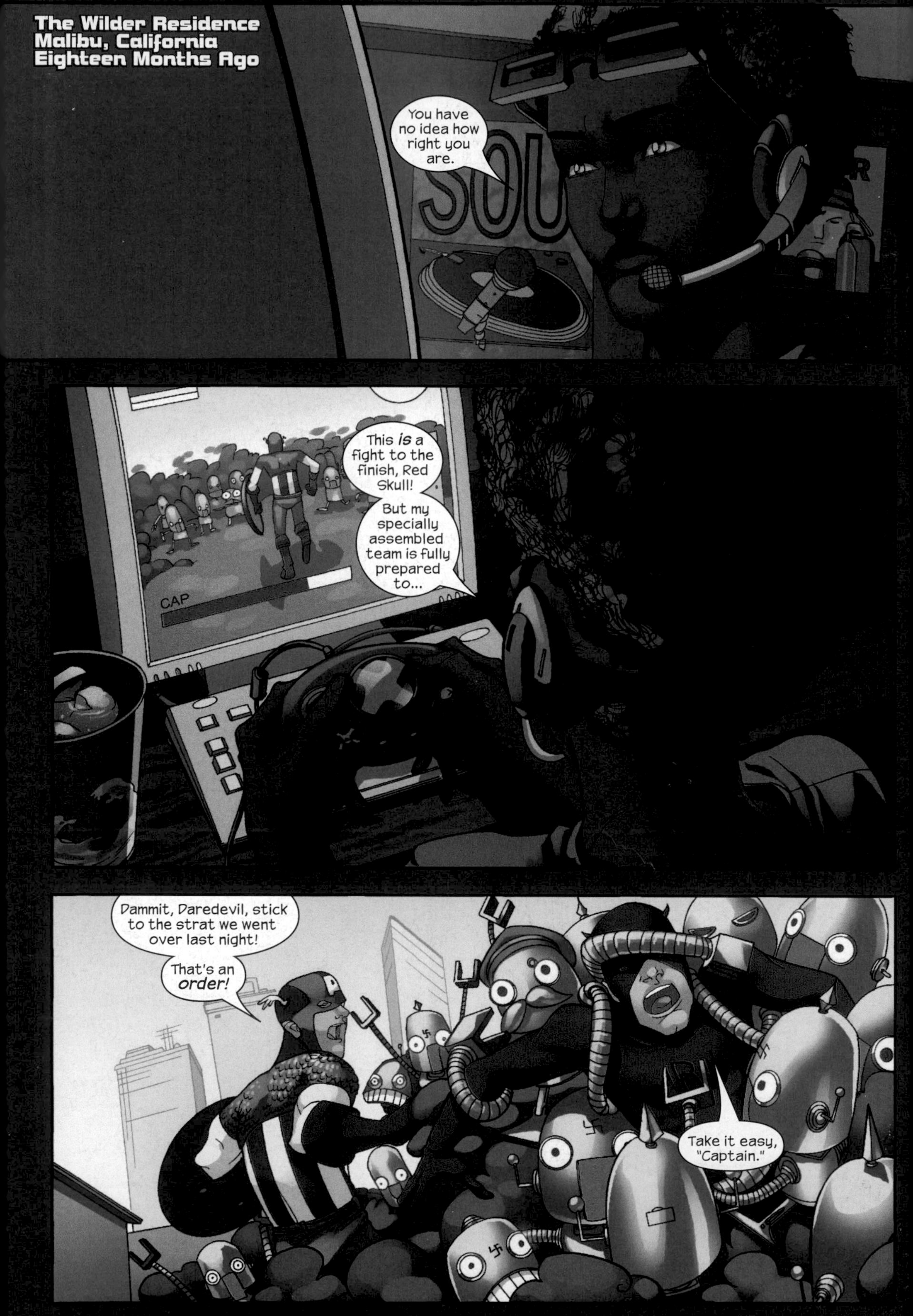
The Wilder Residence
Malibu, California
Eighteen Months Ago
You have no idea how right you are.
This *is* a fight to the finish, Red Skull!
But my specially assembled team is fully prepared to...
CAP
Dammit, Daredevil, stick to the strat we went over last night!
That's an *order!*
Take it easy, "Captain."

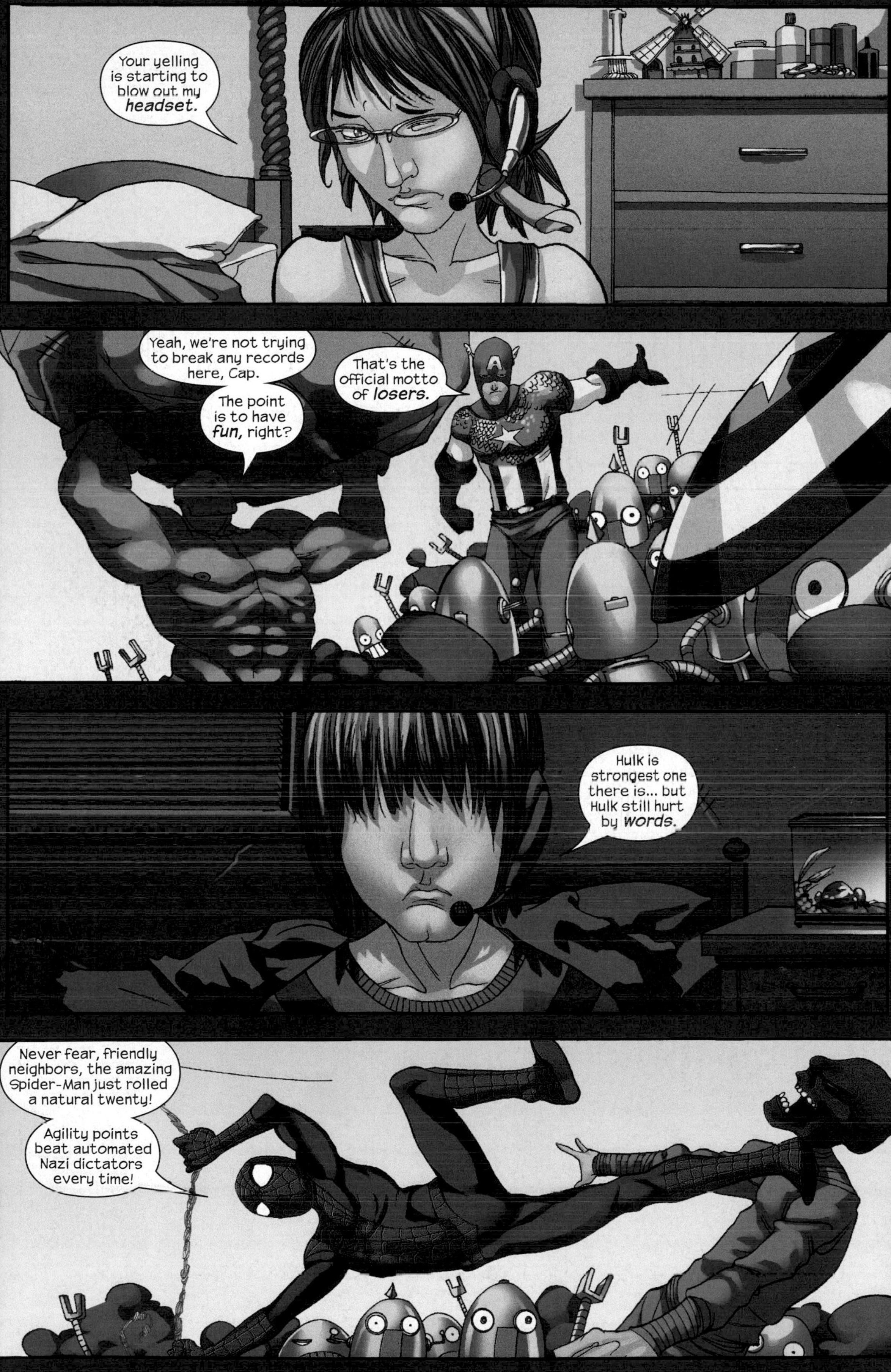
Your yelling is starting to blow out my *headset.*
Yeah, we're not trying to break any records here, Cap.
The point is to have *fun,* right?
That's the official motto of *losers.*
Hulk is strongest one there is... but Hulk still hurt by *words.*
Never fear, friendly neighbors, the amazing Spider-Man just rolled a natural twenty!
Agility points beat automated Nazi dictators every time!

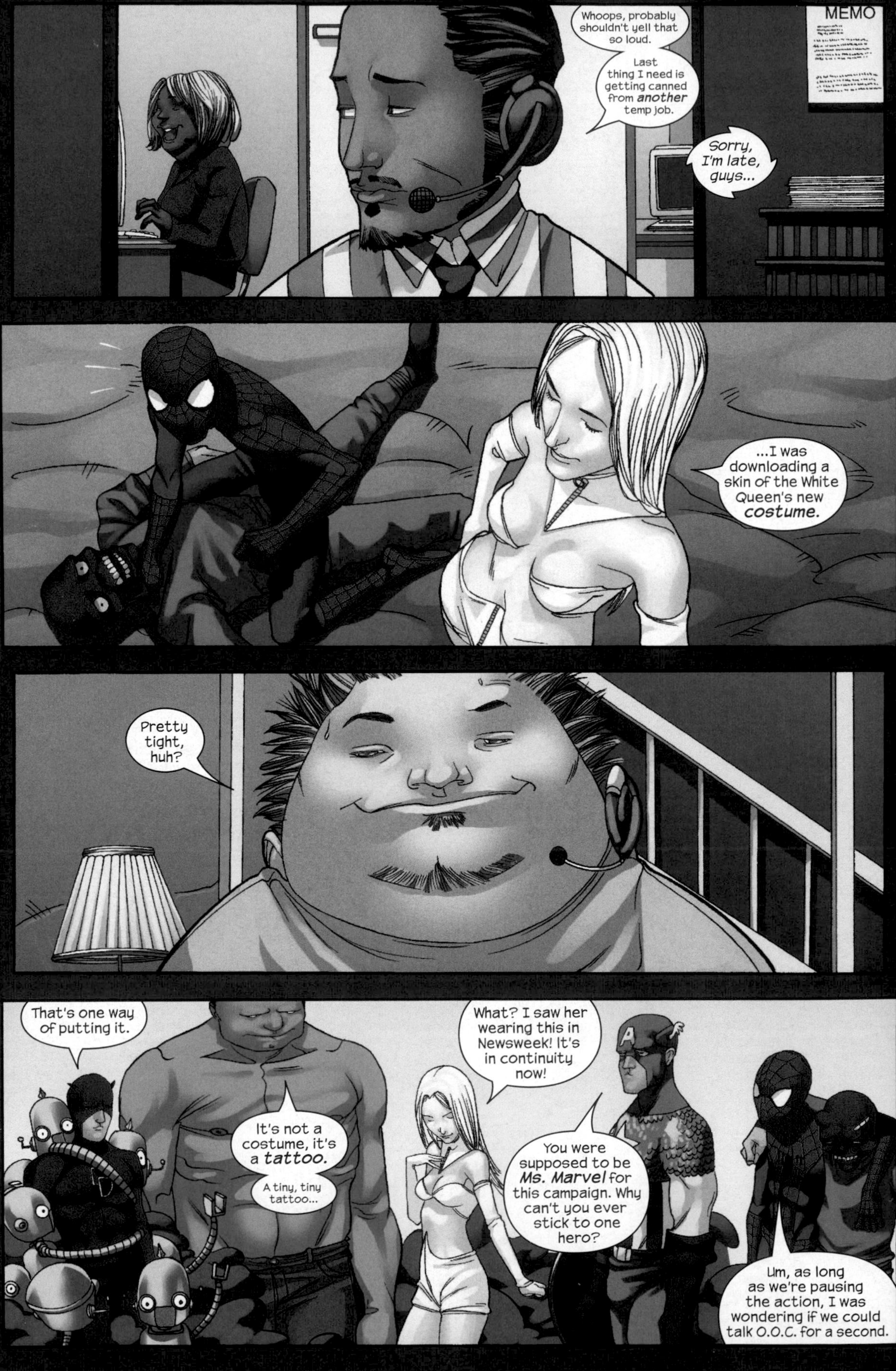
MEMO
Whoops, probably shouldn't yell that so loud.
Last thing I need is getting canned from *another* temp job.
Sorry, I'm late, guys...
...I was downloading a skin of the White Queen's new *costume.*
Pretty tight, huh?
That's one way of putting it.
It's not a costume, it's a *tattoo.*
A tiny, tiny tattoo...
What? I saw her wearing this in Newsweek! It's in continuity now!
You were supposed to be *Ms. Marvel* for this campaign. Why can't you ever stick to one hero?
Um, as long as we're pausing the action, I was wondering if we could talk O.O.C. for a second.

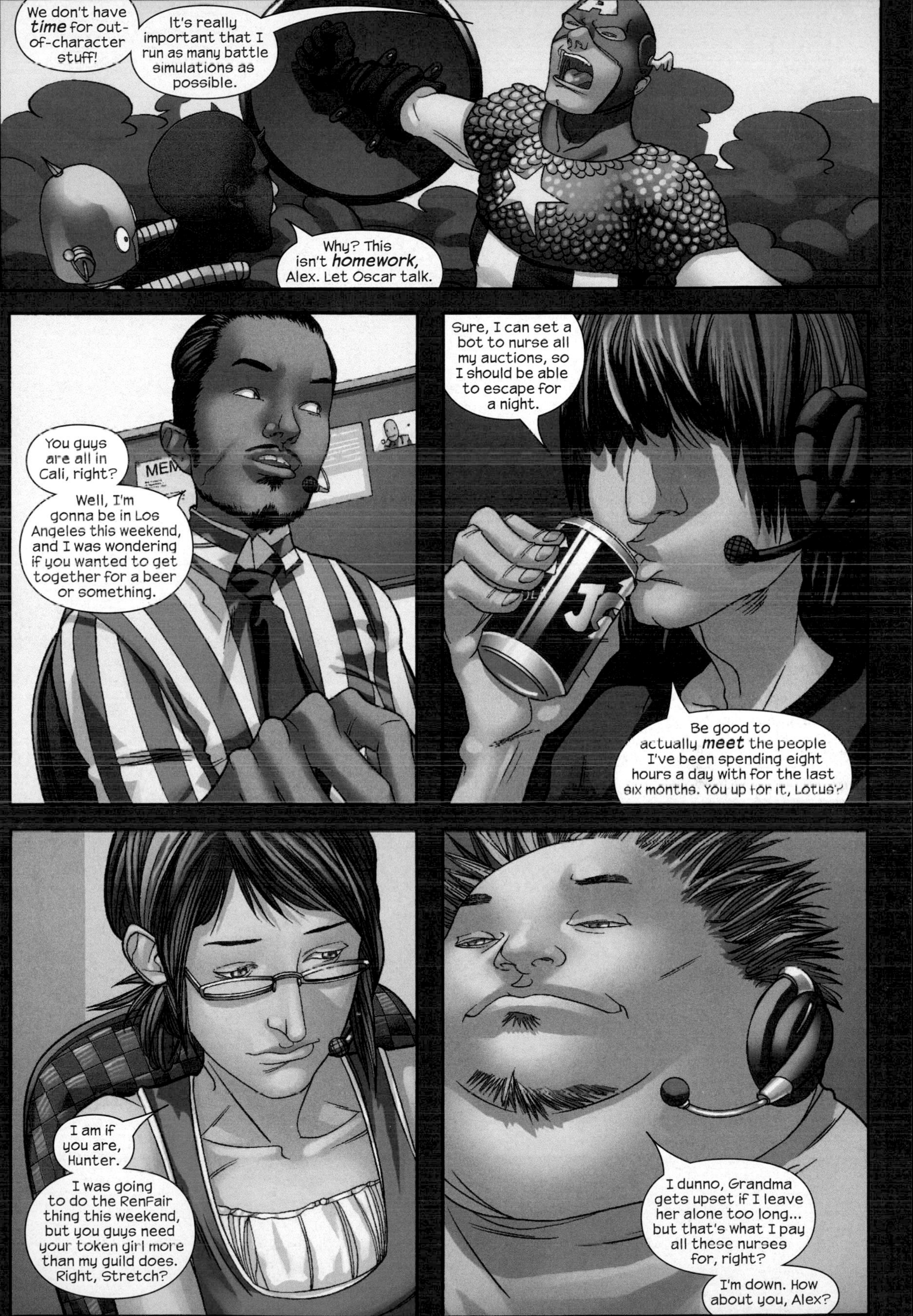
We don't have *time* for out-of-character stuff!
It's really important that I run as many battle simulations as possible.
Why? This isn't *homework*, Alex. Let Oscar talk.
You guys are all in Cali, right?
Well, I'm gonna be in Los Angeles this weekend, and I was wondering if you wanted to get together for a beer or something.
Sure, I can set a bot to nurse all my auctions, so I should be able to escape for a night.
Be good to actually *meet* the people I've been spending eight hours a day with for the last six months. You up for it, Lotus?
I am if you are, Hunter.
I was going to do the RenFair thing this weekend, but you guys need your token girl more than my guild does. Right, Stretch?
I dunno, Grandma gets upset if I leave her alone too long... but that's what I pay all these nurses for, right?
I'm down. How about you, Alex?

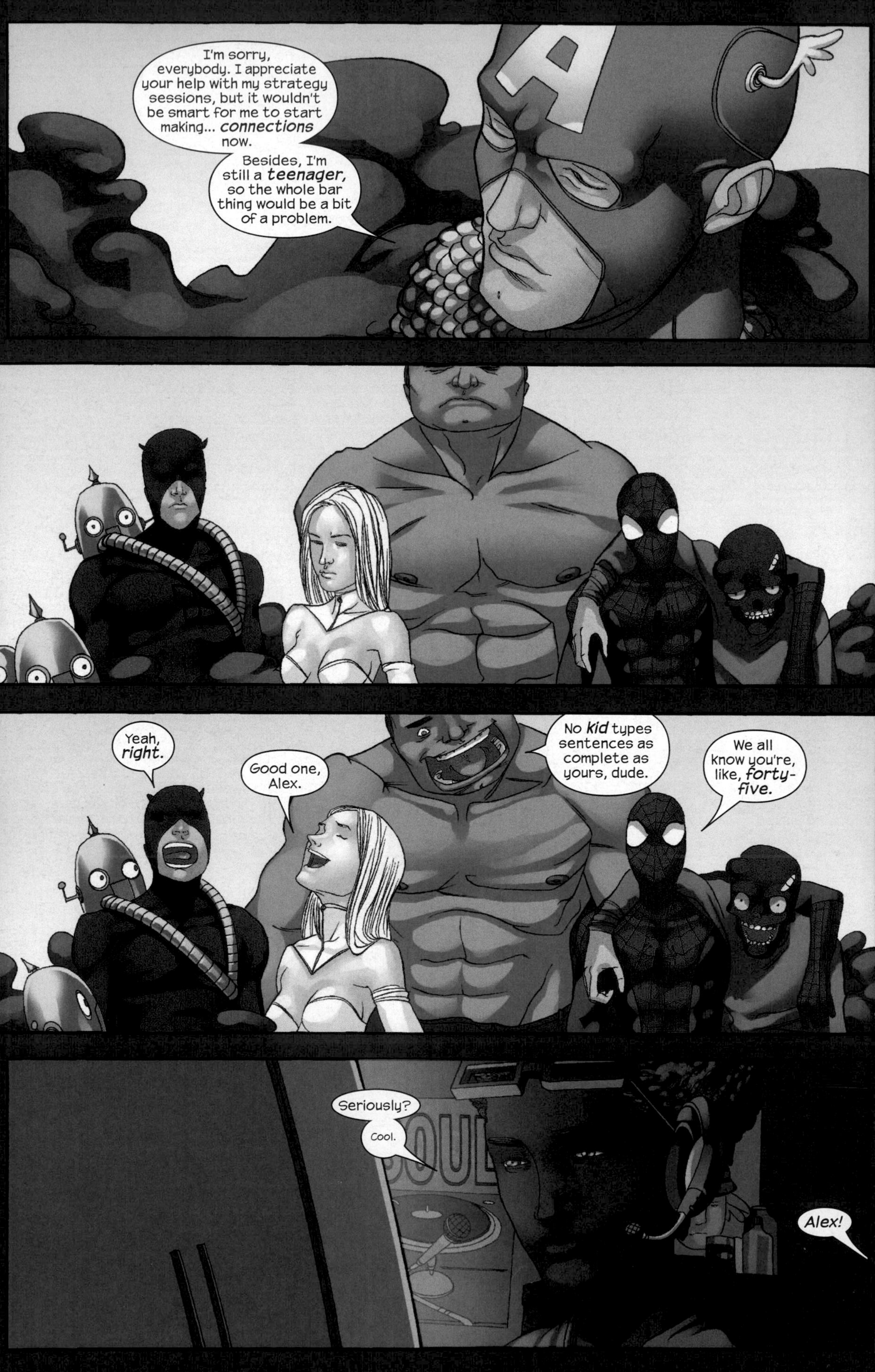
I'm sorry, everybody. I appreciate your help with my strategy sessions, but it wouldn't be smart for me to start making... connections now.
Besides, I'm still a teenager, so the whole bar thing would be a bit of a problem.
Yeah, right.
Good one, Alex.
No kid types sentences as complete as yours, dude.
We all know you're, like, forty-five.
Seriously?
Cool.
Alex!

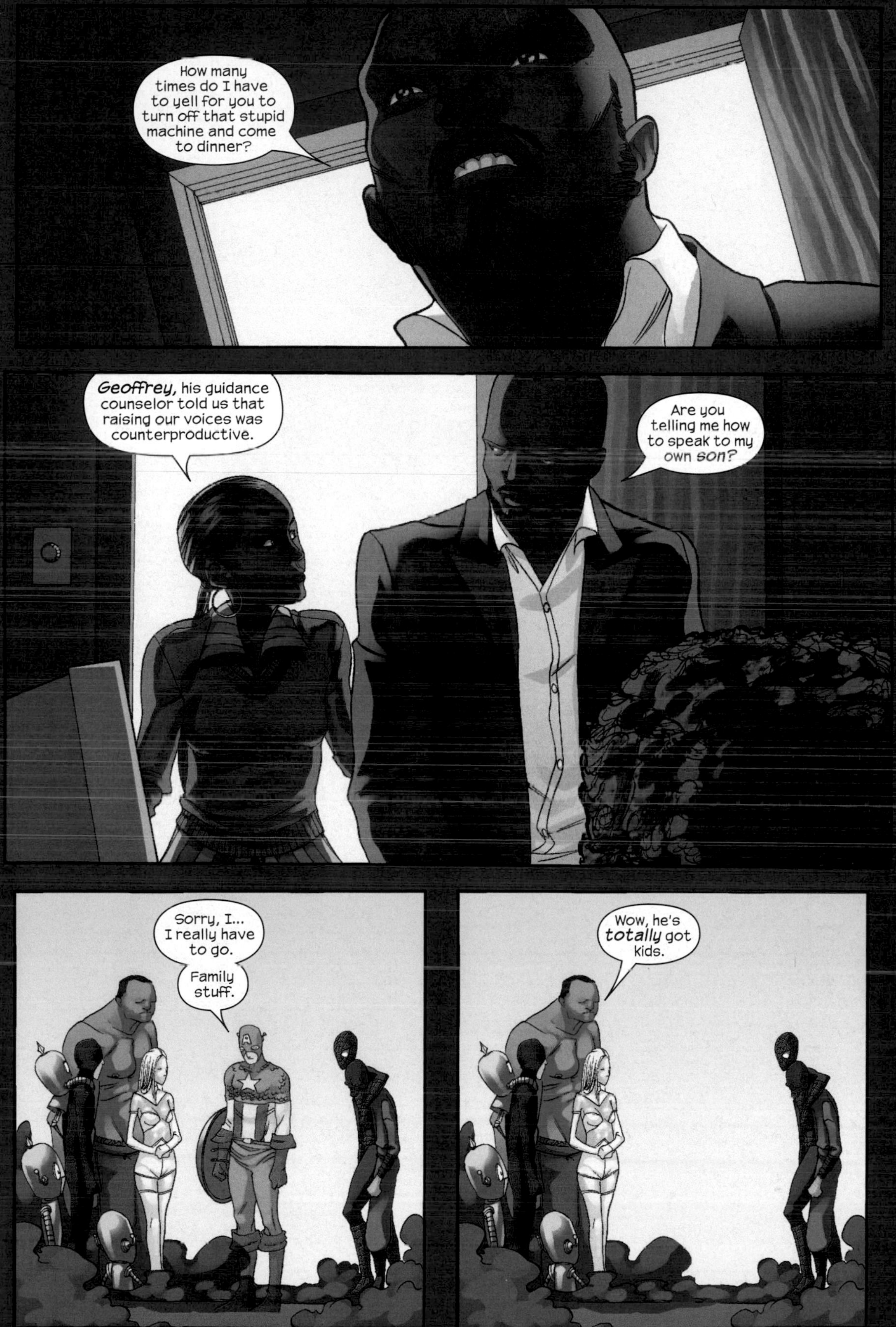
How many times do I have to yell for you to turn off that stupid machine and come to dinner?
Geoffrey, his guidance counselor told us that raising our voices was counterproductive.
Are you telling me how to speak to my own son?
Sorry, I... I really have to go.
Family stuff.
Wow, he's totally got kids.

Los Angeles
Months Later

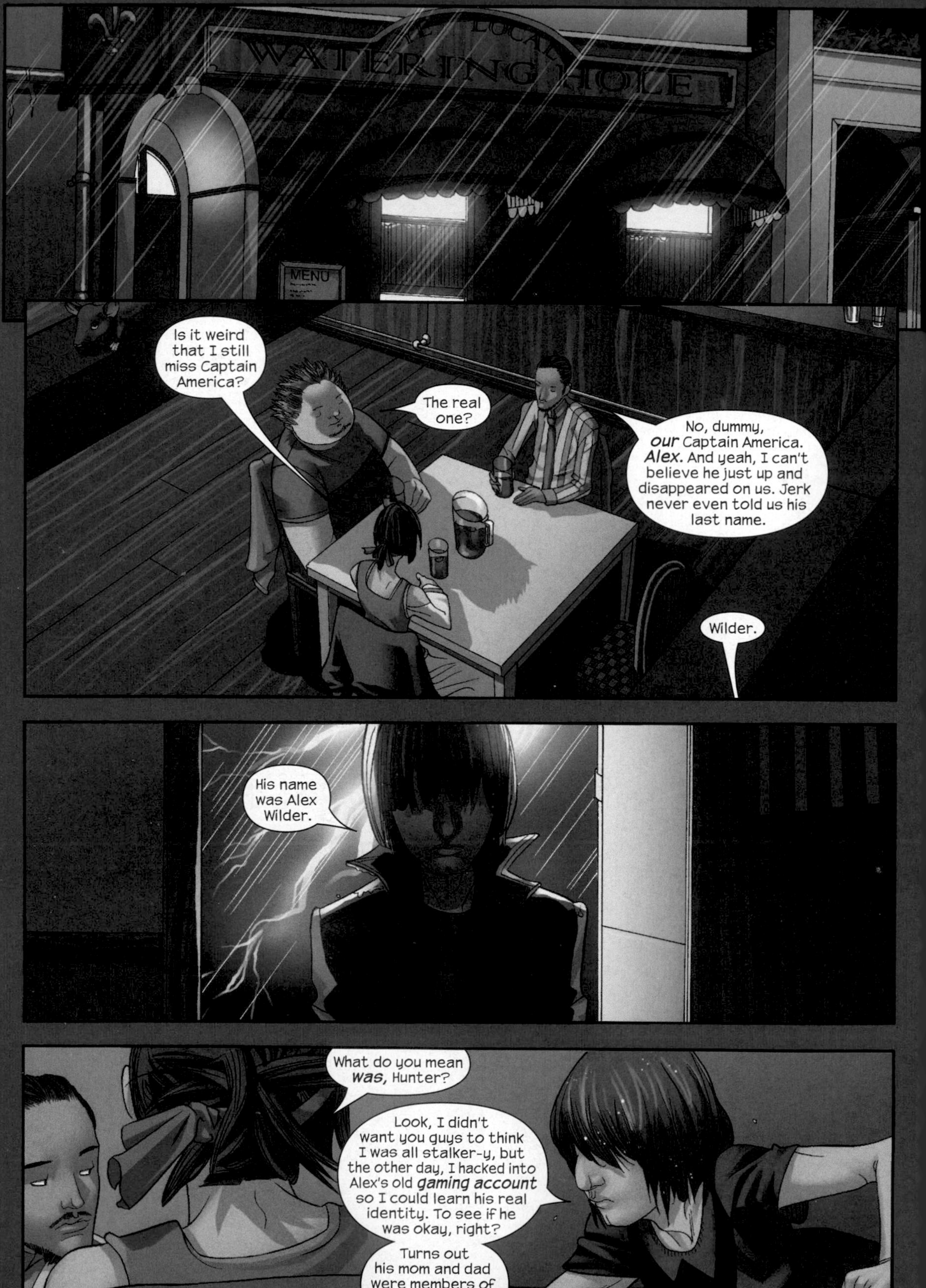

THE LOCAL WATERING HOLE
MENU
Is it weird that I still miss Captain America?
The real one?
No, dummy, *our* Captain America. *Alex.* And yeah, I can't believe he just up and disappeared on us. Jerk never even told us his last name.
Wilder.
His name was Alex Wilder.
What do you mean *was,* Hunter?
Look, I didn't want you guys to think I was all stalker-y, but the other day, I hacked into Alex's old *gaming account* so I could learn his real identity. To see if he was okay, right?
Turns out his mom and dad were members of this group called *The Pride...*

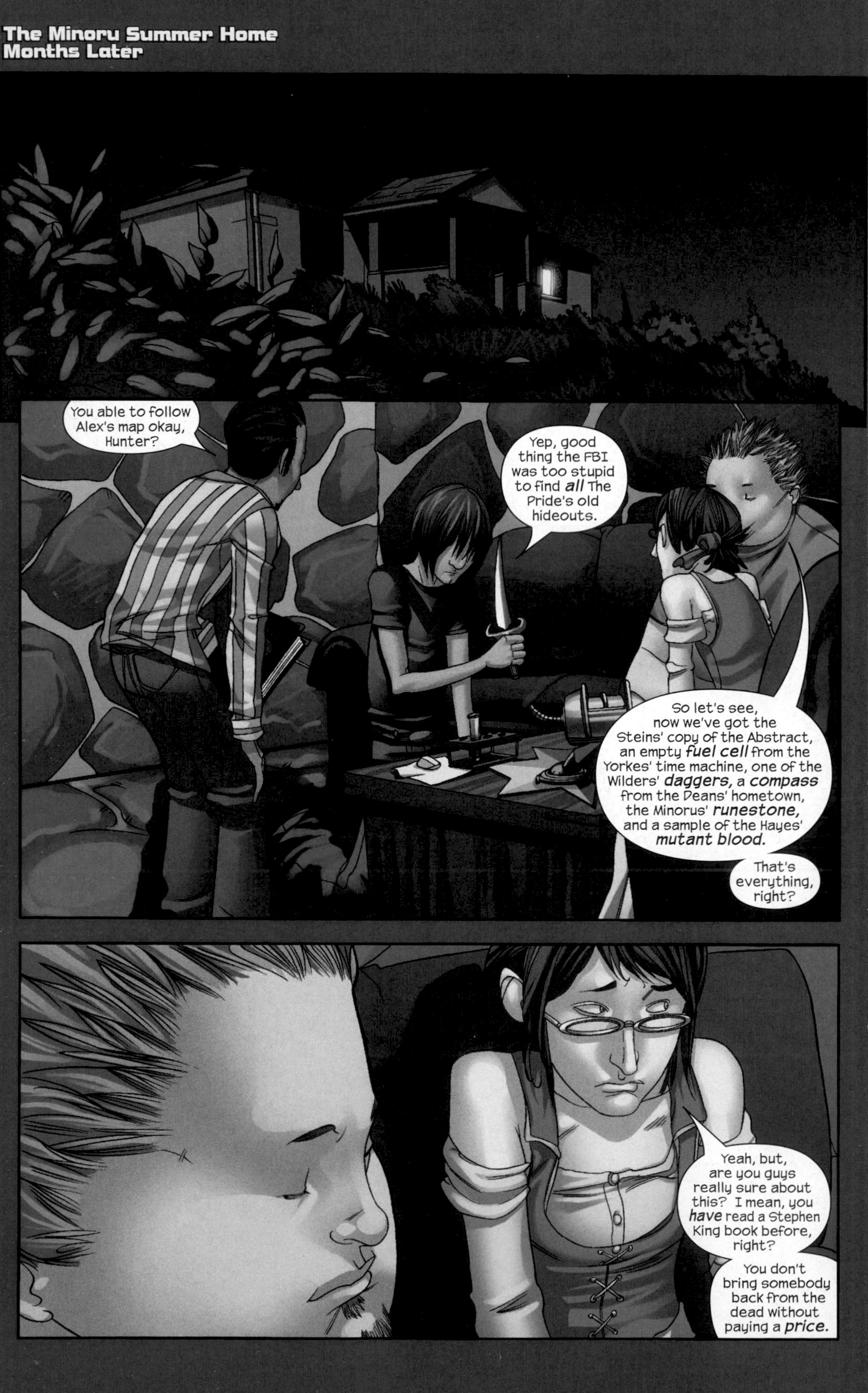
The Minoru Summer Home
Months Later
You able to follow Alex's map okay, Hunter?
Yep, good thing the FBI was too stupid to find *all* The Pride's old hideouts.
So let's see, now we've got the Steins' copy of the Abstract, an empty *fuel cell* from the Yorkes' time machine, one of the Wilders' *daggers*, a *compass* from the Deans' hometown, the Minorus' *runestone*, and a sample of the Hayes' *mutant blood*.
That's everything, right?
Yeah, but, are you guys really sure about this? I mean, you *have* read a Stephen King book before, right?
You don't bring somebody back from the dead without paying a *price*.

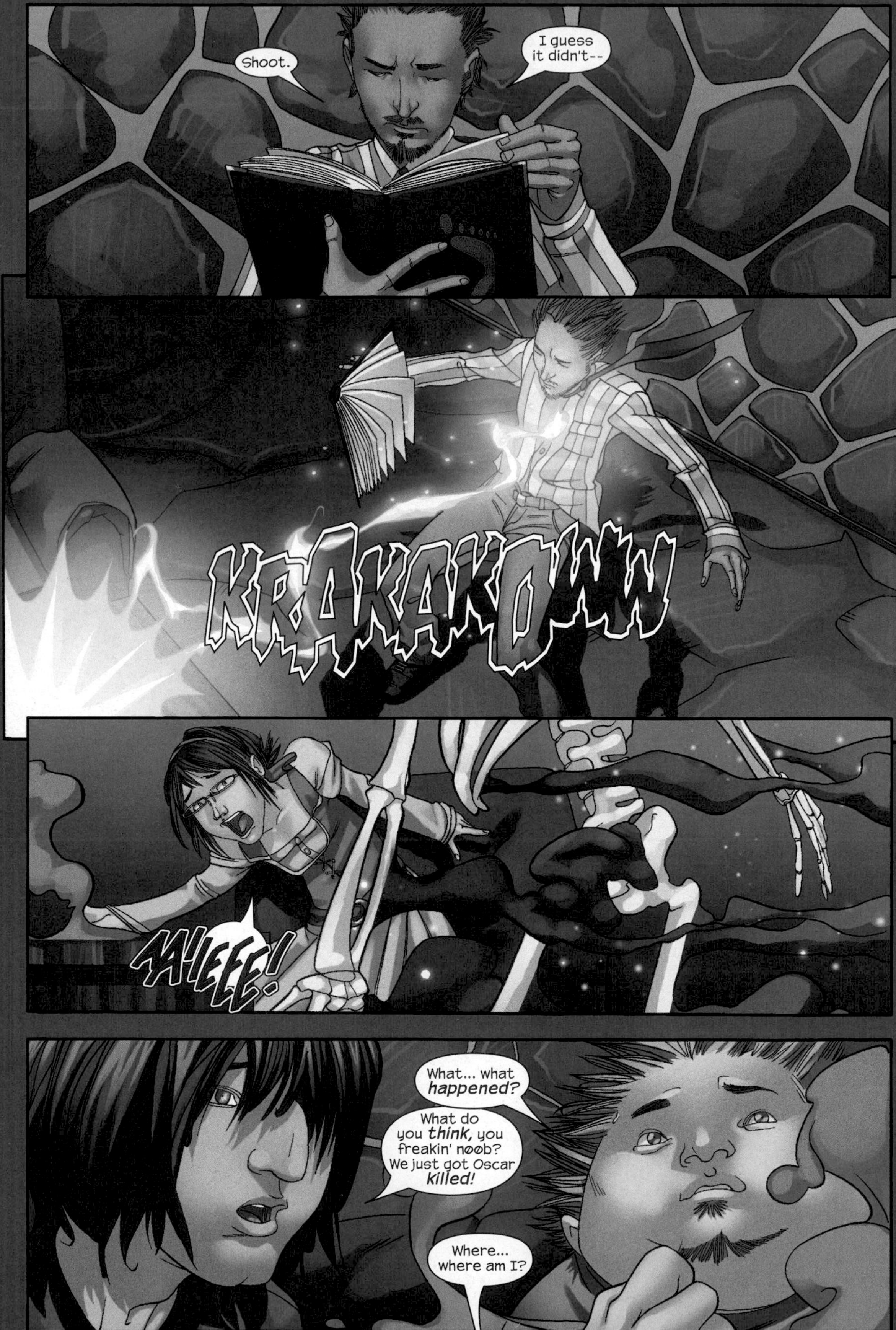
Shoot.
I guess it didn't--
KRAKAKOWW
AAIEEE!
What... what *happened*?
What do you ***think,*** you freakin' nøøb? We just got Oscar ***killed!***
Where... where am I?

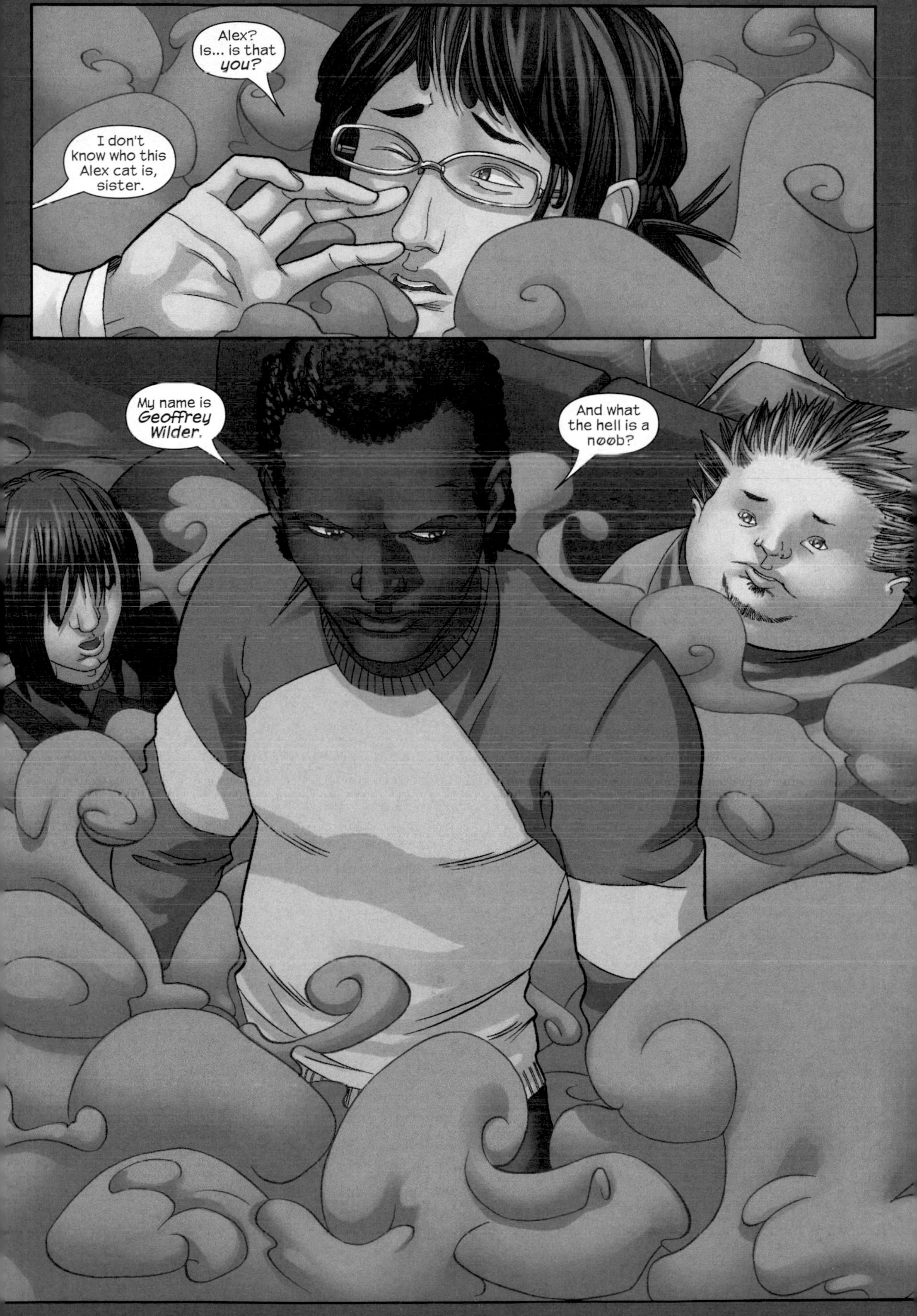
Alex? Is... is that *you?*
I don't know who this Alex cat is, sister.
My name is *Geoffrey Wilder*.
And what the hell is a nøøb?

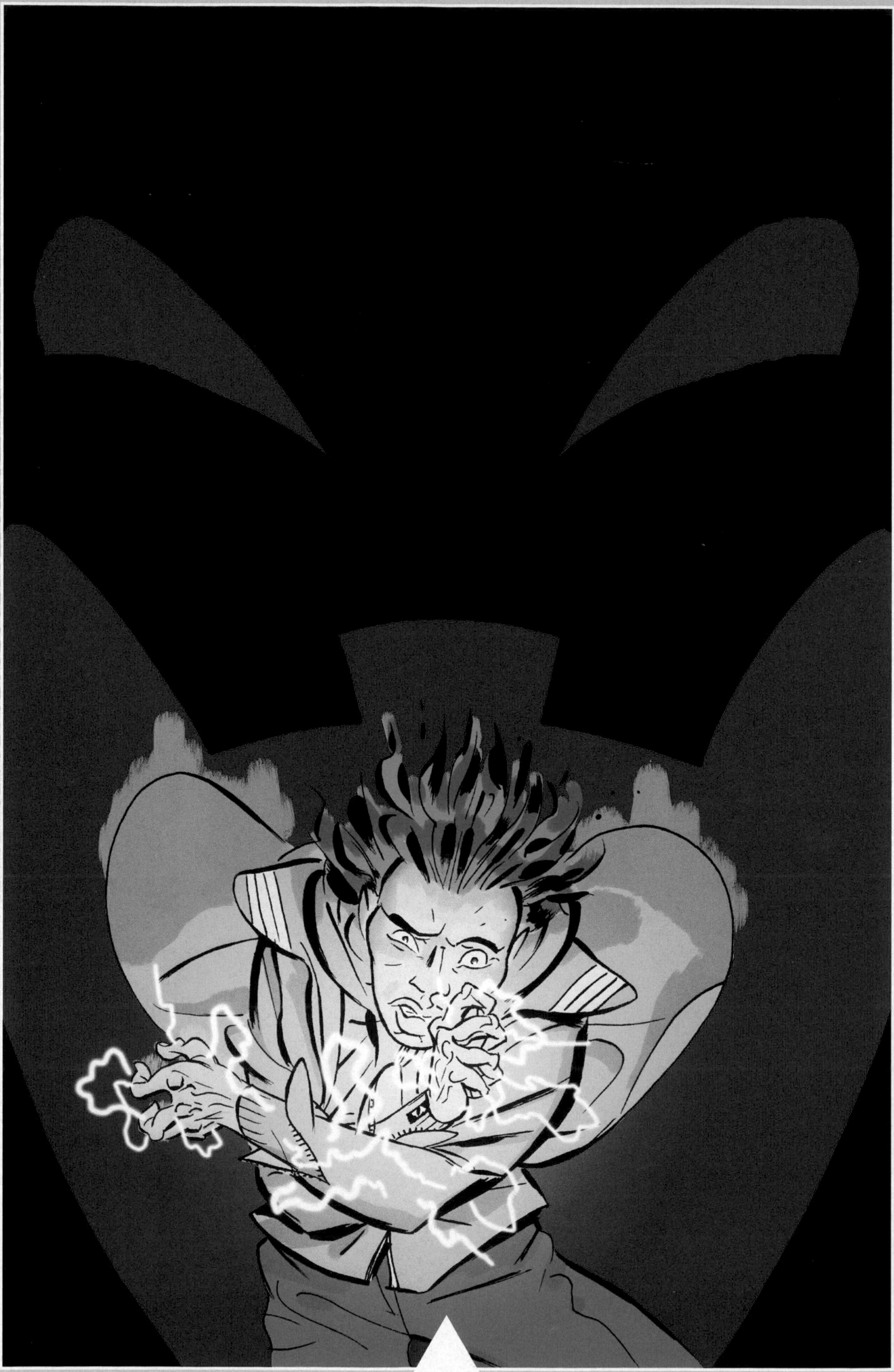

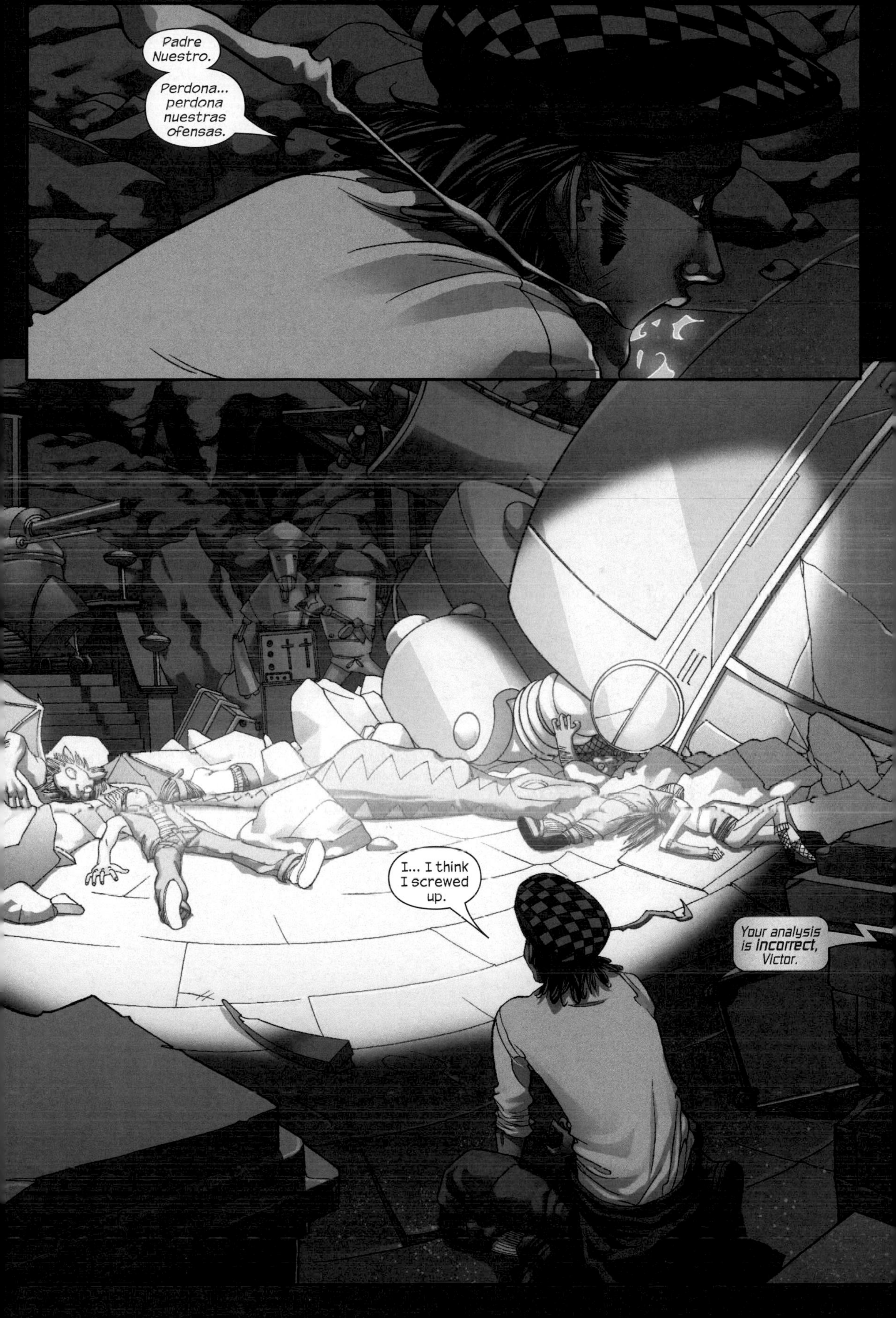

Padre Nuestro.
Perdona... perdona nuestras ofensas.
I... I think I screwed up.
Your analysis is incorrect, Victor.

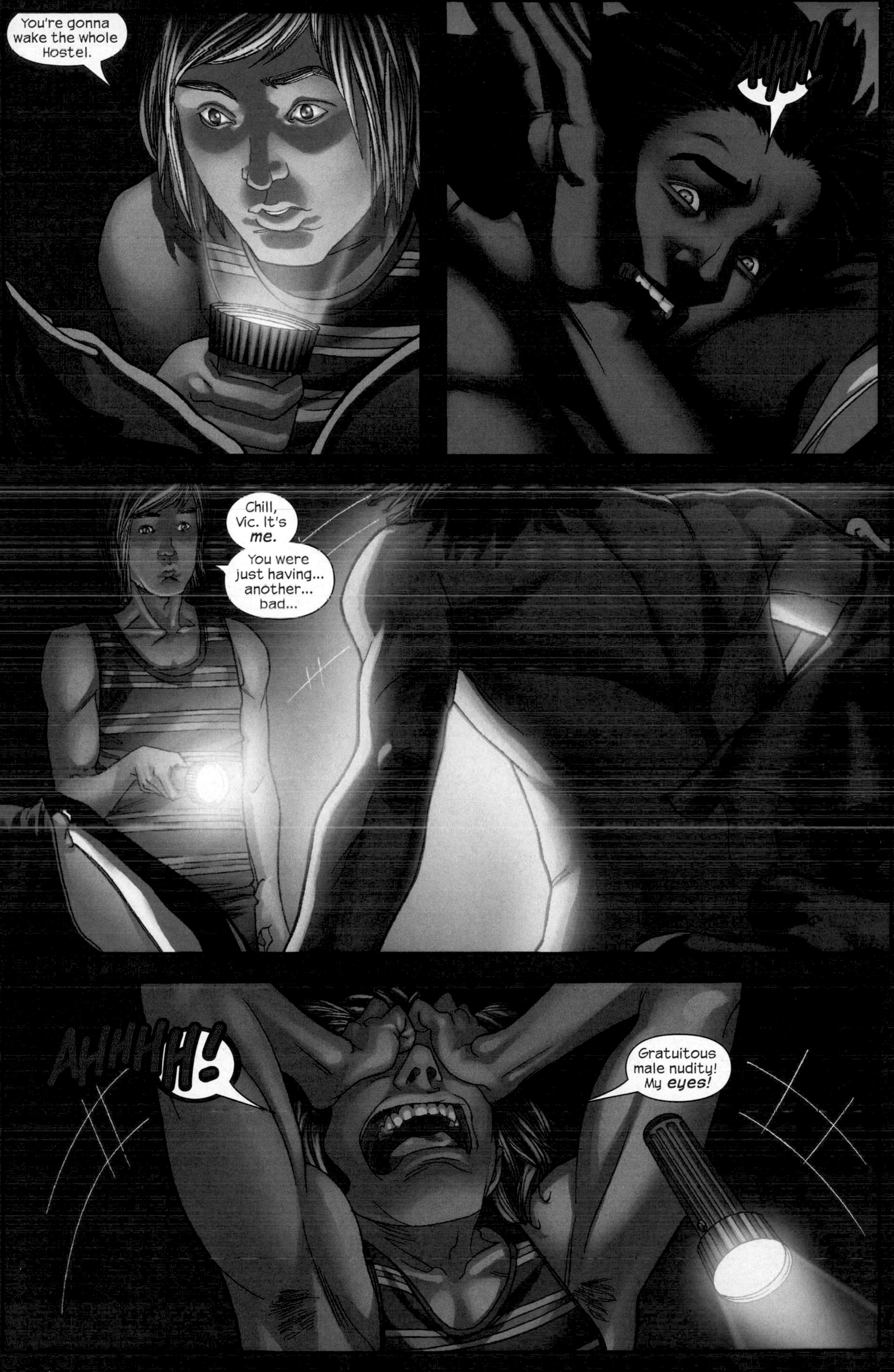
You're gonna wake the whole Hostel.
AHHH!
Chill, Vic. It's *me.*
You were just having... another... bad...
AHHHH!
Gratuitous male nudity! My *eyes!*

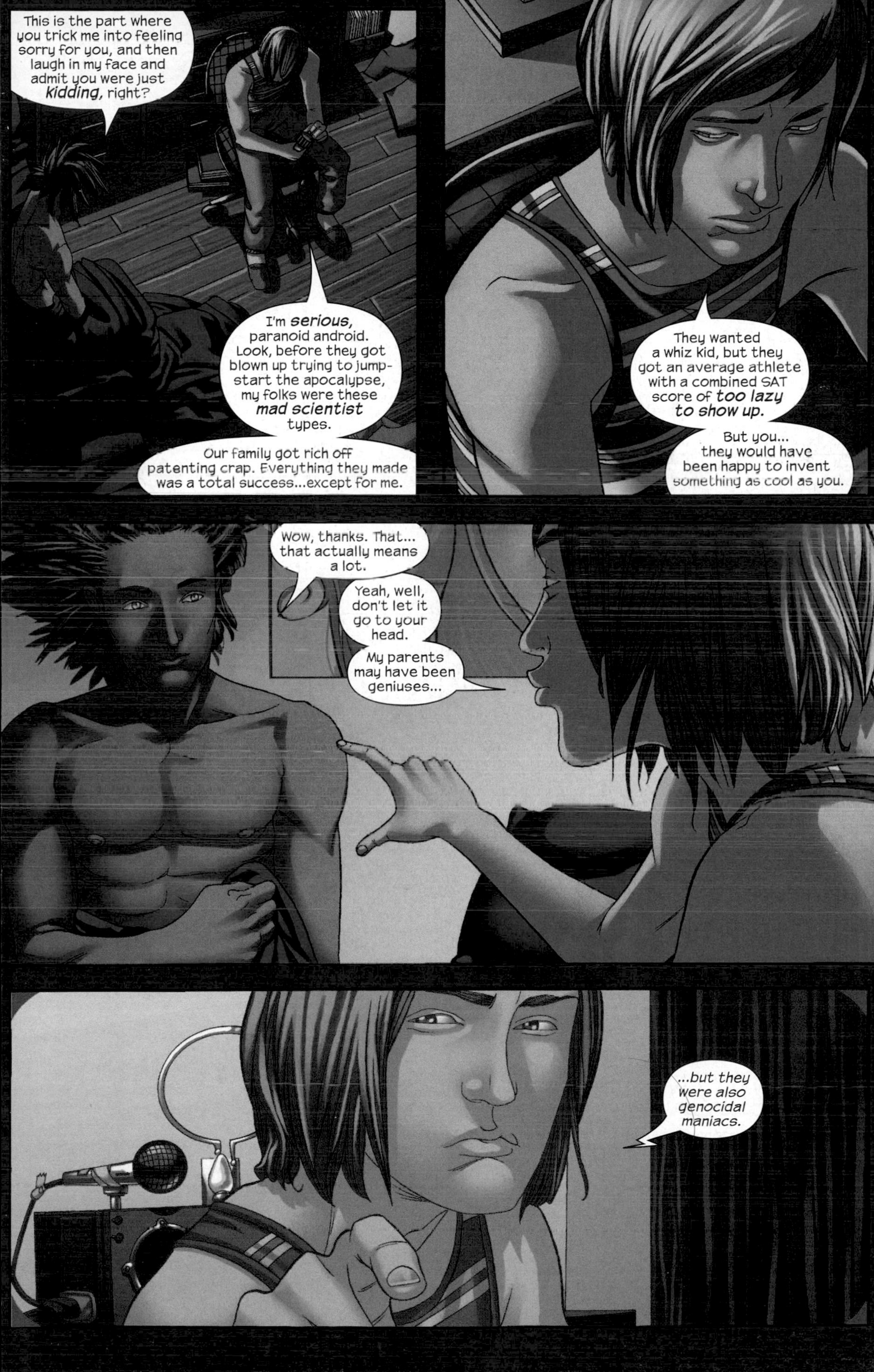

This is the part where you trick me into feeling sorry for you, and then laugh in my face and admit you were just *kidding,* right?
I'm *serious,* paranoid android. Look, before they got blown up trying to jump-start the apocalypse, my folks were these *mad scientist* types.
Our family got rich off patenting crap. Everything they made was a total success...except for me.
They wanted a whiz kid, but they got an average athlete with a combined SAT score of *too lazy to show up.*
But you... they would have been happy to invent something as cool as you.
Wow, thanks. That... that actually means a lot.
Yeah, well, don't let it go to your head.
My parents may have been geniuses...
...but they were also genocidal maniacs.

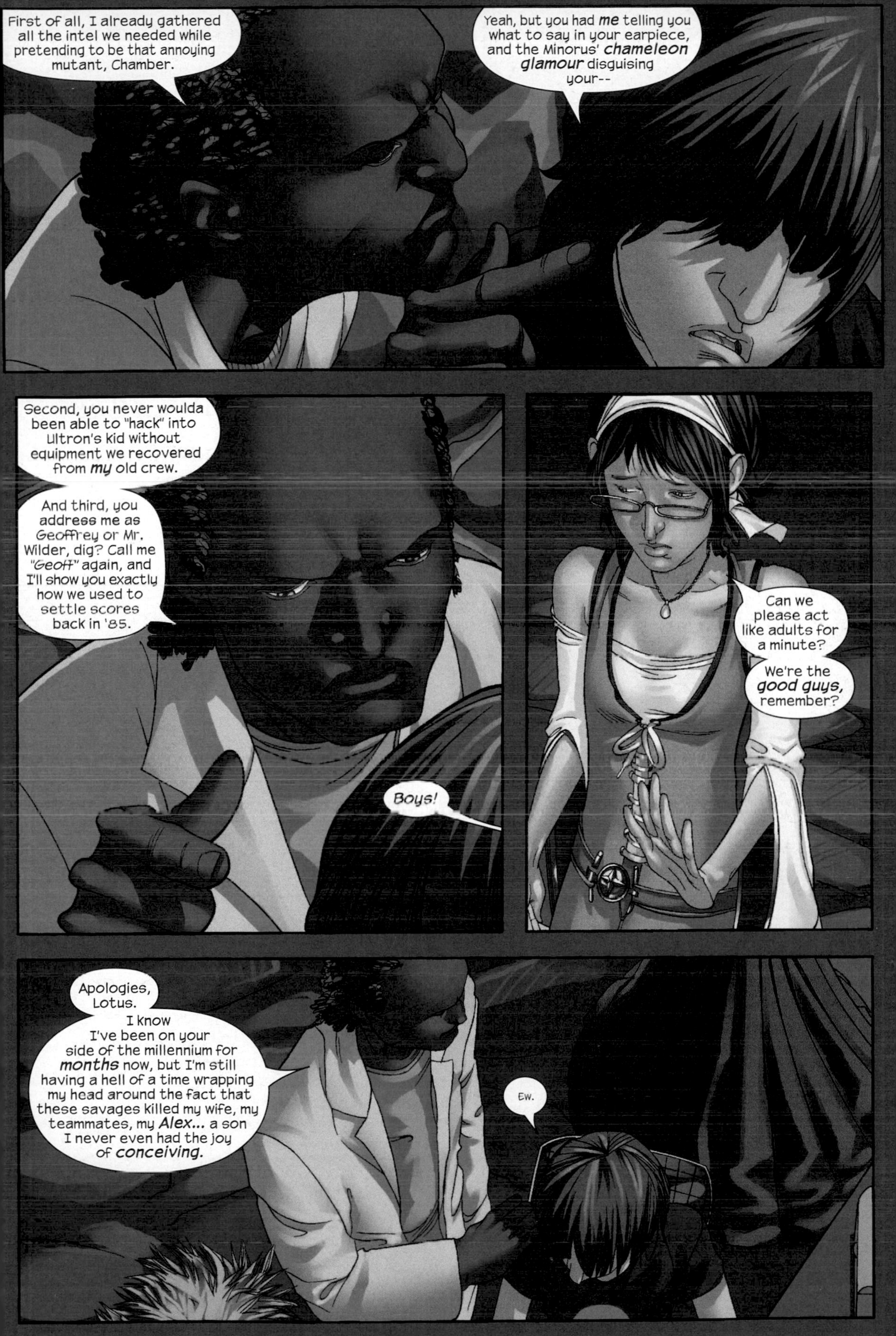
First of all, I already gathered all the intel we needed while pretending to be that annoying mutant, Chamber.
Yeah, but you had *me* telling you what to say in your earpiece, and the Minorus' ***chameleon glamour*** disguising your--
Second, you never woulda been able to "hack" into Ultron's kid without equipment we recovered from *my* old crew.
And third, you address me as Geoffrey or Mr. Wilder, dig? Call me *"Geoff"* again, and I'll show you exactly how we used to settle scores back in '85.
Can we please act like adults for a minute?
We're the ***good guys,*** remember?
Boys!
Apologies, Lotus.
I know I've been on your side of the millennium for *months* now, but I'm still having a hell of a time wrapping my head around the fact that these savages killed my wife, my teammates, my *Alex...* a son I never even had the joy of ***conceiving.***
Ew.

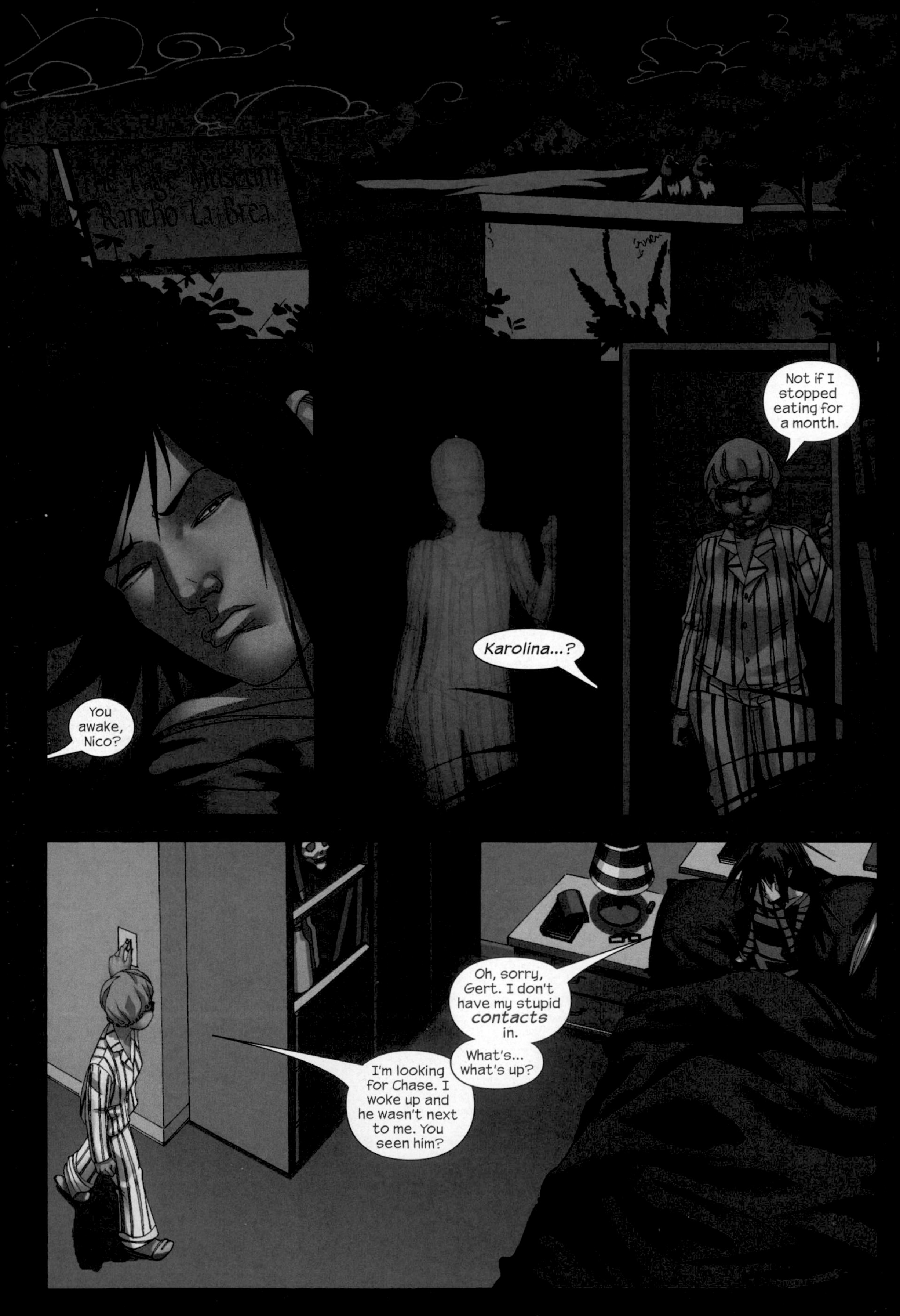

You awake, Nico?
Karolina...?
Not if I stopped eating for a month.
Oh, sorry, Gert. I don't have my stupid *contacts* in.
What's... what's up?
I'm looking for Chase. I woke up and he wasn't next to me. You seen him?

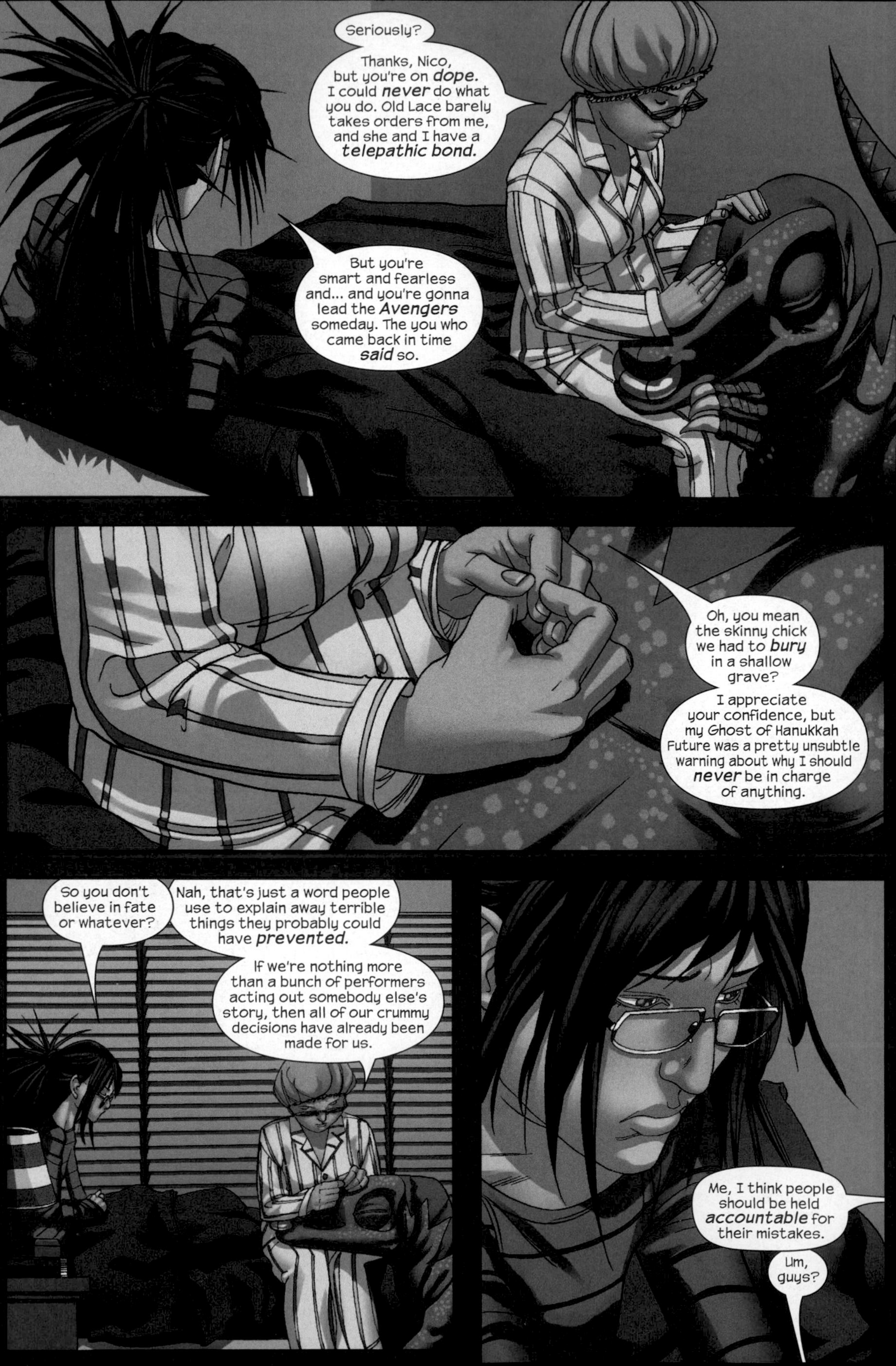
Seriously?
Thanks, Nico, but you're on dope. I could never do what you do. Old Lace barely takes orders from me, and she and I have a telepathic bond.
But you're smart and fearless and... and you're gonna lead the Avengers someday. The you who came back in time said so.
Oh, you mean the skinny chick we had to bury in a shallow grave?
I appreciate your confidence, but my Ghost of Hanukkah Future was a pretty unsubtle warning about why I should never be in charge of anything.
So you don't believe in fate or whatever?
Nah, that's just a word people use to explain away terrible things they probably could have prevented.
If we're nothing more than a bunch of performers acting out somebody else's story, then all of our crummy decisions have already been made for us.
Me, I think people should be held accountable for their mistakes.
Um, guys?

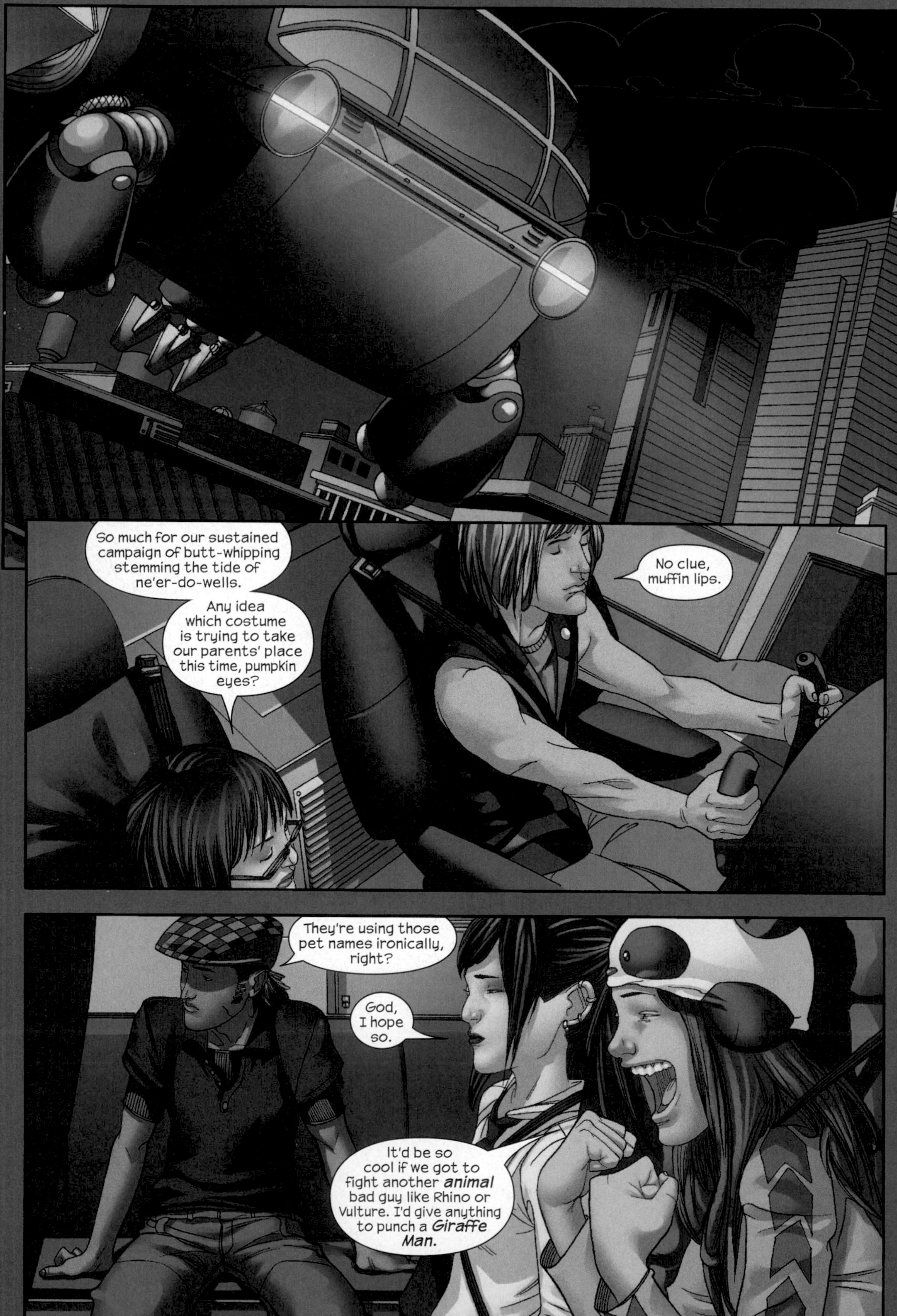
So much for our sustained campaign of butt-whipping stemming the tide of ne'er-do-wells.
Any idea which costume is trying to take our parents' place this time, pumpkin eyes?
No clue, muffin lips.
They're using those pet names ironically, right?
God, I hope so.
It'd be so cool if we got to fight another *animal* bad guy like Rhino or Vulture. I'd give anything to punch a *Giraffe Man*.

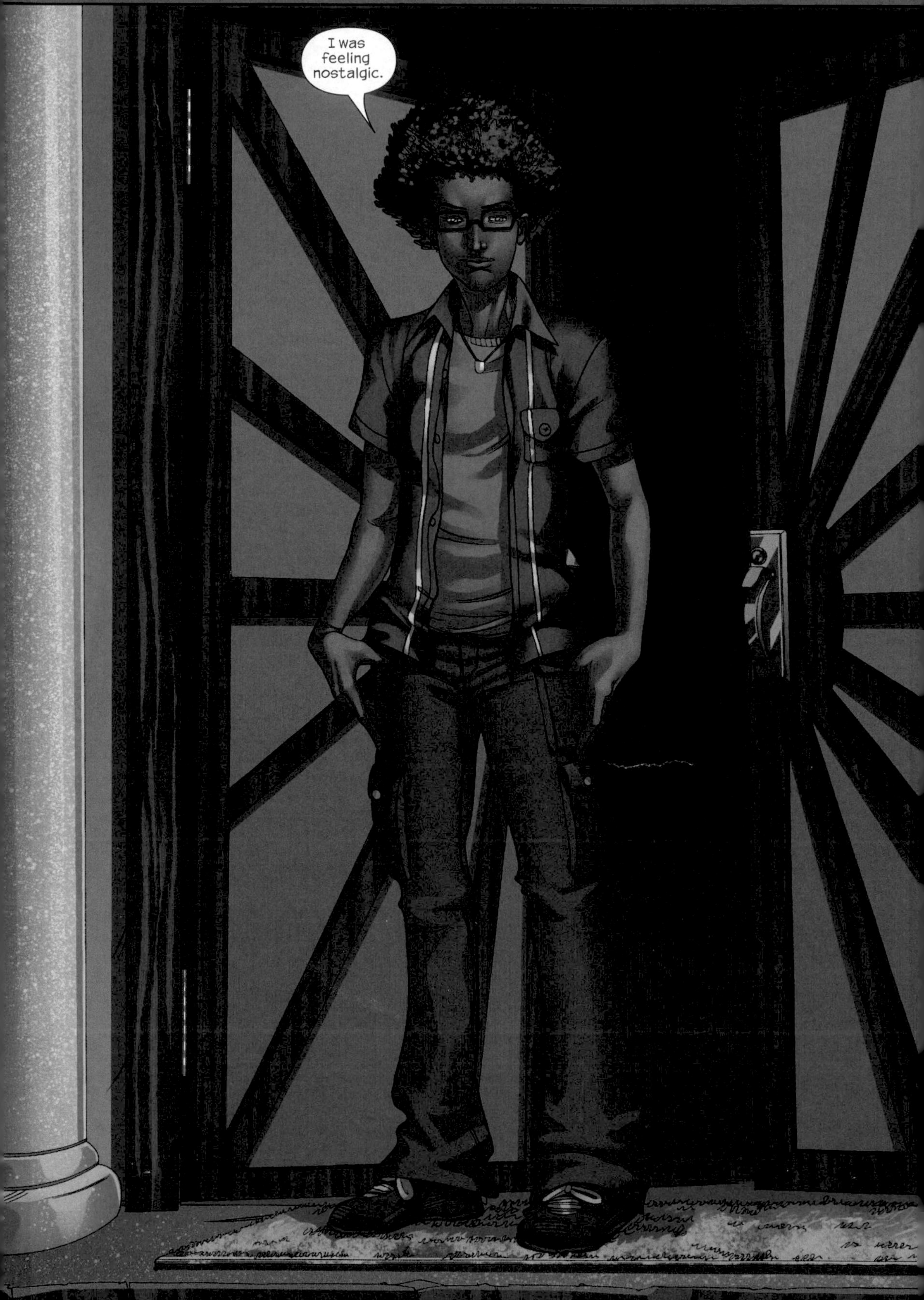
I was feeling nostalgic.

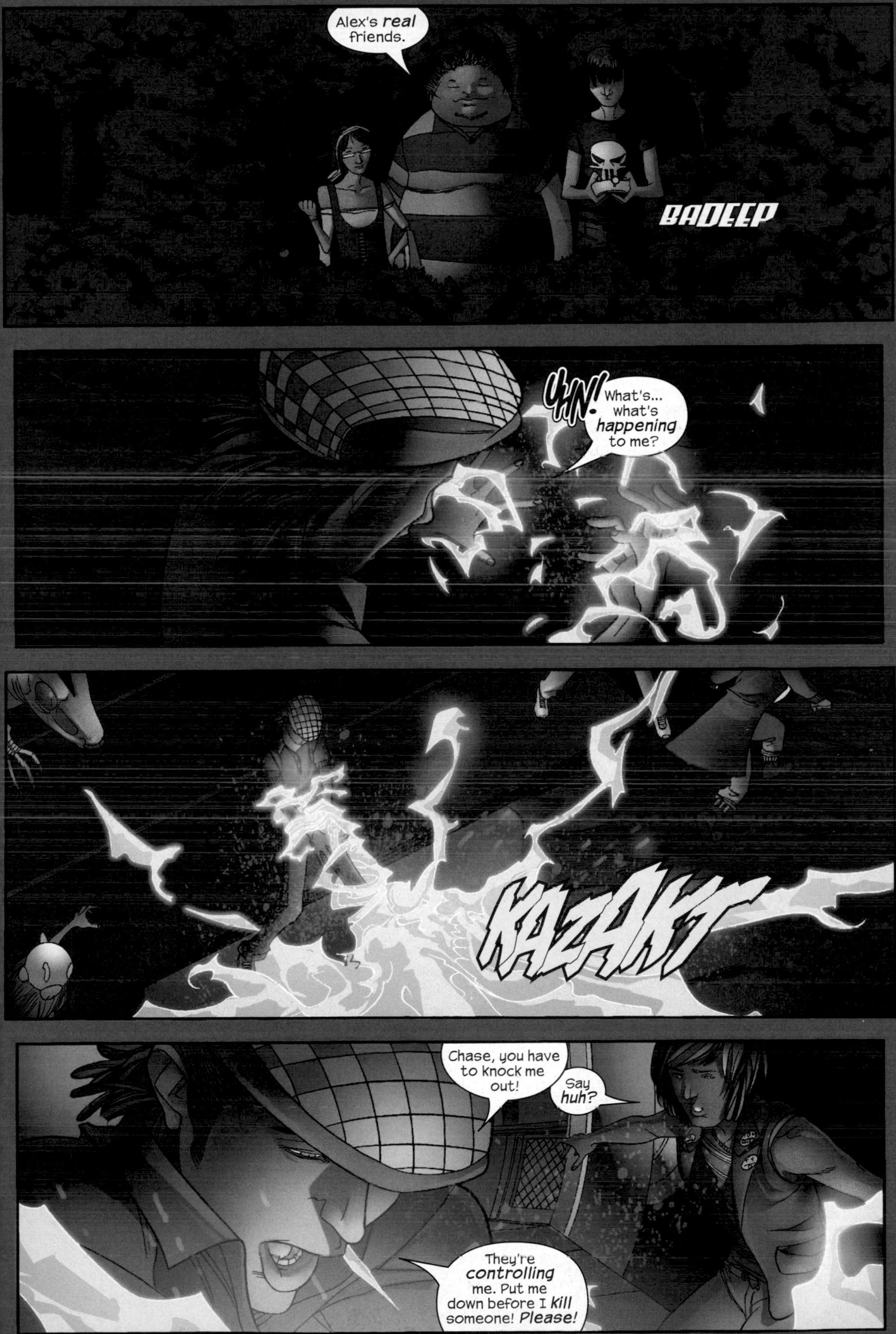
Alex's *real* friends.
BADEEP
UHN! What's... what's *happening* to me?
KAZAK!
Chase, you have to knock me out!
Say *huh*?
They're *controlling* me. Put me down before I *kill* someone! *Please!*

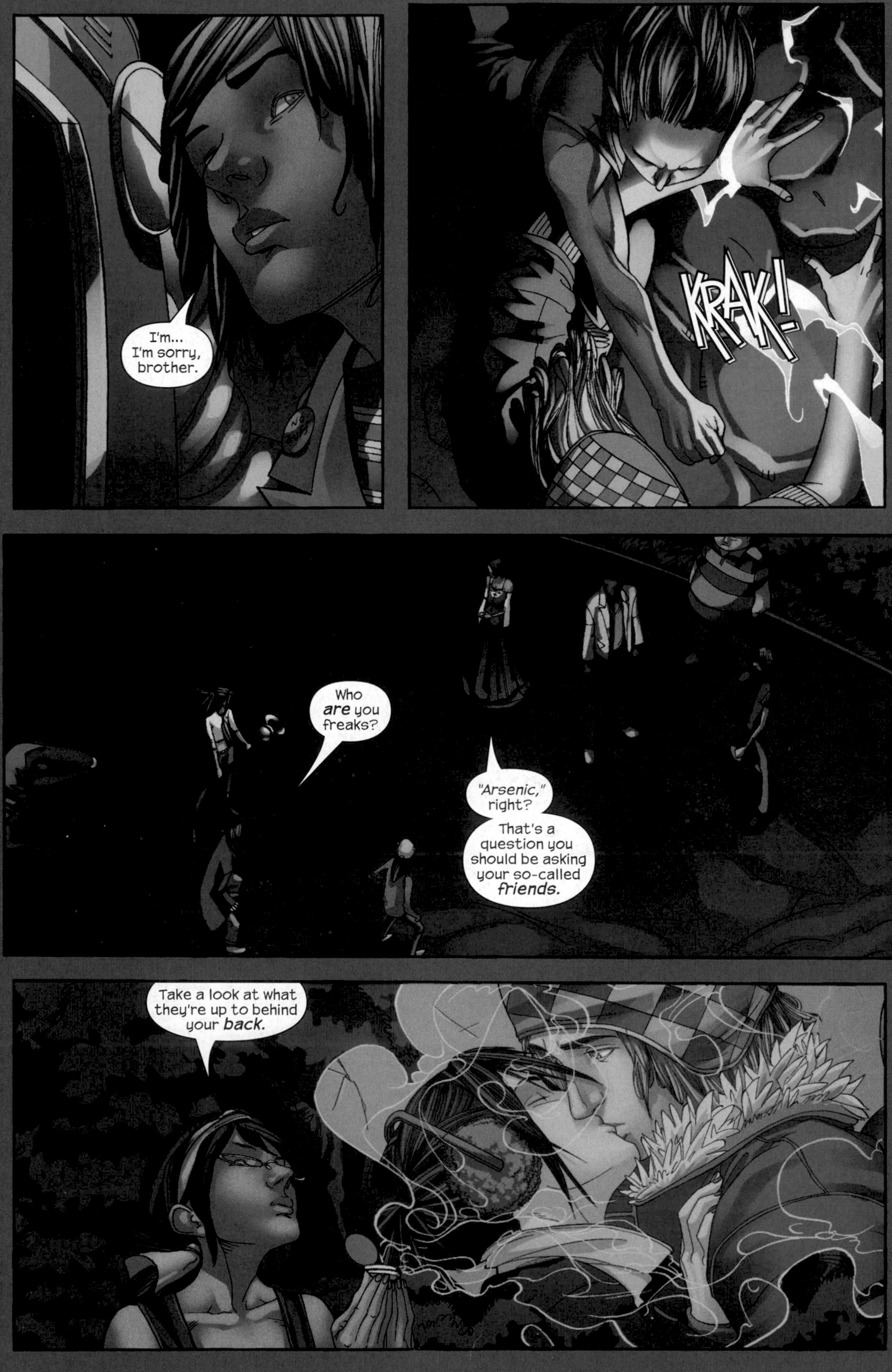
I'm... I'm sorry, brother.
KRAK!
Who *are* you freaks?
"Arsenic," right?
That's a question you should be asking your so-called *friends.*
Take a look at what they're up to behind your *back.*

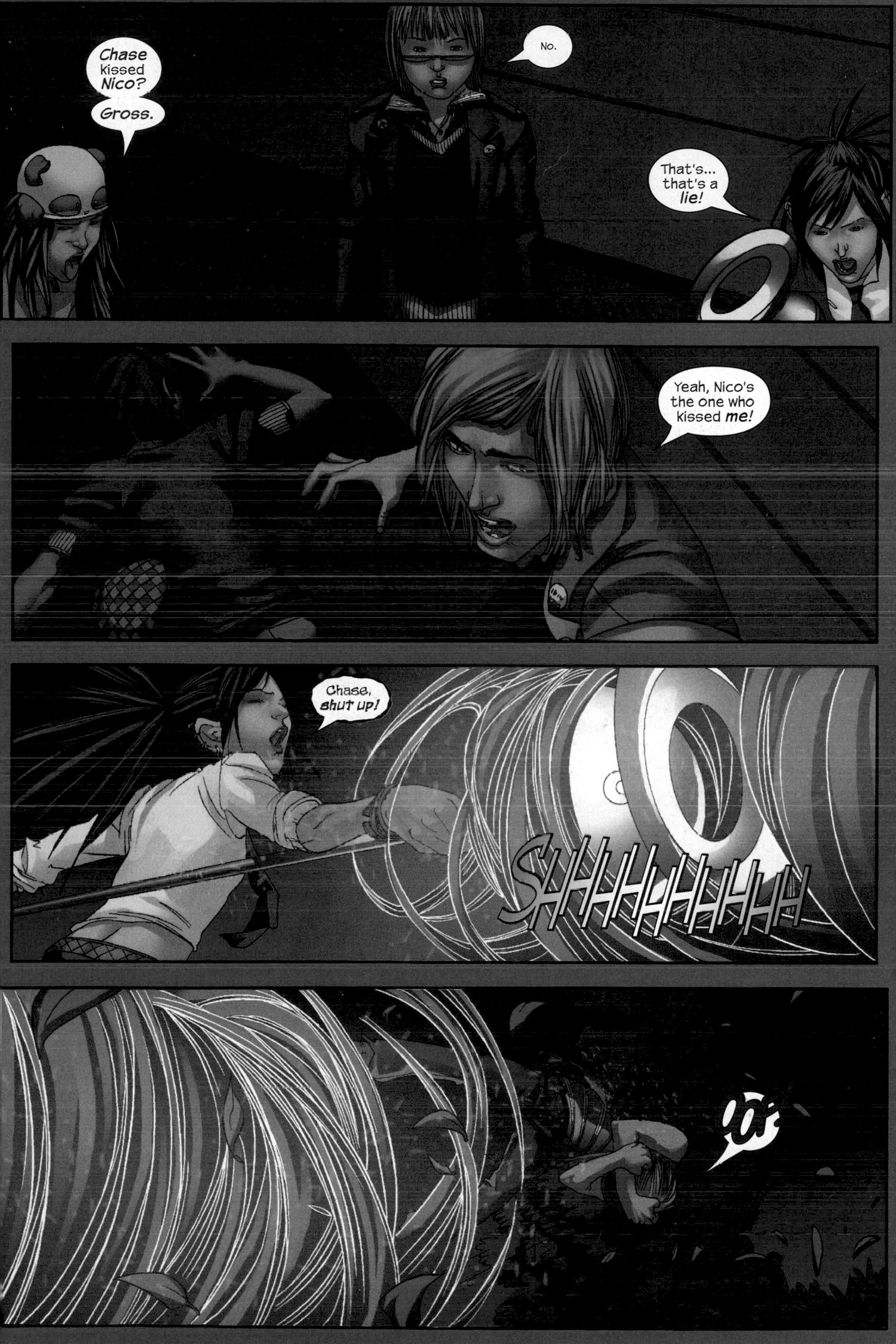

Chase kissed Nico?
Gross.
No.
That's... that's a lie!
Yeah, Nico's the one who kissed me!
Chase, shut up!
SHHHHHHHHH

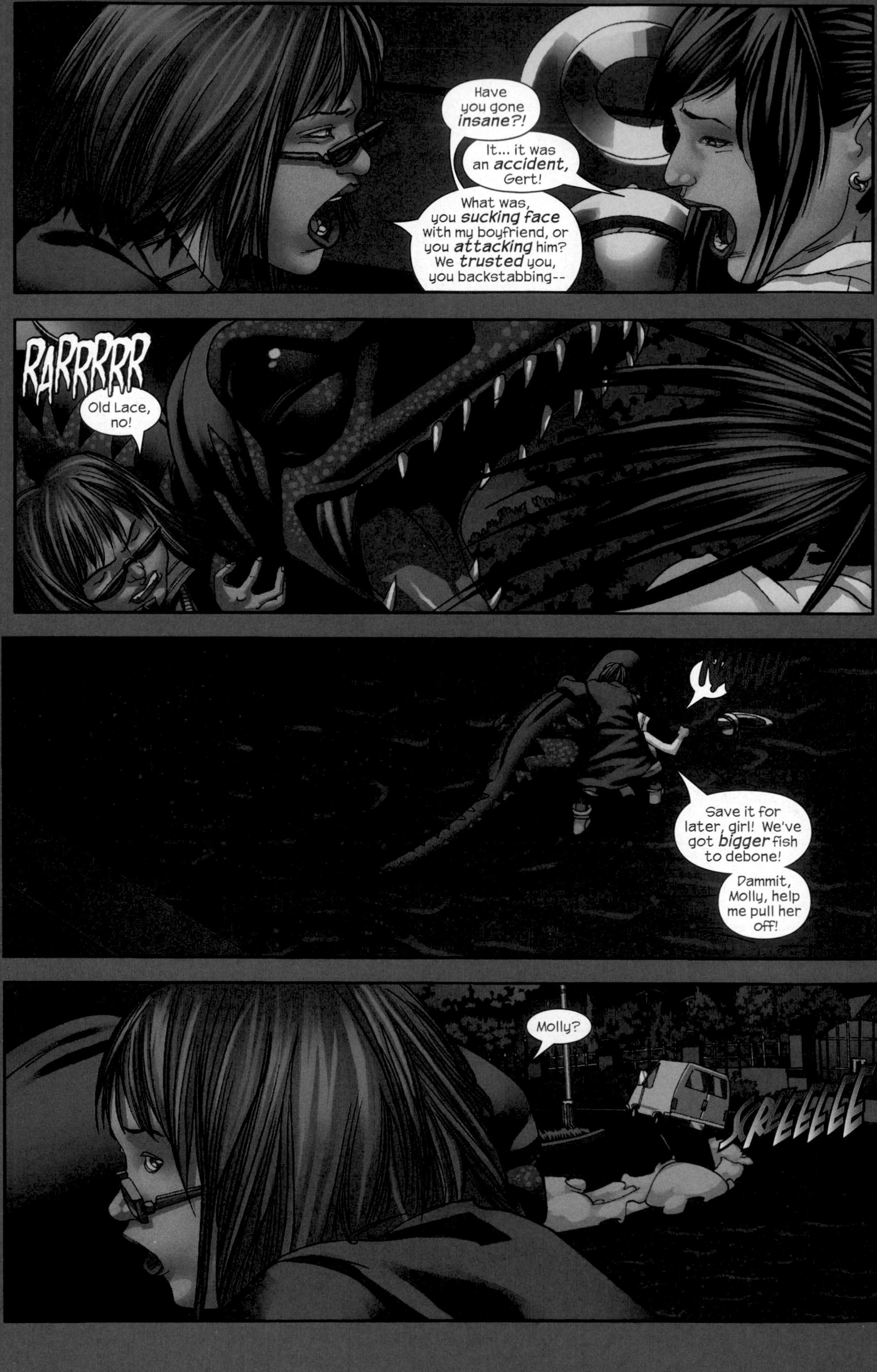
Have you gone insane?!
It... it was an accident, Gert!
What was, you sucking face with my boyfriend, or you attacking him? We trusted you, you backstabbing--
RARRRRR
Old Lace, no!
Save it for later, girl! We've got bigger fish to debone!
Dammit, Molly, help me pull her off!
Molly?
SCREEEEEE

"Molly!"

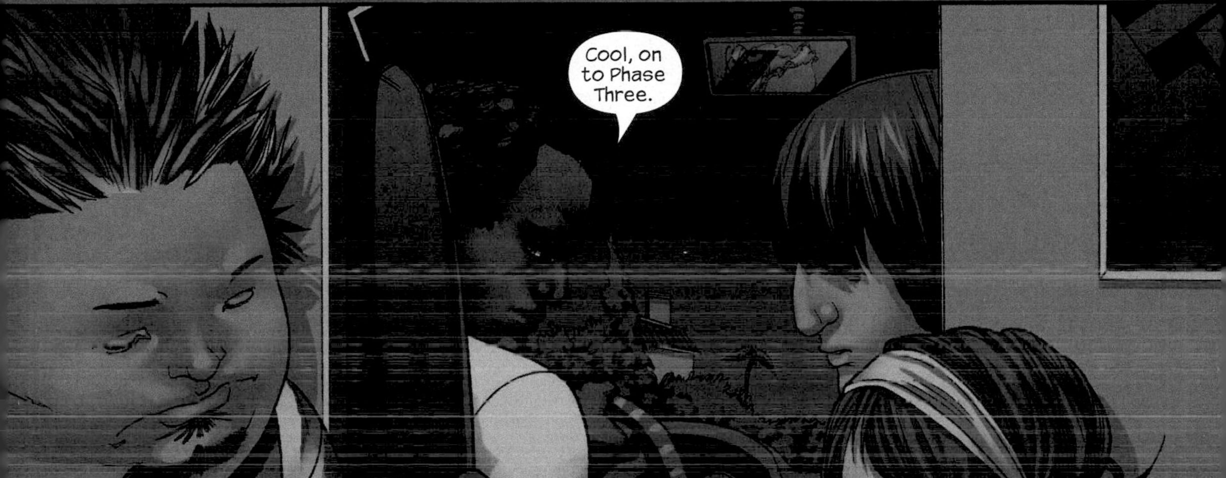
Cool, on to Phase Three.

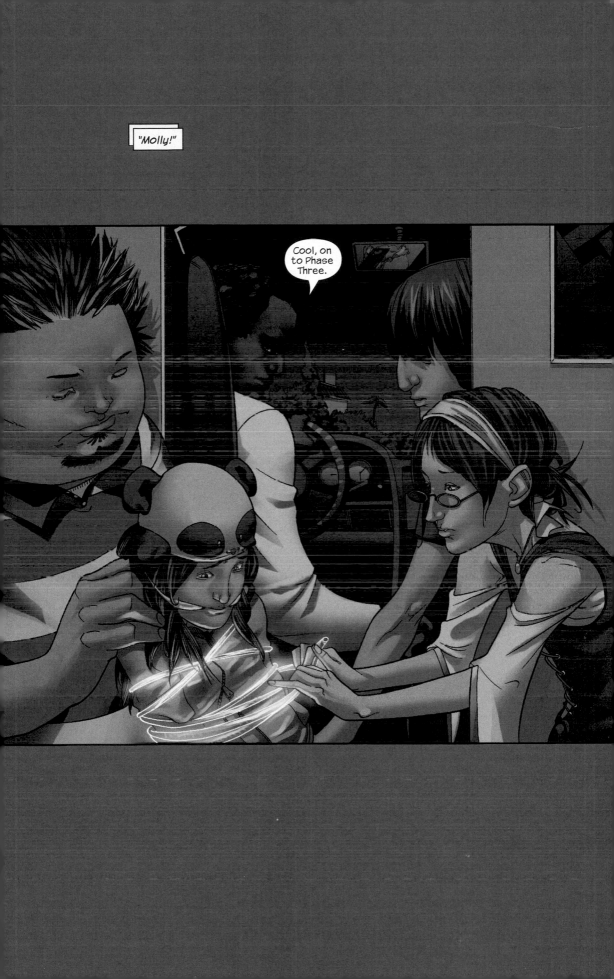

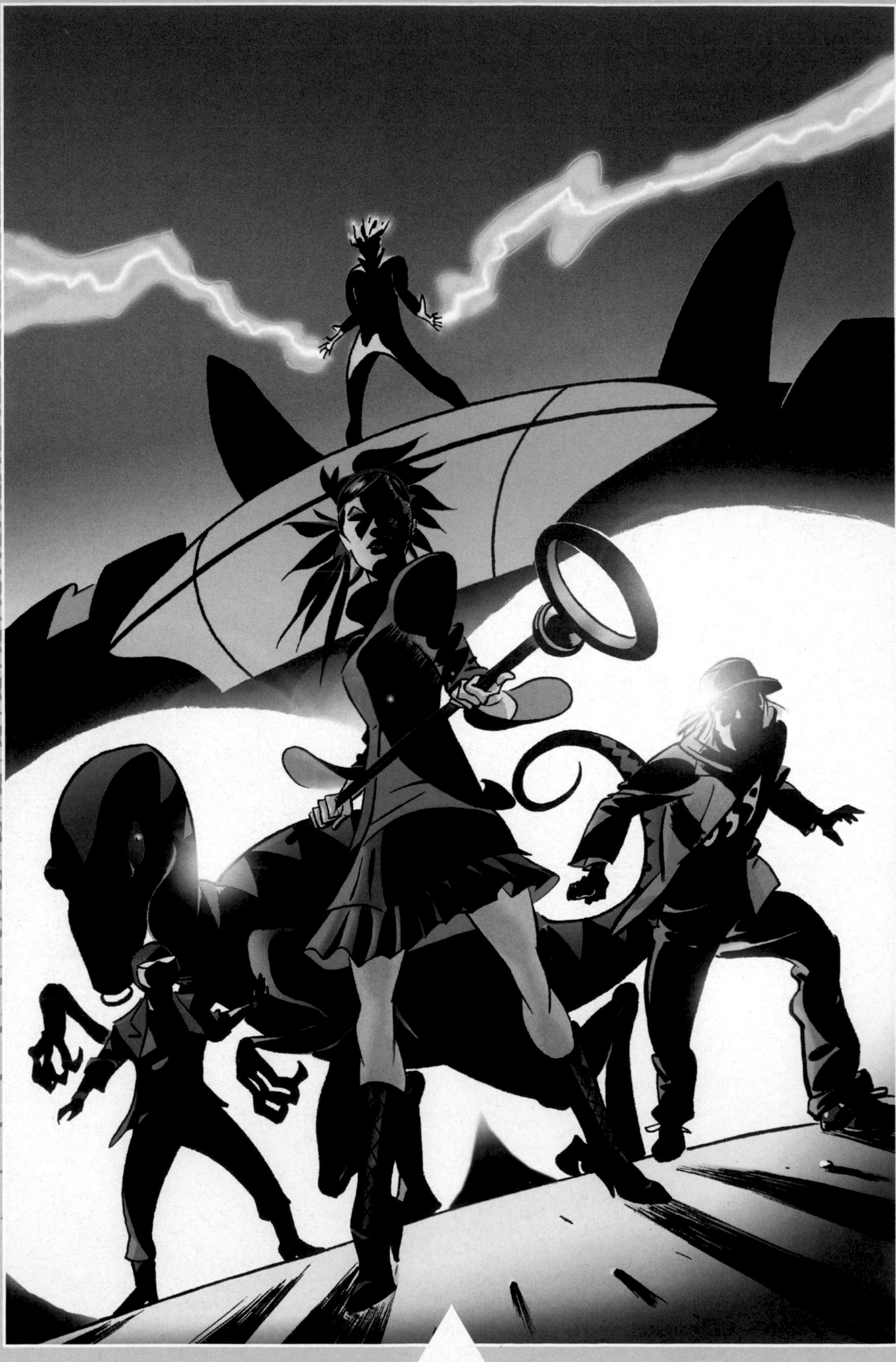

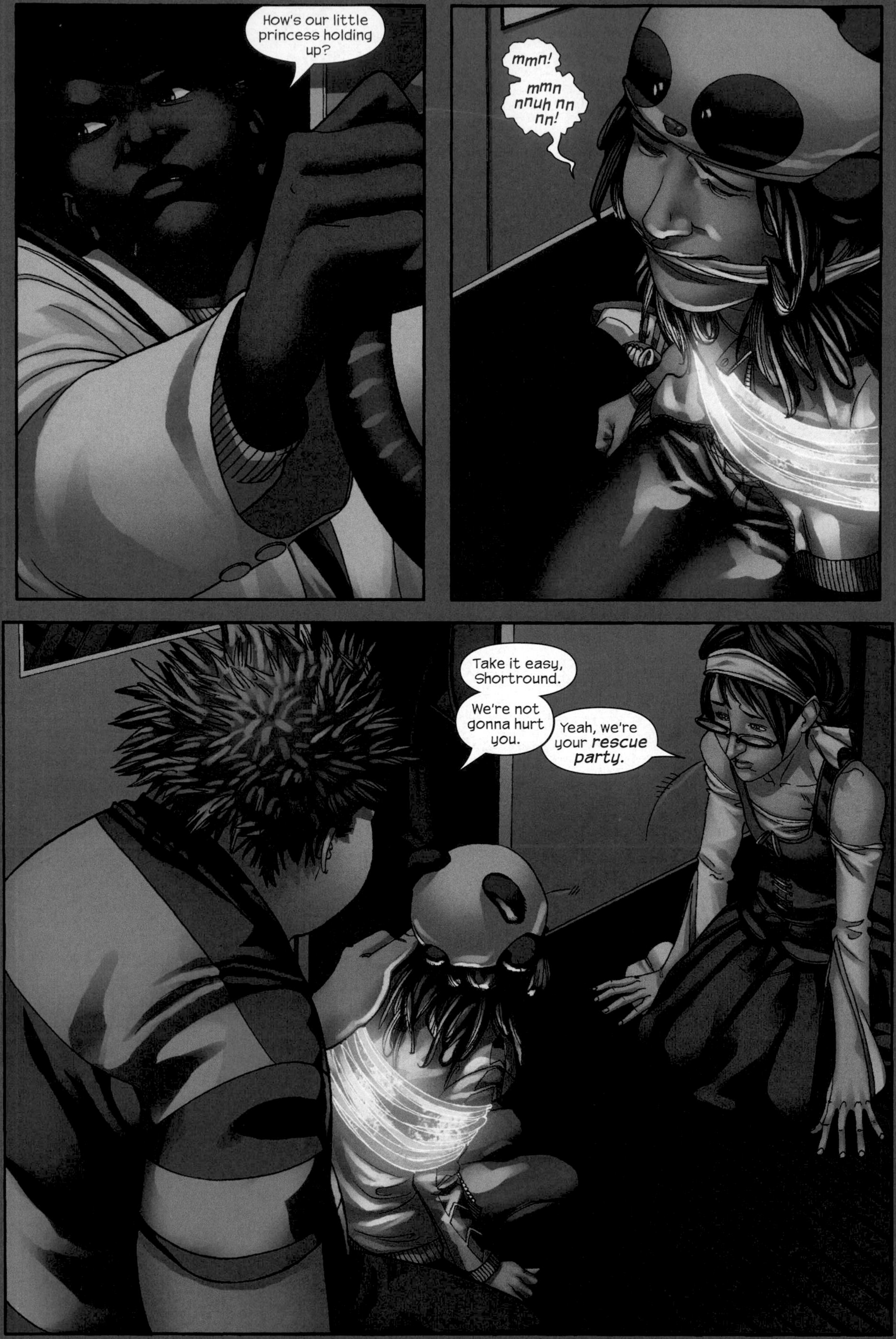
How's our little princess holding up?
mmn!
mmn nnuh nn nn!
Take it easy, Shortround.
We're not gonna hurt you.
Yeah, we're your *rescue party.*

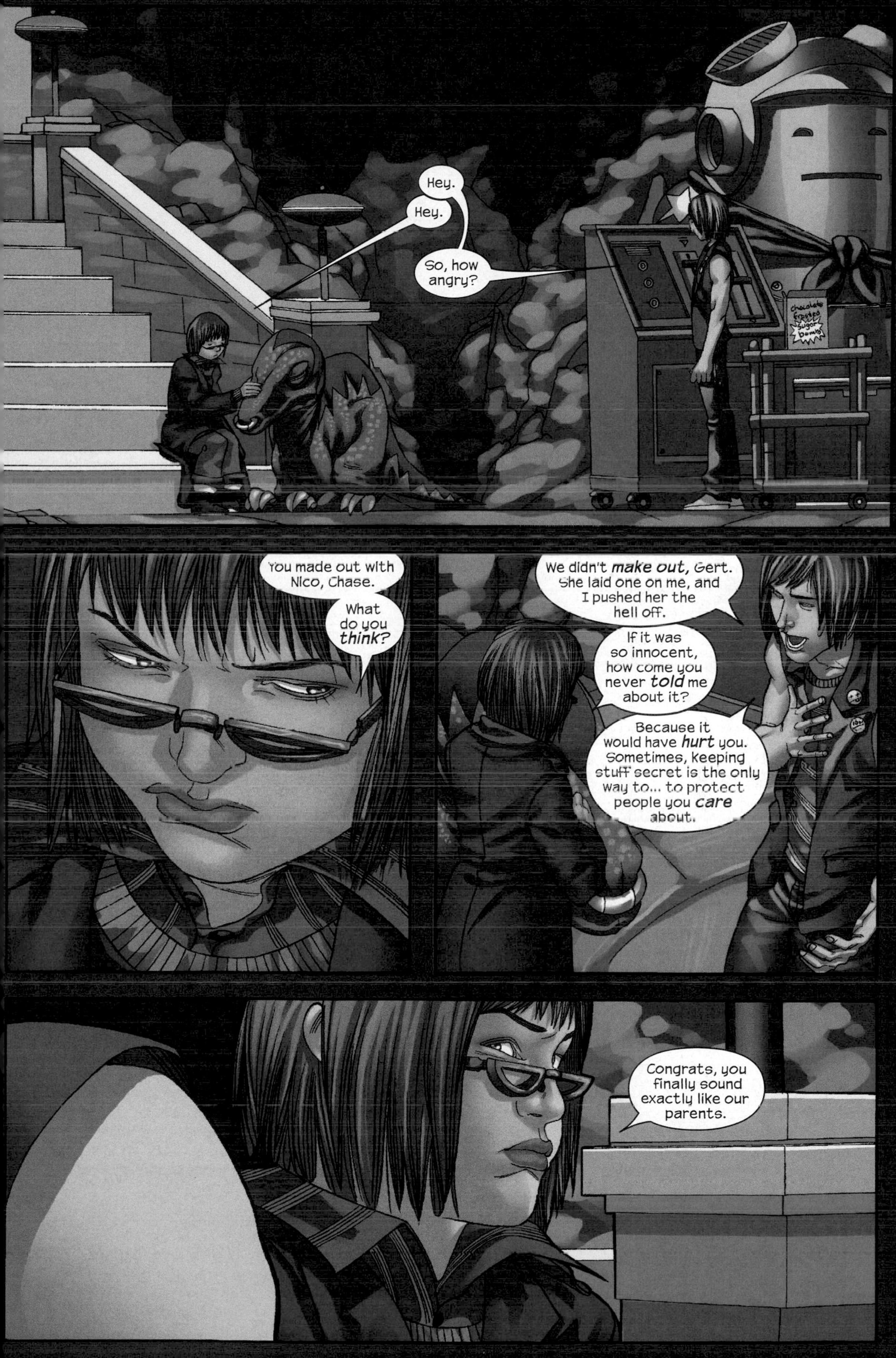
Hey.
Hey.
So, how angry?
You made out with Nico, Chase.
What do you *think?*
We didn't *make out,* Gert. She laid one on me, and I pushed her the hell off.
If it was so innocent, how come you never *told* me about it?
Because it would have *hurt* you. Sometimes, keeping stuff secret is the only way to... to protect people you *care* about.
Congrats, you finally sound exactly like our parents.
Chocolate Frosted Sugar Bombs

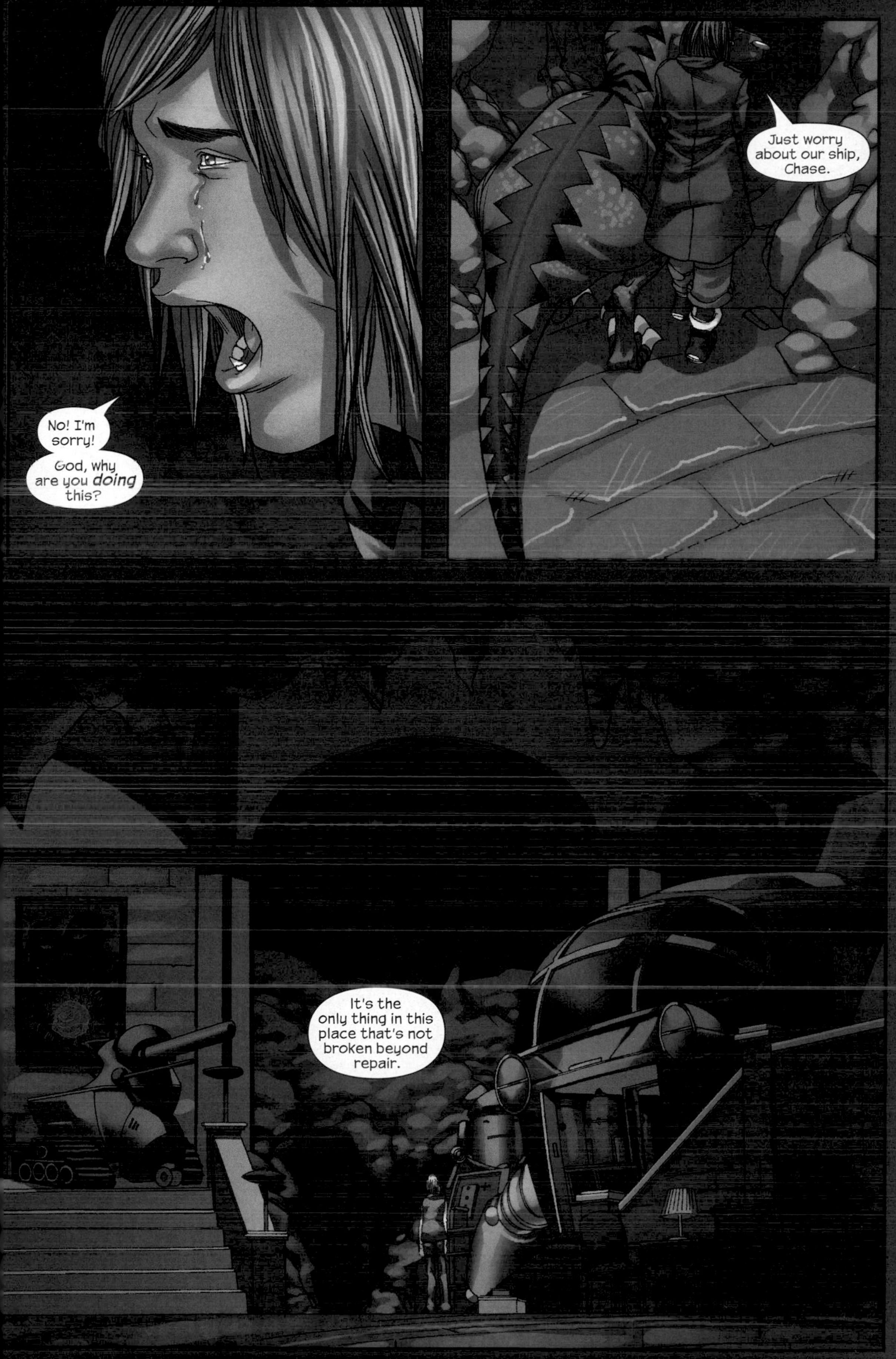
No! I'm sorry!
God, why are you *doing* this?
Just worry about our ship, Chase.
It's the only thing in this place that's not broken beyond repair.

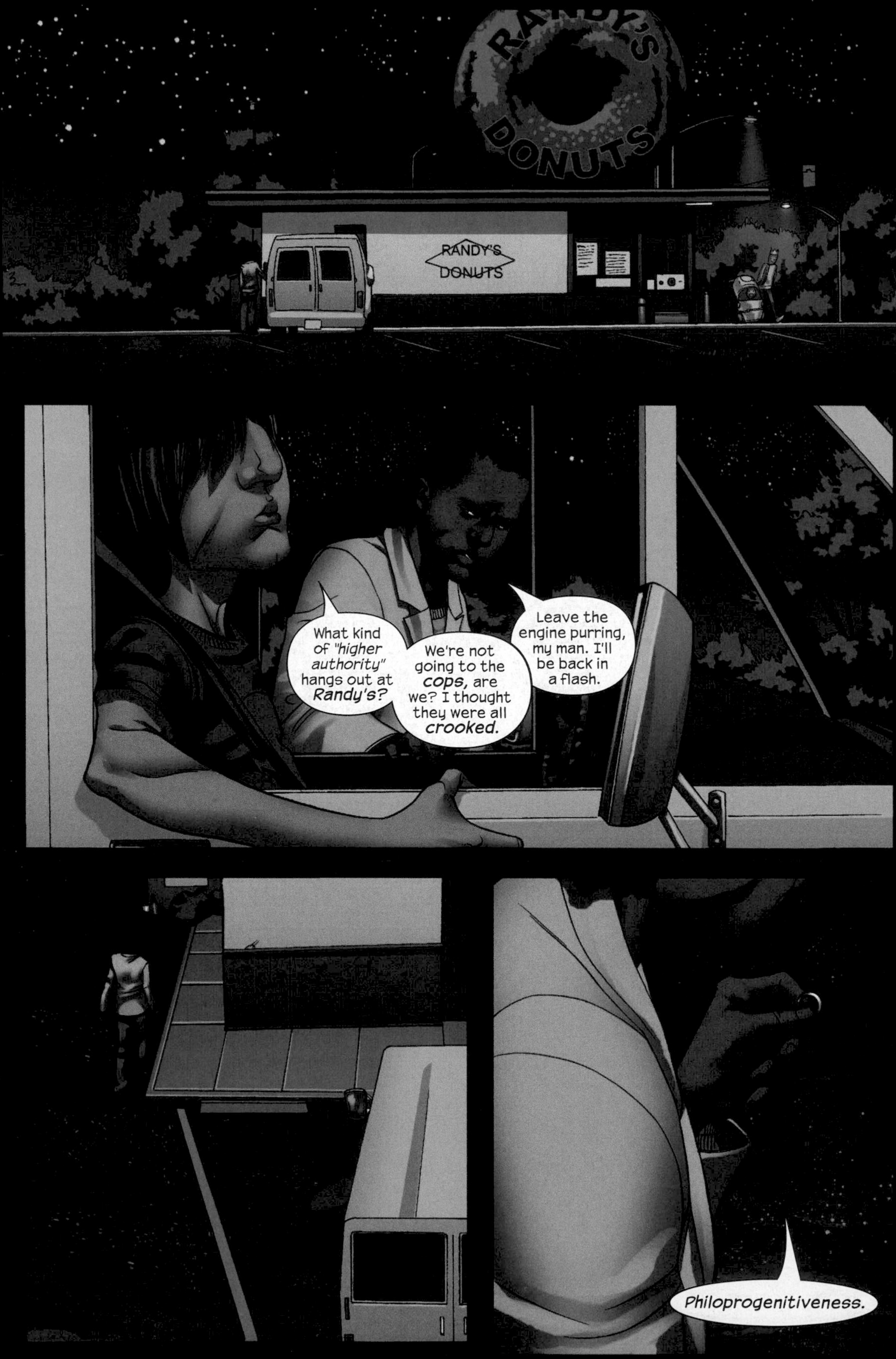
RANDY'S DONUTS
RANDY'S DONUTS
What kind of "higher authority" hangs out at Randy's?
We're not going to the cops, are we? I thought they were all crooked.
Leave the engine purring, my man. I'll be back in a flash.
Philoprogenitiveness.

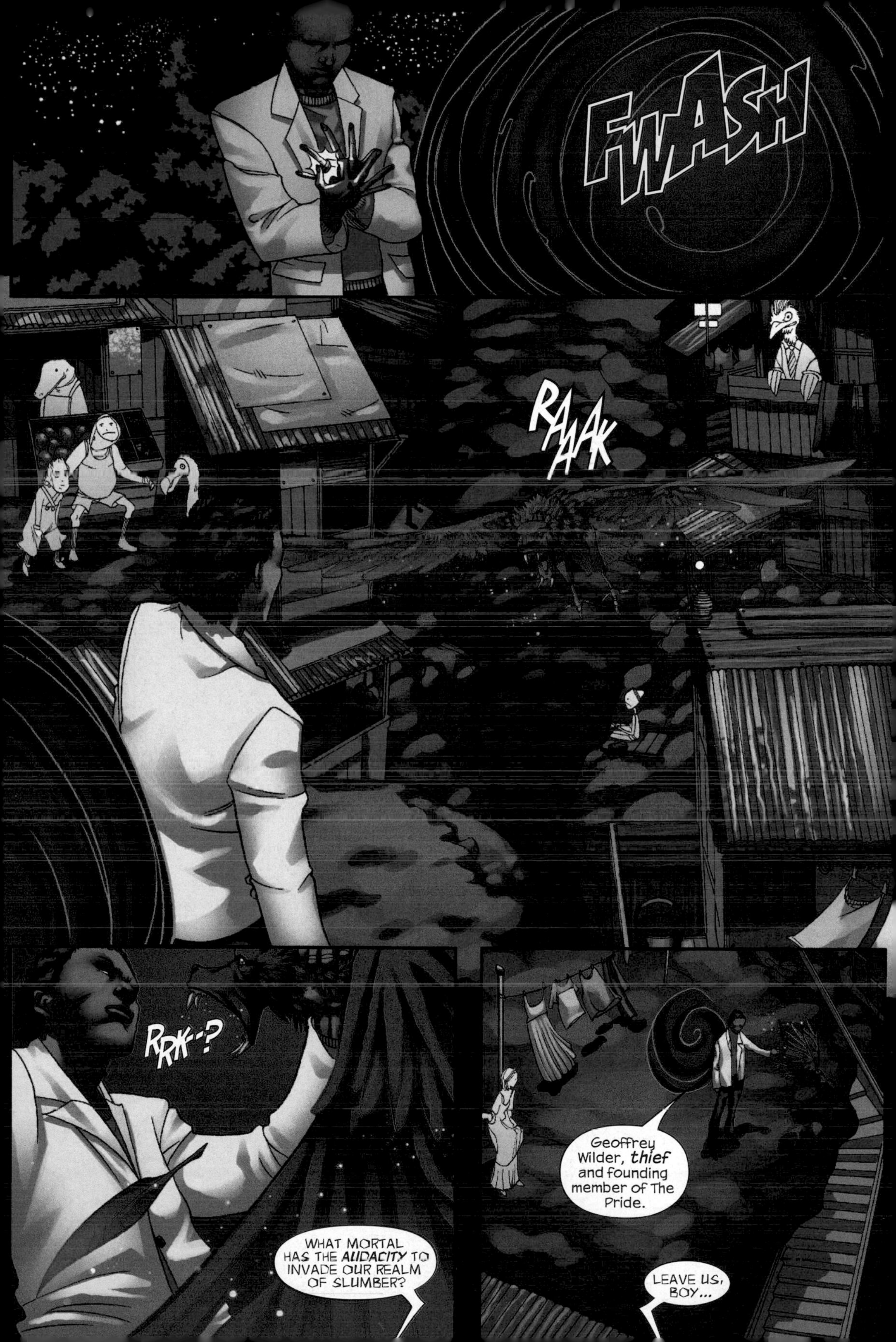
FWASH
RAAAAK
RRK-?
WHAT MORTAL HAS THE AUDACITY TO INVADE OUR REALM OF SLUMBER?
Geoffrey Wilder, thief and founding member of The Pride.
LEAVE US, BOY...

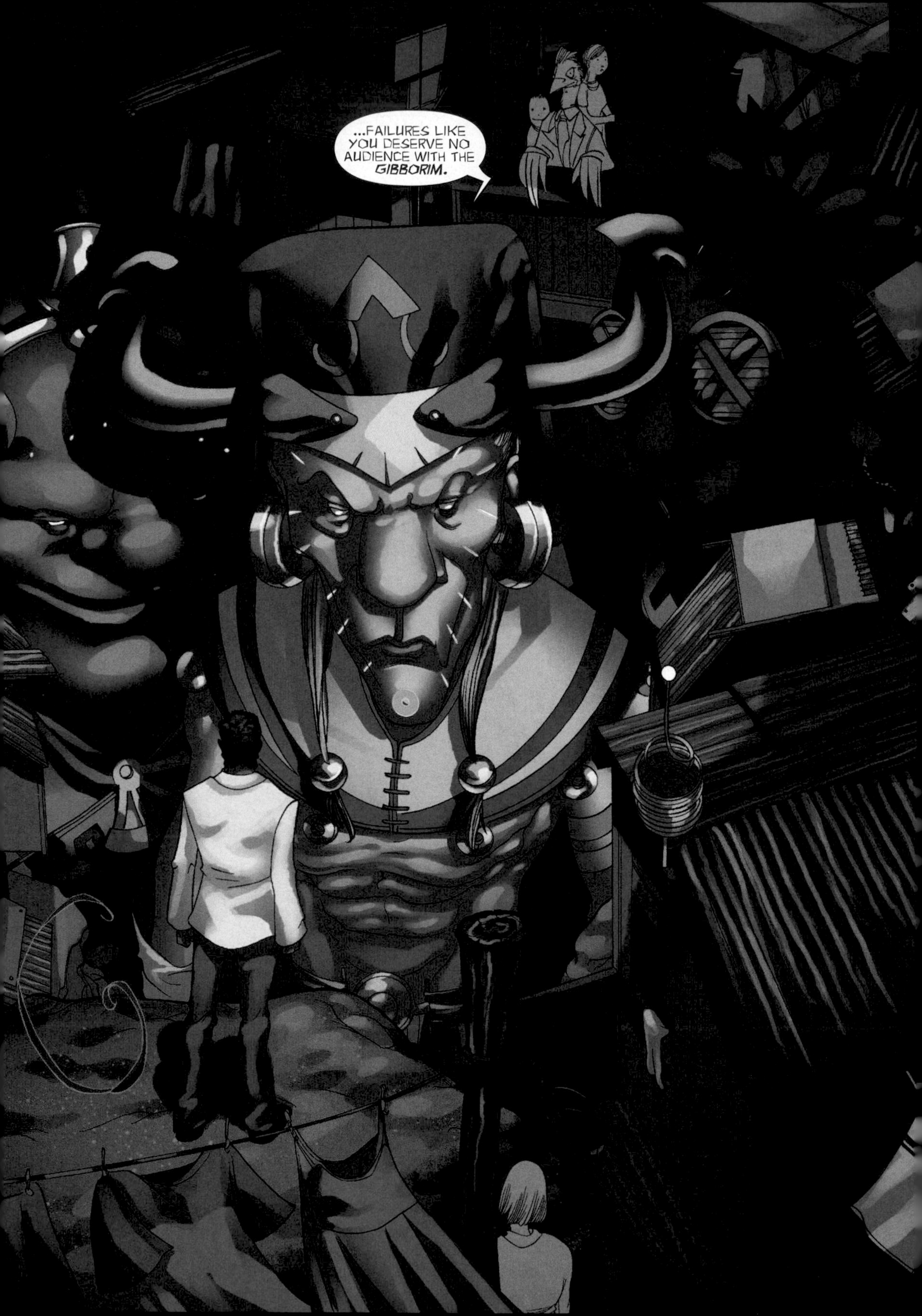
...FAILURES LIKE YOU DESERVE NO AUDIENCE WITH THE GIBBORIM.

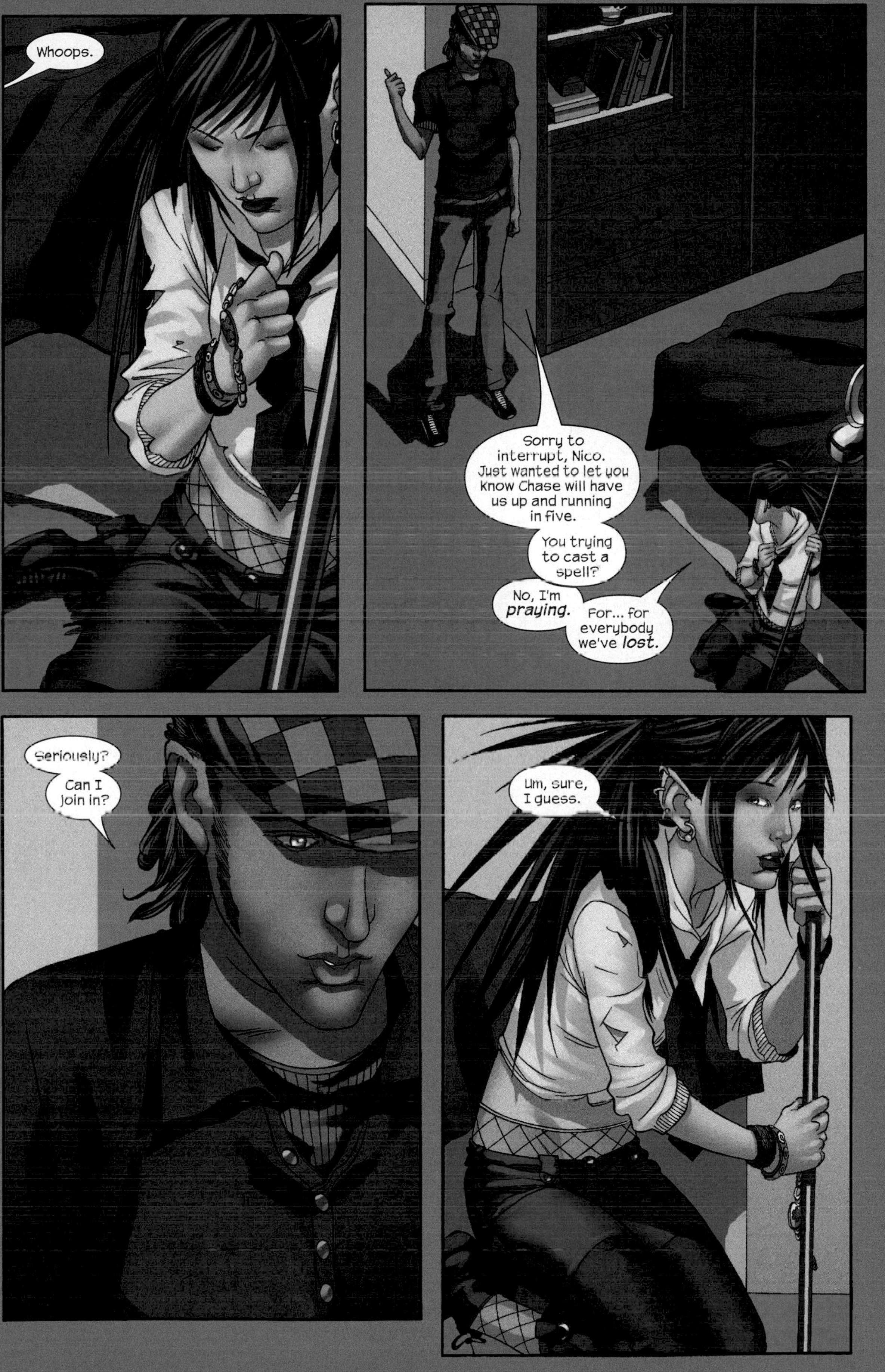
Whoops.
Sorry to interrupt, Nico. Just wanted to let you know Chase will have us up and running in five.
You trying to cast a spell?
No, I'm *praying.*
For... for everybody we've *lost.*
Seriously?
Can I join in?
Um, sure, I guess.

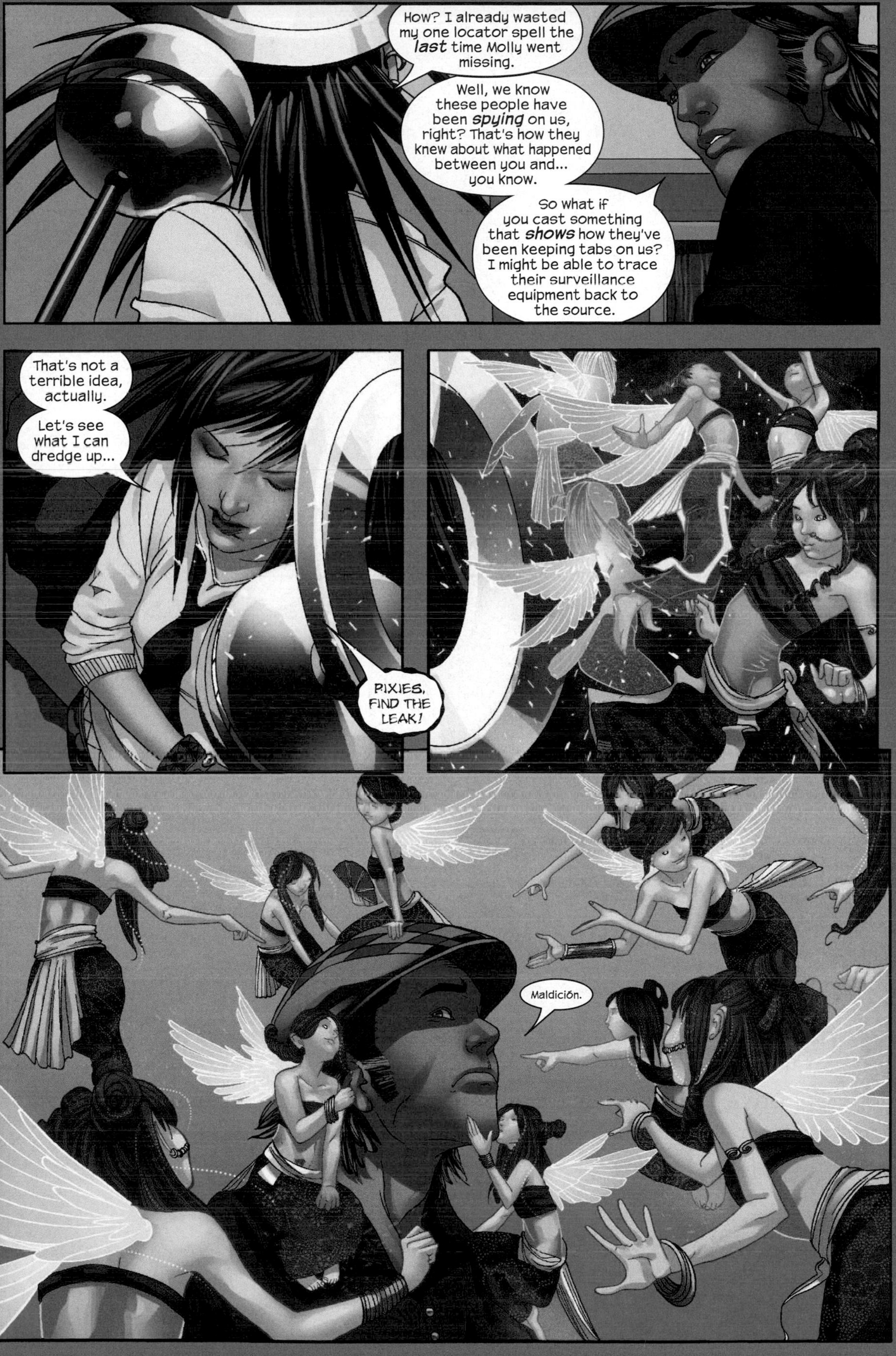
How? I already wasted my one locator spell the *last* time Molly went missing.
Well, we know these people have been *spying* on us, right? That's how they knew about what happened between you and... you know.
So what if you cast something that *shows* how they've been keeping tabs on us? I might be able to trace their surveillance equipment back to the source.
That's not a terrible idea, actually.
Let's see what I can dredge up...
PIXIES, FIND THE LEAK!
Maldición.

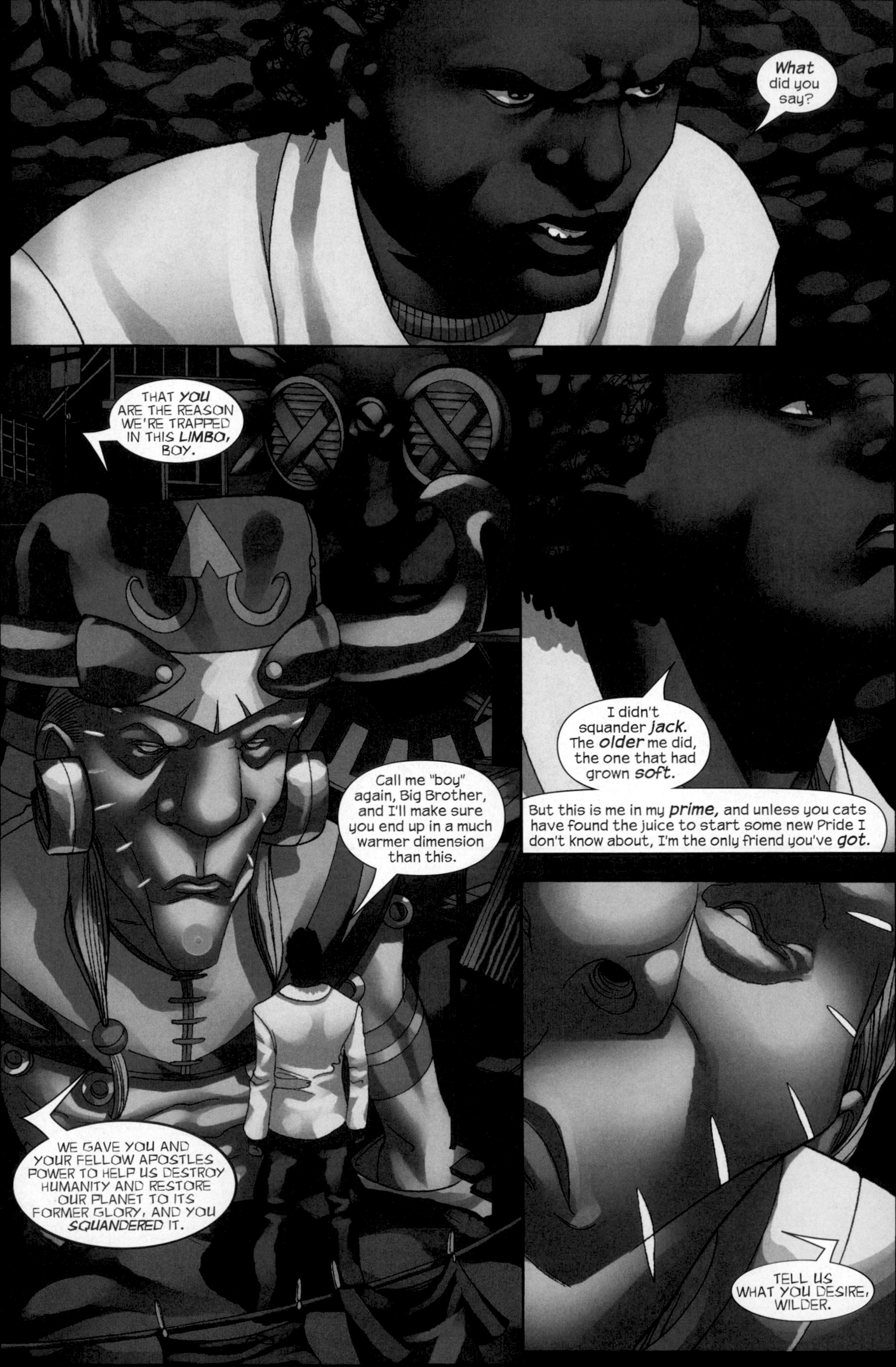
What did you say?
THAT YOU ARE THE REASON WE'RE TRAPPED IN THIS LIMBO, BOY.
I didn't squander jack. The older me did, the one that had grown soft.
But this is me in my prime, and unless you cats have found the juice to start some new Pride I don't know about, I'm the only friend you've got.
Call me "boy" again, Big Brother, and I'll make sure you end up in a much warmer dimension than this.
WE GAVE YOU AND YOUR FELLOW APOSTLES POWER TO HELP US DESTROY HUMANITY AND RESTORE OUR PLANET TO ITS FORMER GLORY, AND YOU SQUANDERED IT.
TELL US WHAT YOU DESIRE, WILDER.

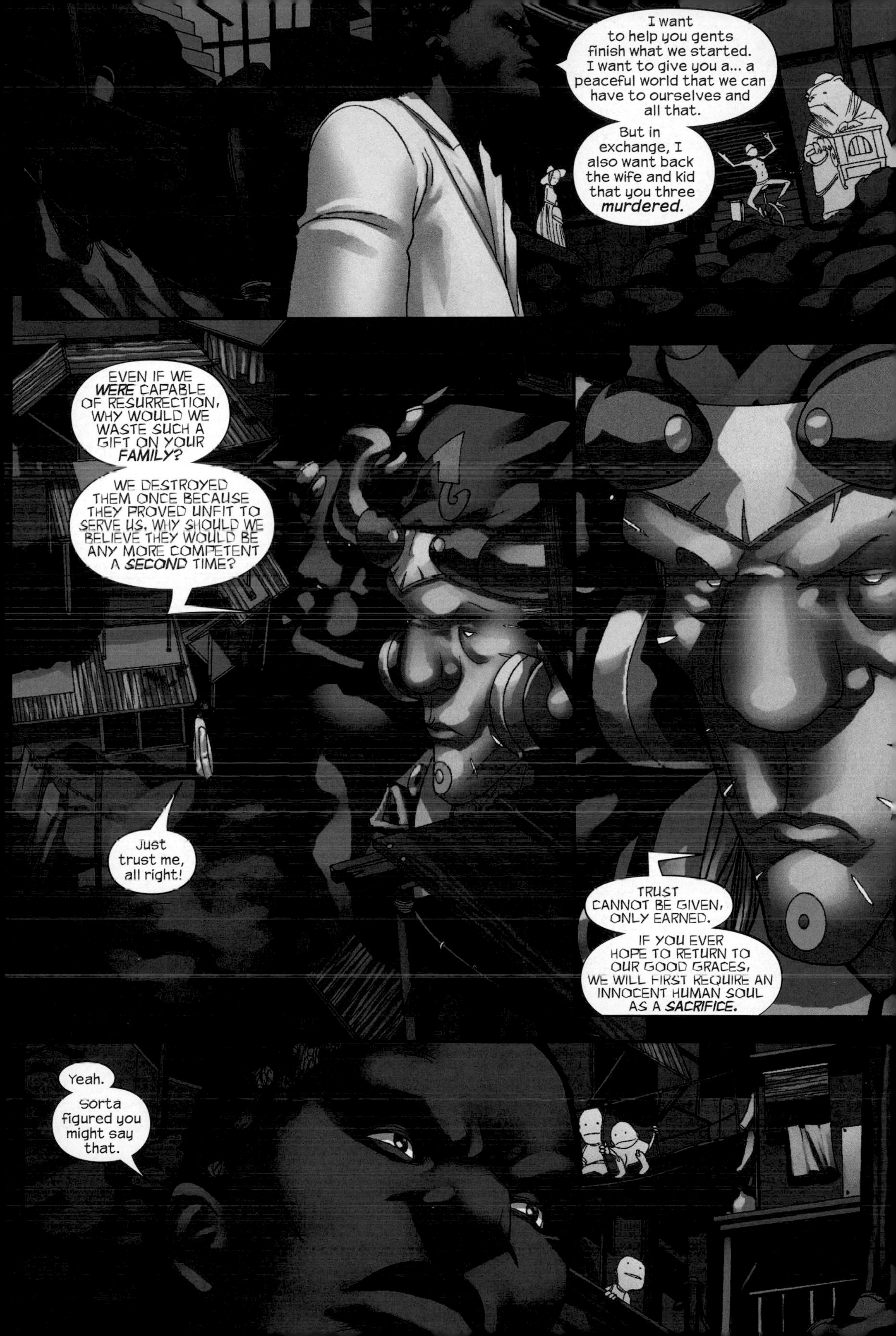
I want to help you gents finish what we started. I want to give you a... a peaceful world that we can have to ourselves and all that.
But in exchange, I also want back the wife and kid that you three *murdered.*
EVEN IF WE *WERE* CAPABLE OF RESURRECTION, WHY WOULD WE WASTE SUCH A GIFT ON YOUR *FAMILY?*
WE DESTROYED THEM ONCE BECAUSE THEY PROVED UNFIT TO SERVE US. WHY SHOULD WE BELIEVE THEY WOULD BE ANY MORE COMPETENT A *SECOND* TIME?
Just trust me, all right!
TRUST CANNOT BE GIVEN, ONLY EARNED.
IF YOU EVER HOPE TO RETURN TO OUR GOOD GRACES, WE WILL FIRST REQUIRE AN INNOCENT HUMAN SOUL AS A *SACRIFICE.*
Yeah.
Sorta figured you might say that.

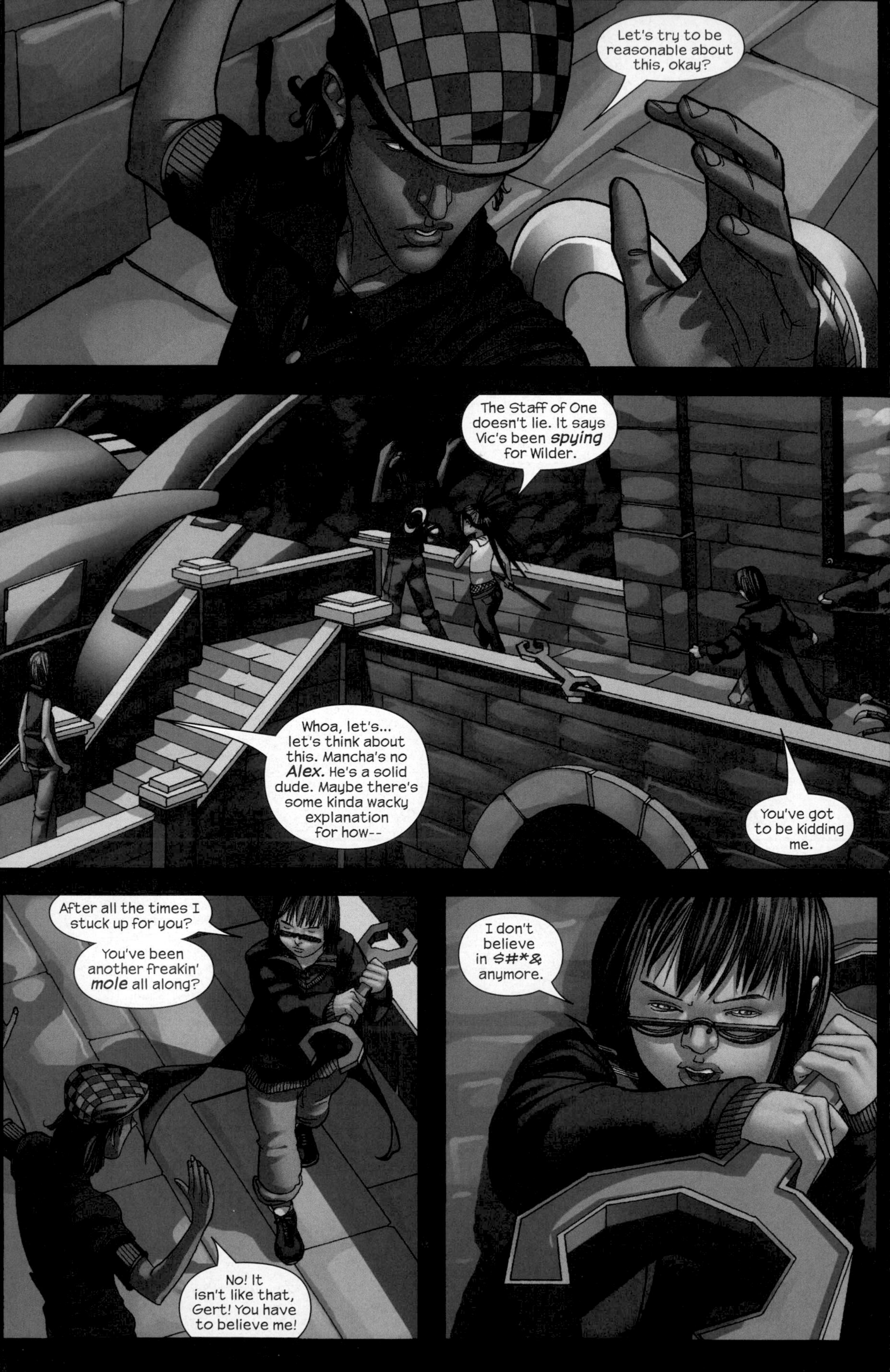
Let's try to be reasonable about this, okay?
The Staff of One doesn't lie. It says Vic's been *spying* for Wilder.
Whoa, let's... let's think about this. Mancha's no *Alex.* He's a solid dude. Maybe there's some kinda wacky explanation for how--
You've got to be kidding me.
After all the times I stuck up for you?
You've been another freakin' *mole* all along?
No! It isn't like that, Gert! You have to believe me!
I don't believe in $#*& anymore.

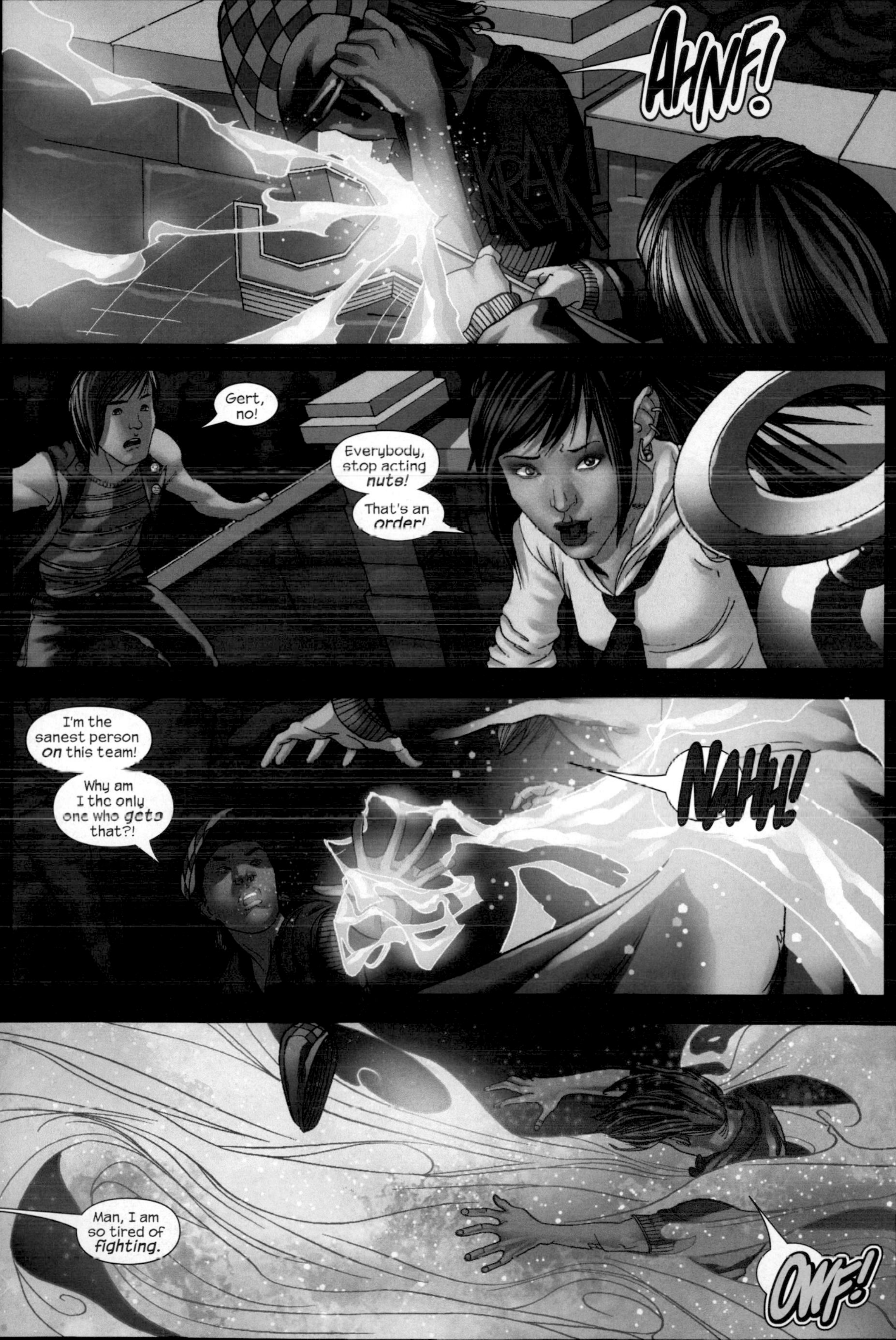
AHNF!
KRAK!
Gert, no!
Everybody, stop acting nuts!
That's an order!
I'm the sanest person on this team!
Why am I the only one who gets that?!
NAHH!
Man, I am so tired of fighting.
OWF!

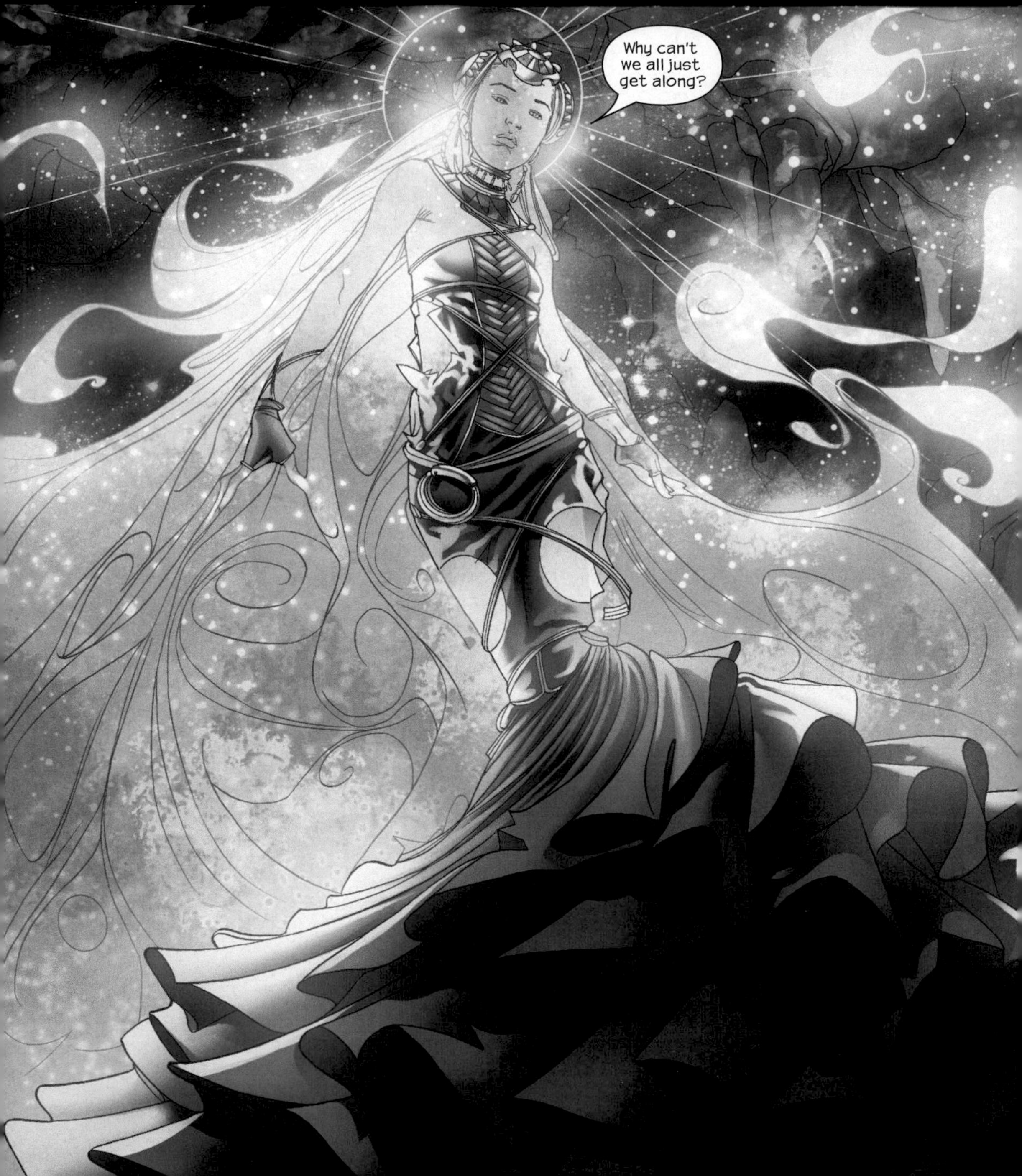
Why can't we all just get along?

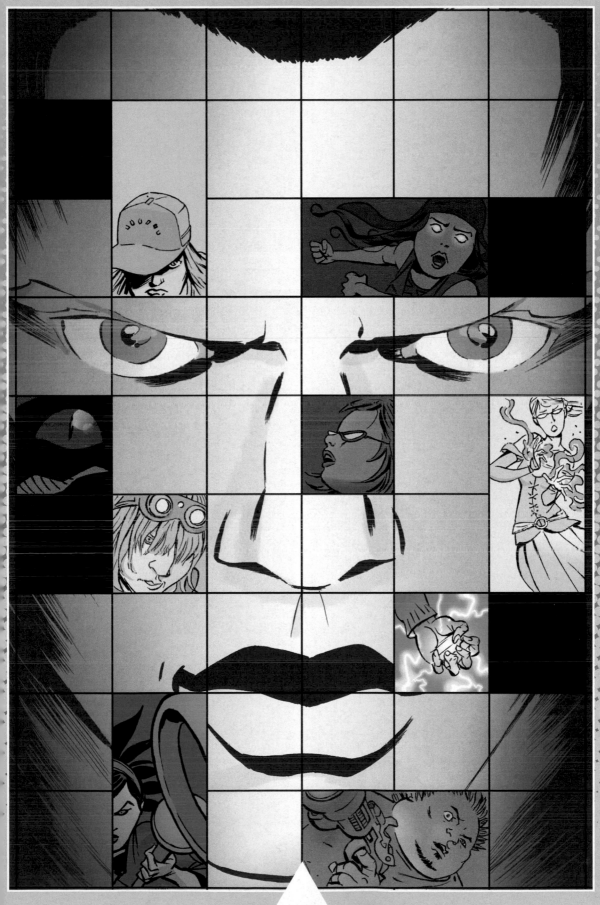

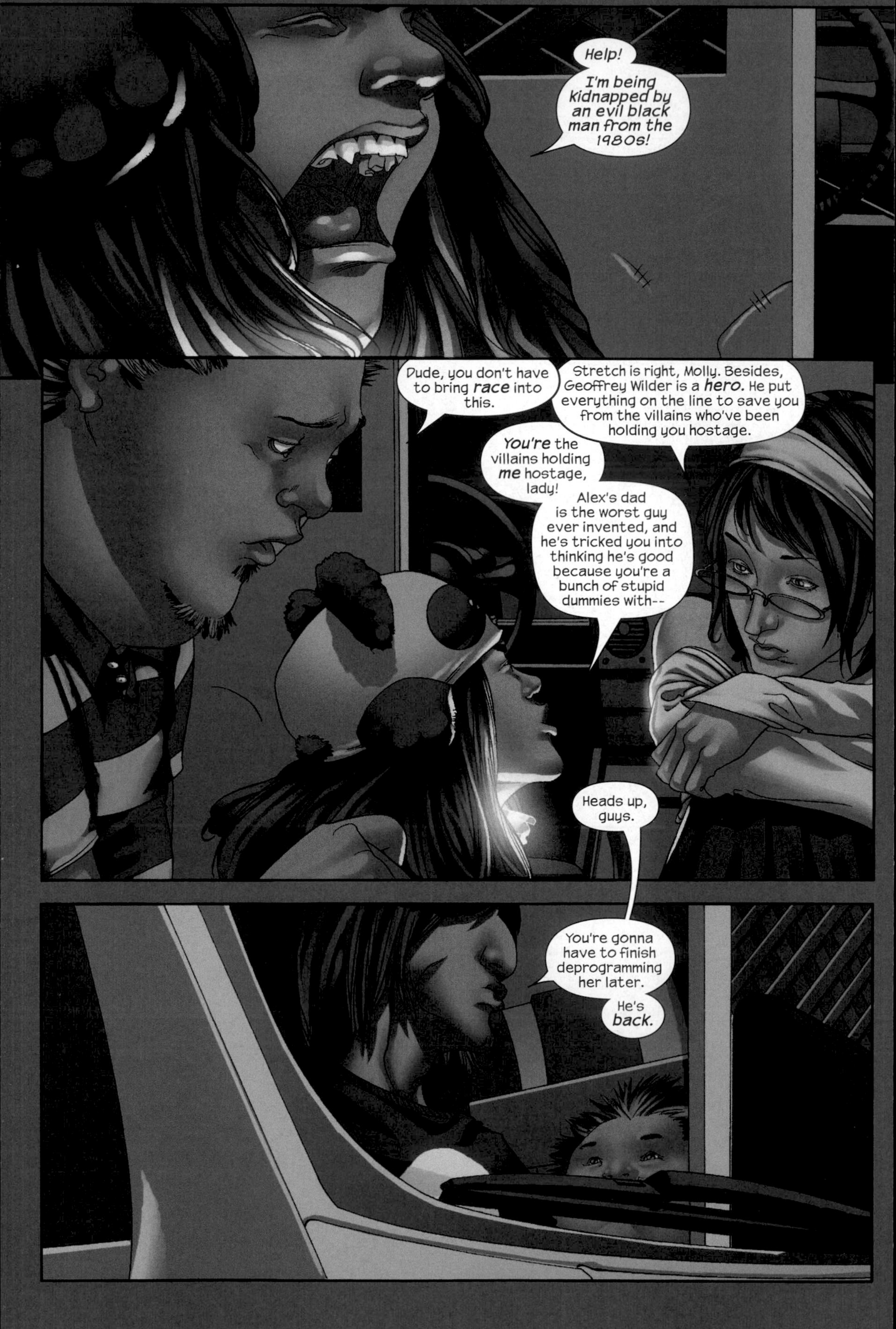
Help!
I'm being kidnapped by an evil black man from the 1980s!
Dude, you don't have to bring *race* into this.
Stretch is right, Molly. Besides, Geoffrey Wilder is a *hero.* He put everything on the line to save you from the villains who've been holding you hostage.
You're the villains holding *me* hostage, lady!
Alex's dad is the worst guy ever invented, and he's tricked you into thinking he's good because you're a bunch of stupid dummies with--
Heads up, guys.
You're gonna have to finish deprogramming her later.
He's *back.*

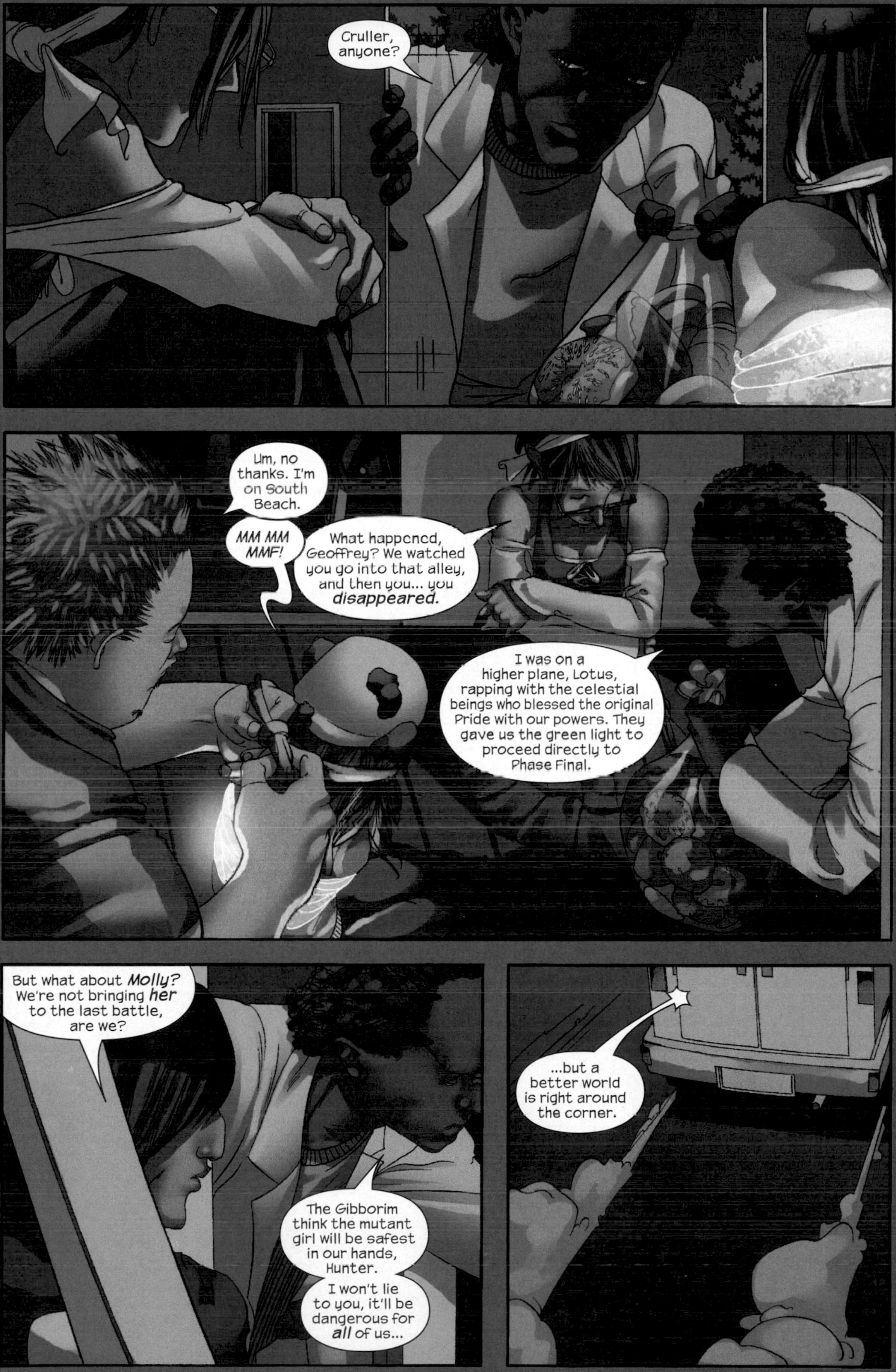
Cruller, anyone?
Um, no thanks. I'm on South Beach.
MM MM MMF!
What happened, Geoffrey? We watched you go into that alley, and then you... you *disappeared.*
I was on a higher plane, Lotus, rapping with the celestial beings who blessed the original Pride with our powers. They gave us the green light to proceed directly to Phase Final.
But what about *Molly?* We're not bringing *her* to the last battle, are we?
The Gibborim think the mutant girl will be safest in our hands, Hunter.
I won't lie to you, it'll be dangerous for *all* of us...
...but a better world is right around the corner.

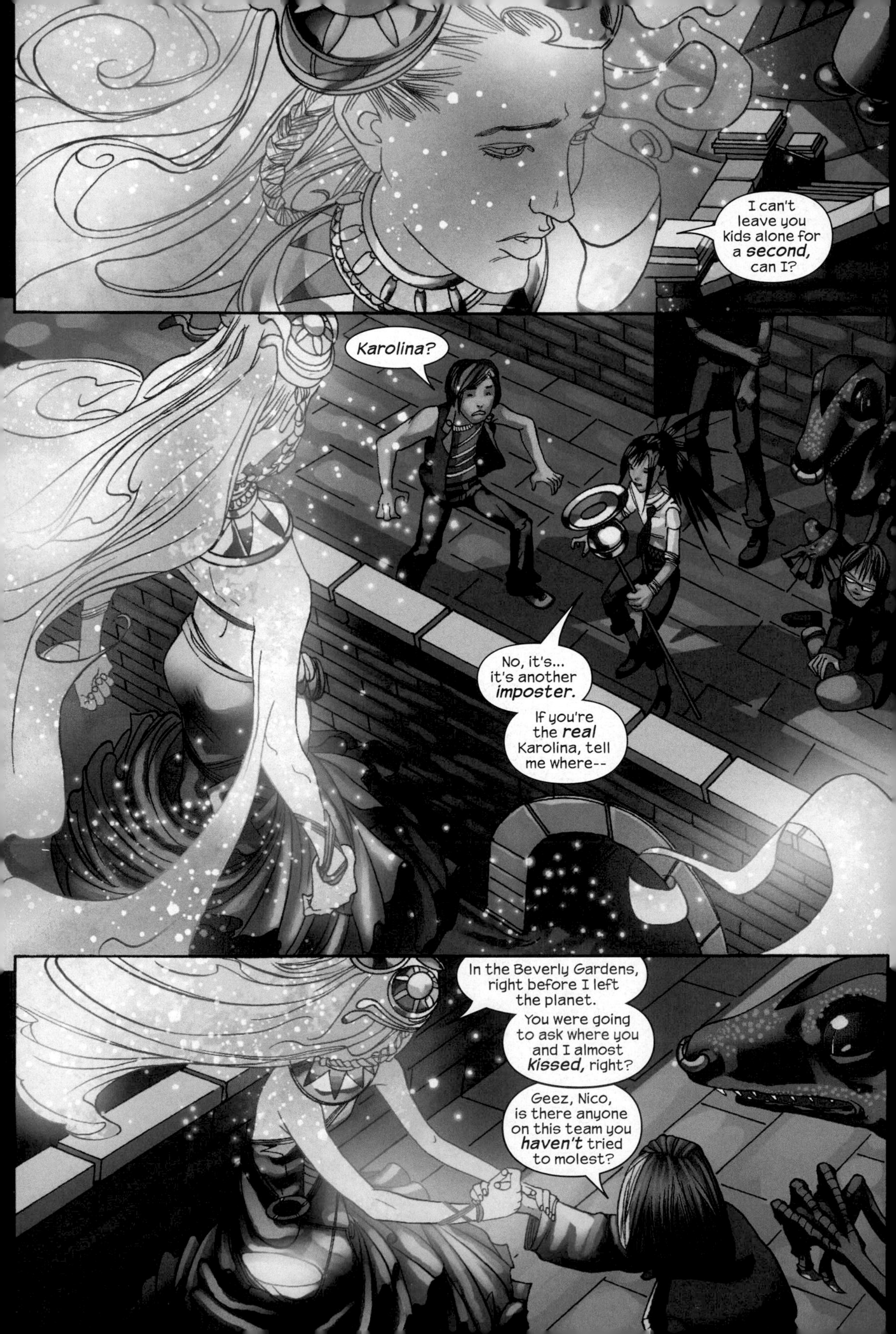
I can't leave you kids alone for a *second,* can I?
Karolina?
No, it's... it's another ***imposter.***
If you're the ***real*** Karolina, tell me where--
In the Beverly Gardens, right before I left the planet.
You were going to ask where you and I almost ***kissed,*** right?
Geez, Nico, is there anyone on this team you ***haven't*** tried to molest?

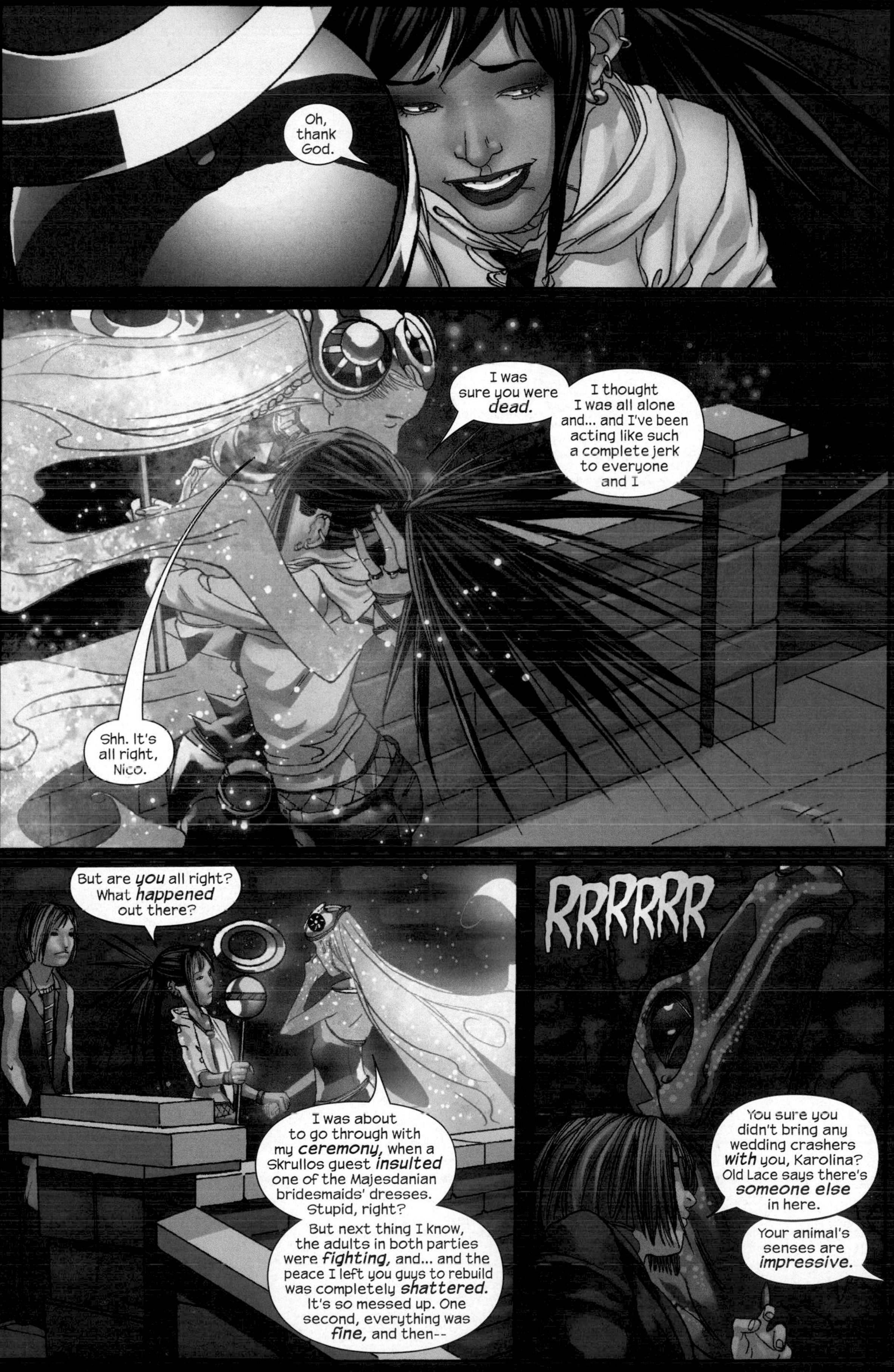
Oh, thank God.
I was sure you were dead.
I thought I was all alone and... and I've been acting like such a complete jerk to everyone and I
Shh. It's all right, Nico.
But are you all right? What happened out there?
I was about to go through with my ceremony, when a Skrullos guest insulted one of the Majesdanian bridesmaids' dresses. Stupid, right?
But next thing I know, the adults in both parties were fighting, and... and the peace I left you guys to rebuild was completely shattered. It's so messed up. One second, everything was fine, and then--
RRRRRR
You sure you didn't bring any wedding crashers with you, Karolina? Old Lace says there's someone else in here.
Your animal's senses are impressive.

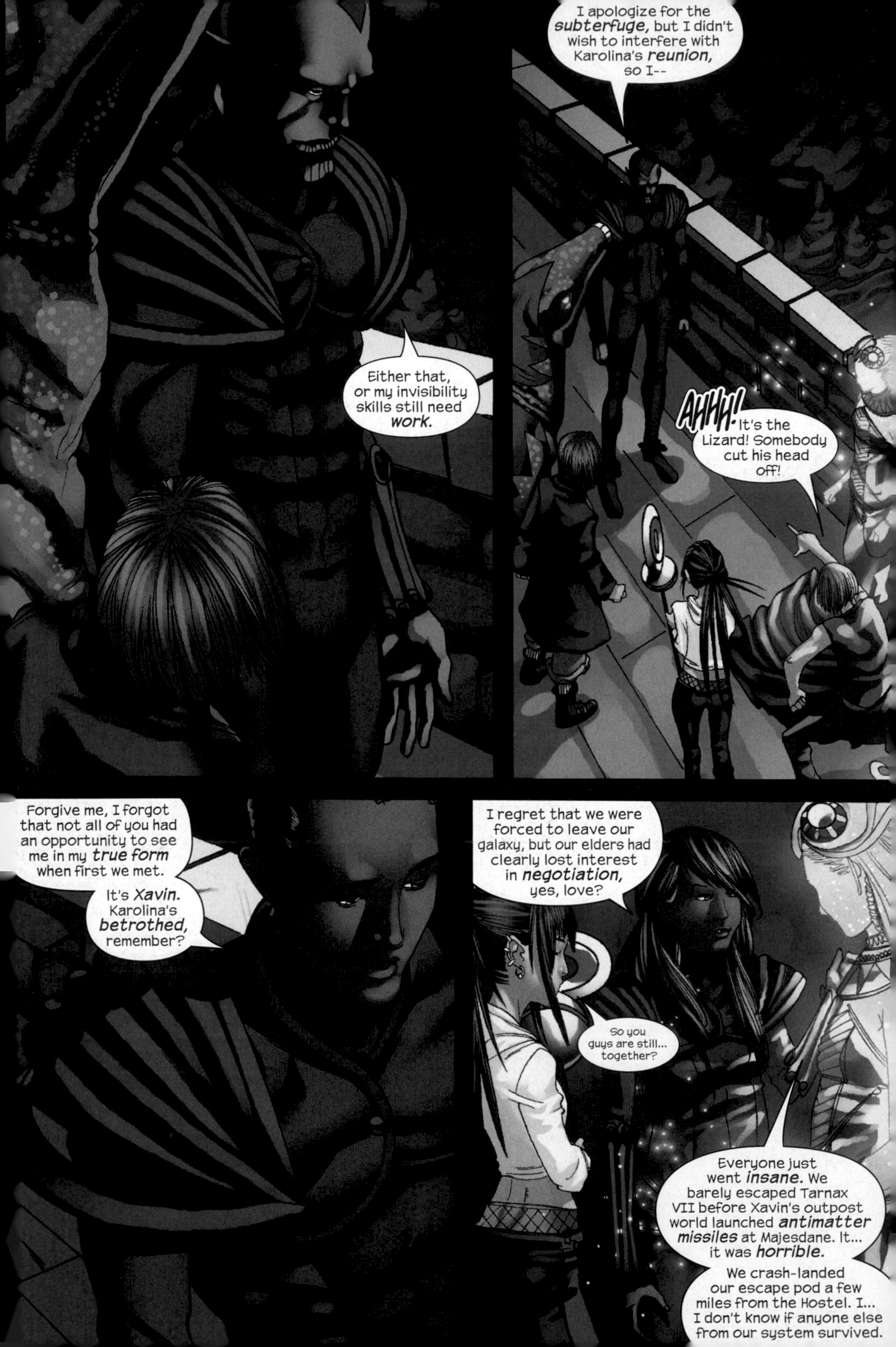

I apologize for the subterfuge, but I didn't wish to interfere with Karolina's reunion, so I--
Either that, or my invisibility skills still need work.
AHHH!
It's the Lizard! Somebody cut his head off!
Forgive me, I forgot that not all of you had an opportunity to see me in my true form when first we met.
It's Xavin. Karolina's betrothed, remember?
I regret that we were forced to leave our galaxy, but our elders had clearly lost interest in negotiation, yes, love?
So you guys are still... together?
Everyone just went insane. We barely escaped Tarnax VII before Xavin's outpost world launched antimatter missiles at Majesdane. It... it was horrible.
We crash-landed our escape pod a few miles from the Hostel. I... I don't know if anyone else from our system survived.

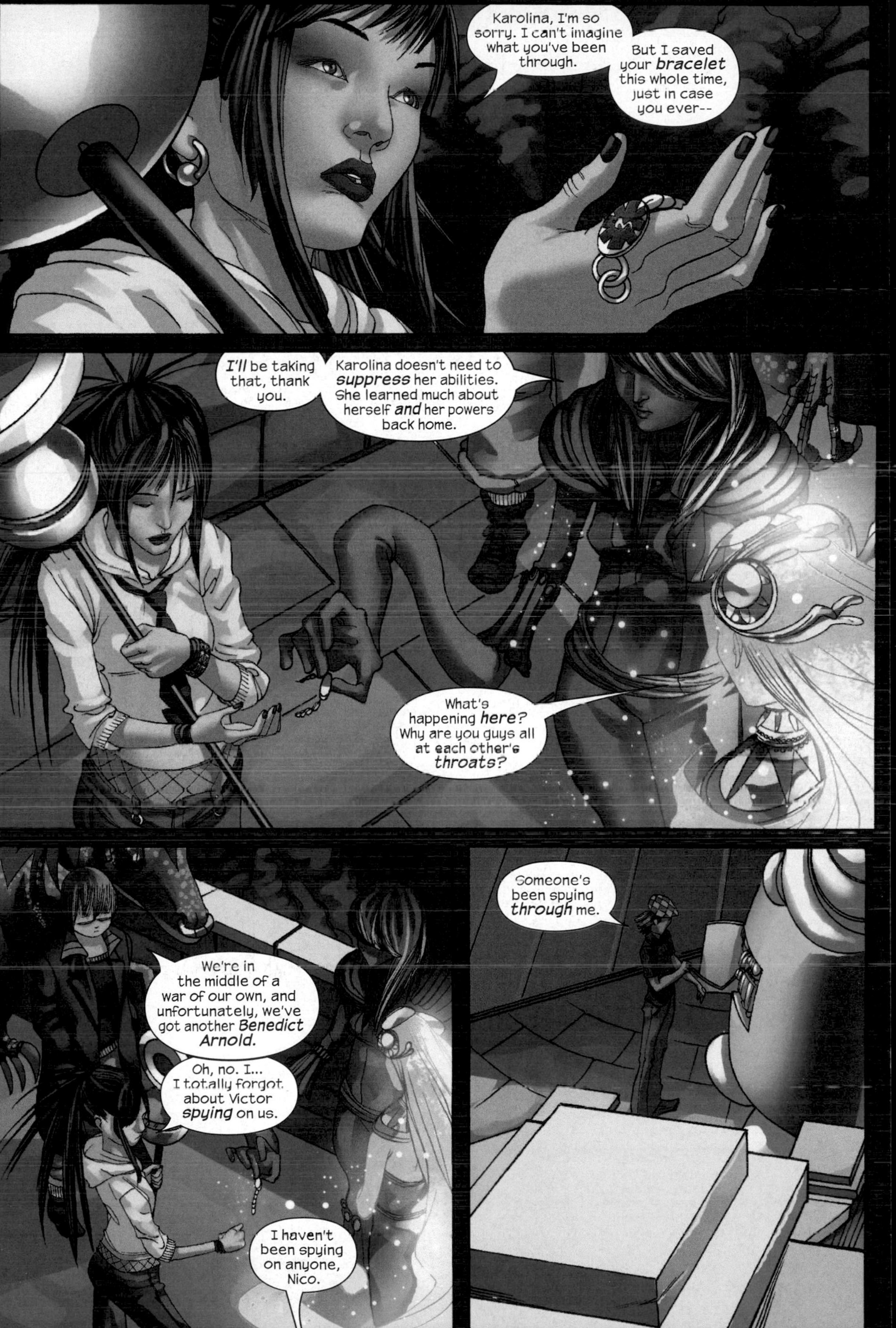
Karolina, I'm so sorry. I can't imagine what you've been through.
But I saved your *bracelet* this whole time, just in case you ever--
I'll be taking that, thank you.
Karolina doesn't need to *suppress* her abilities. She learned much about herself *and* her powers back home.
What's happening *here?* Why are you guys all at each other's *throats?*
We're in the middle of a war of our own, and unfortunately, we've got another *Benedict Arnold.*
Oh, no. I... I totally forgot about Victor *spying* on us.
I haven't been spying on anyone, Nico.
Someone's been spying *through* me.

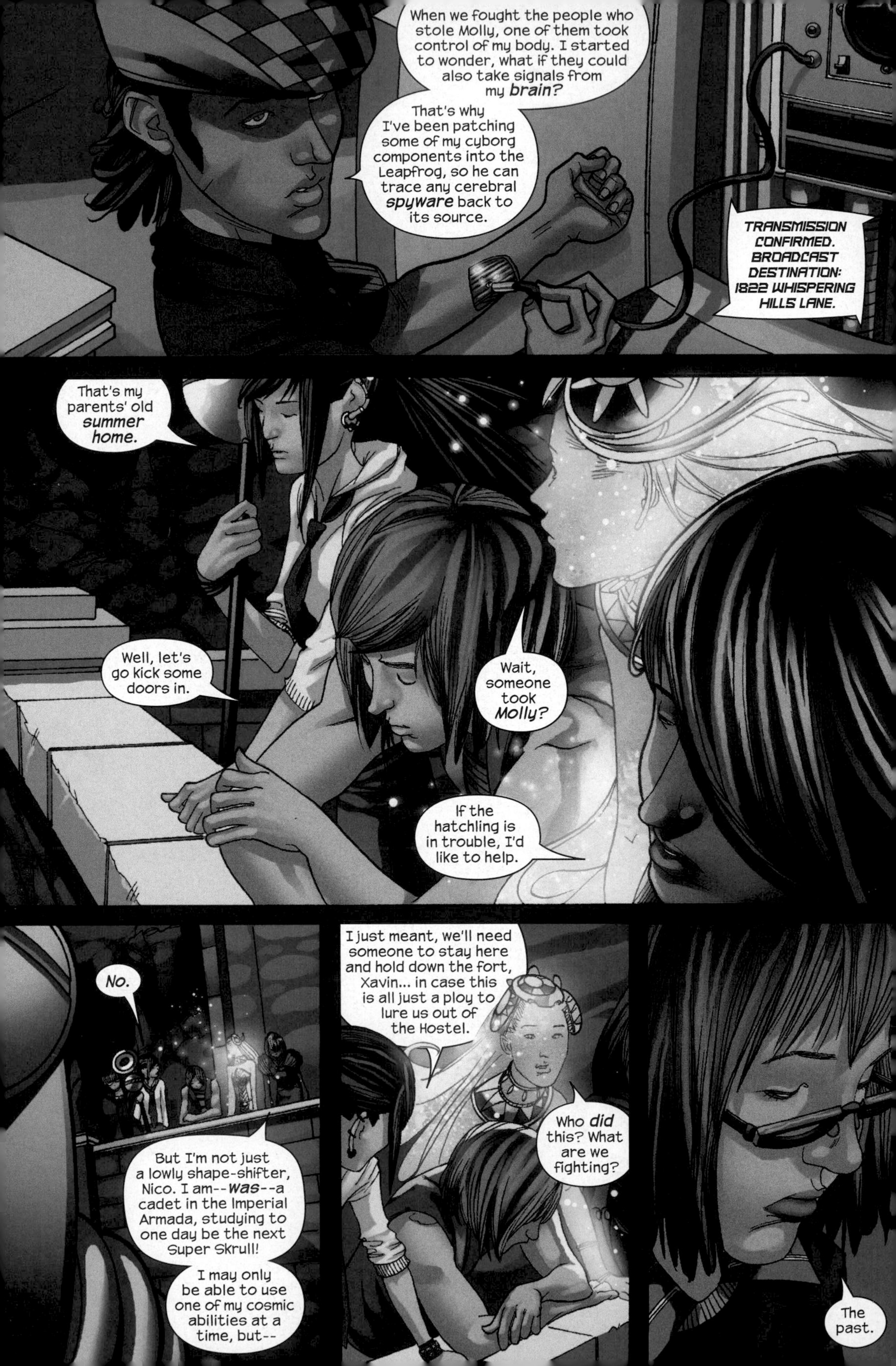
When we fought the people who stole Molly, one of them took control of my body. I started to wonder, what if they could also take signals from my brain?
That's why I've been patching some of my cyborg components into the Leapfrog, so he can trace any cerebral spyware back to its source.
TRANSMISSION CONFIRMED. BROADCAST DESTINATION: 1822 WHISPERING HILLS LANE.
That's my parents' old summer home.
Well, let's go kick some doors in.
Wait, someone took Molly?
If the hatchling is in trouble, I'd like to help.
No.
But I'm not just a lowly shape-shifter, Nico. I am--was--a cadet in the Imperial Armada, studying to one day be the next Super Skrull!
I may only be able to use one of my cosmic abilities at a time, but--
I just meant, we'll need someone to stay here and hold down the fort, Xavin... in case this is all just a ploy to lure us out of the Hostel.
Who did this? What are we fighting?
The past.

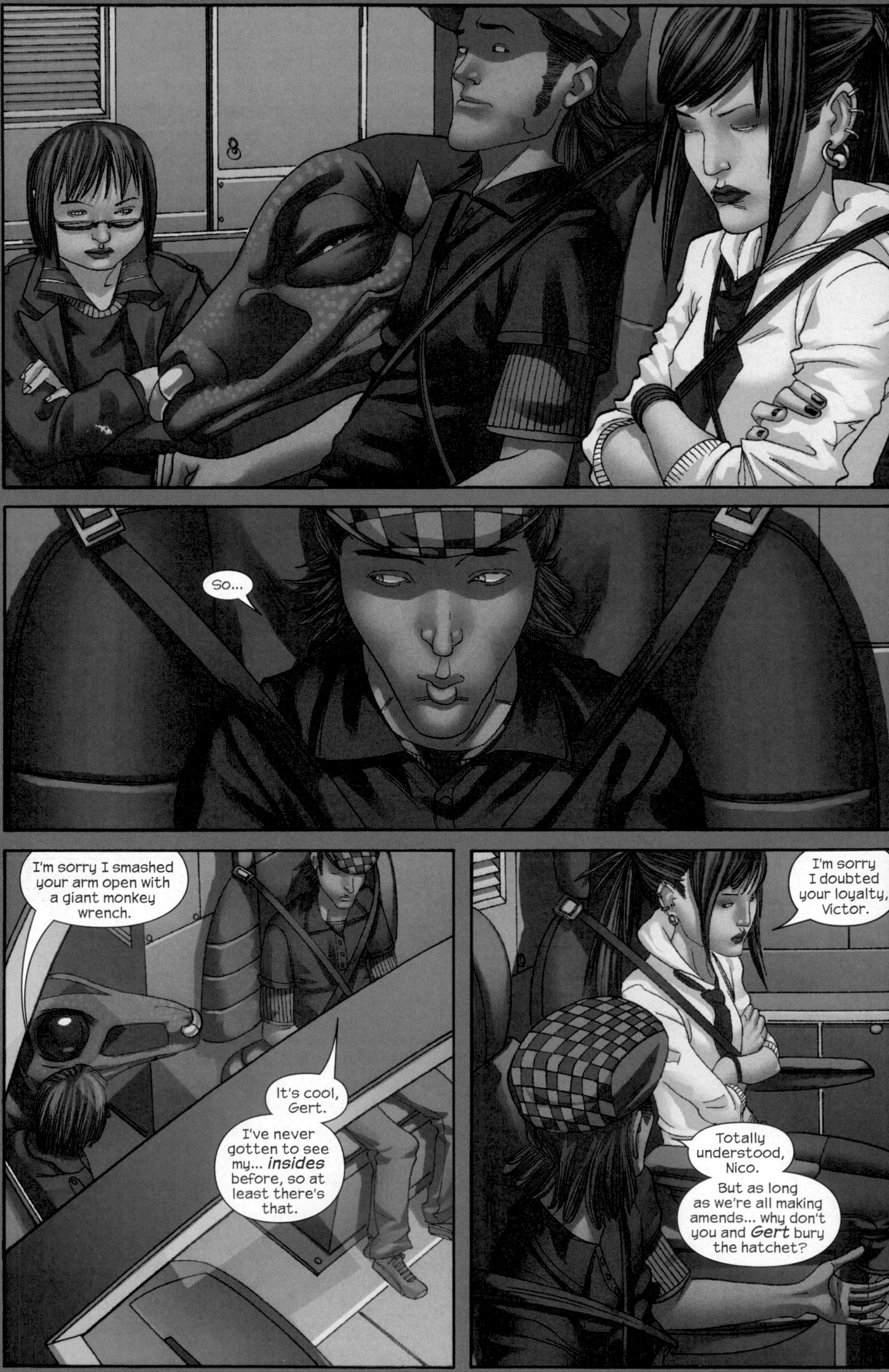
So...
I'm sorry I smashed your arm open with a giant monkey wrench.
It's cool, Gert.
I've never gotten to see my... *insides* before, so at least there's that.
I'm sorry I doubted your loyalty, Victor.
Totally understood, Nico.
But as long as we're all making amends... why don't you and *Gert* bury the hatchet?

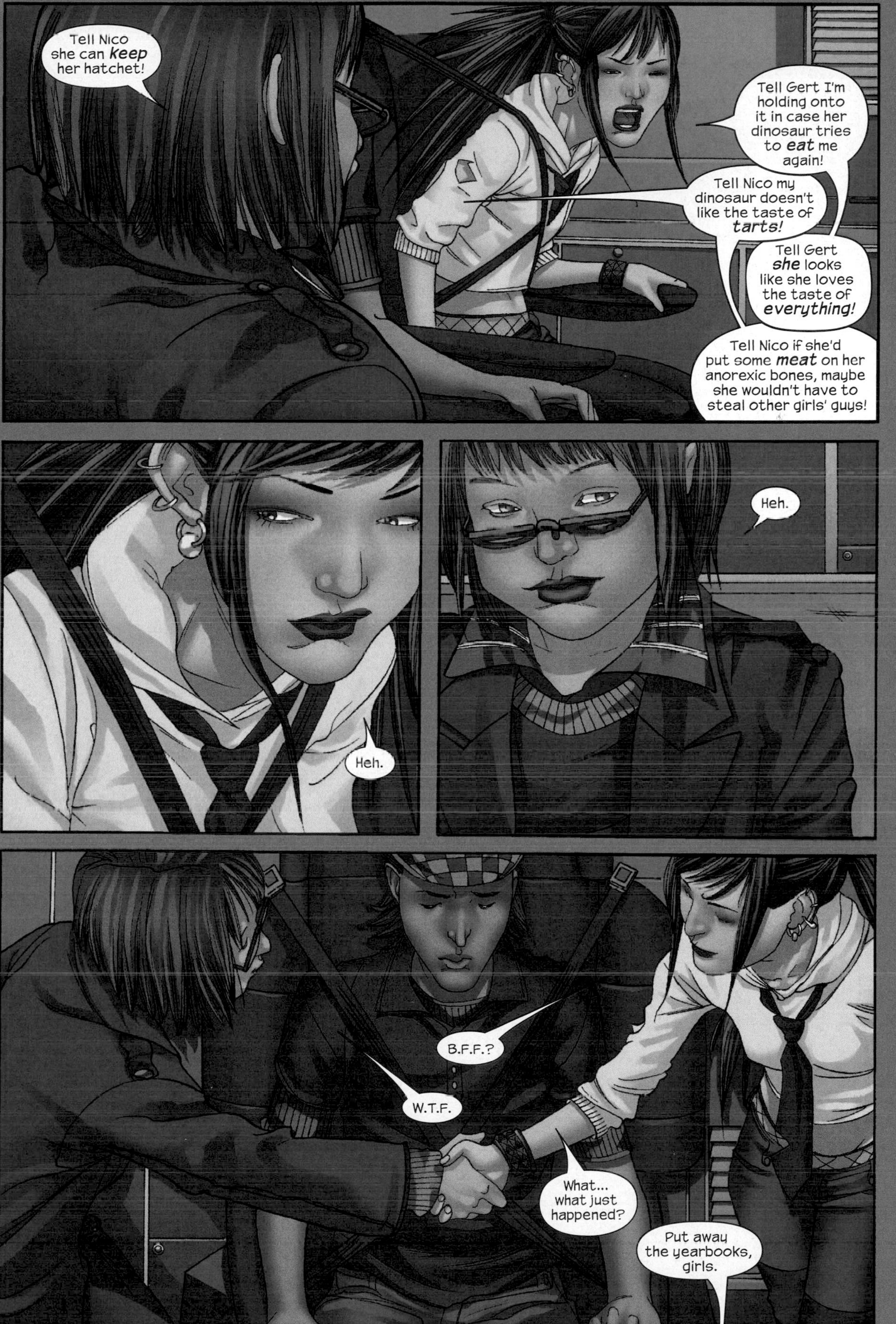
Tell Nico
she can *keep*
her hatchet!
Tell Gert I'm holding onto it in case her dinosaur tries to *eat* me again!
Tell Nico my dinosaur doesn't like the taste of *tarts!*
Tell Gert *she* looks like she loves the taste of *everything!*
Tell Nico if she'd put some *meat* on her anorexic bones, maybe she wouldn't have to steal other girls' guys!
Heh.
Heh.
B.F.F.?
W.T.F.
What... what just happened?
Put away the yearbooks, girls.

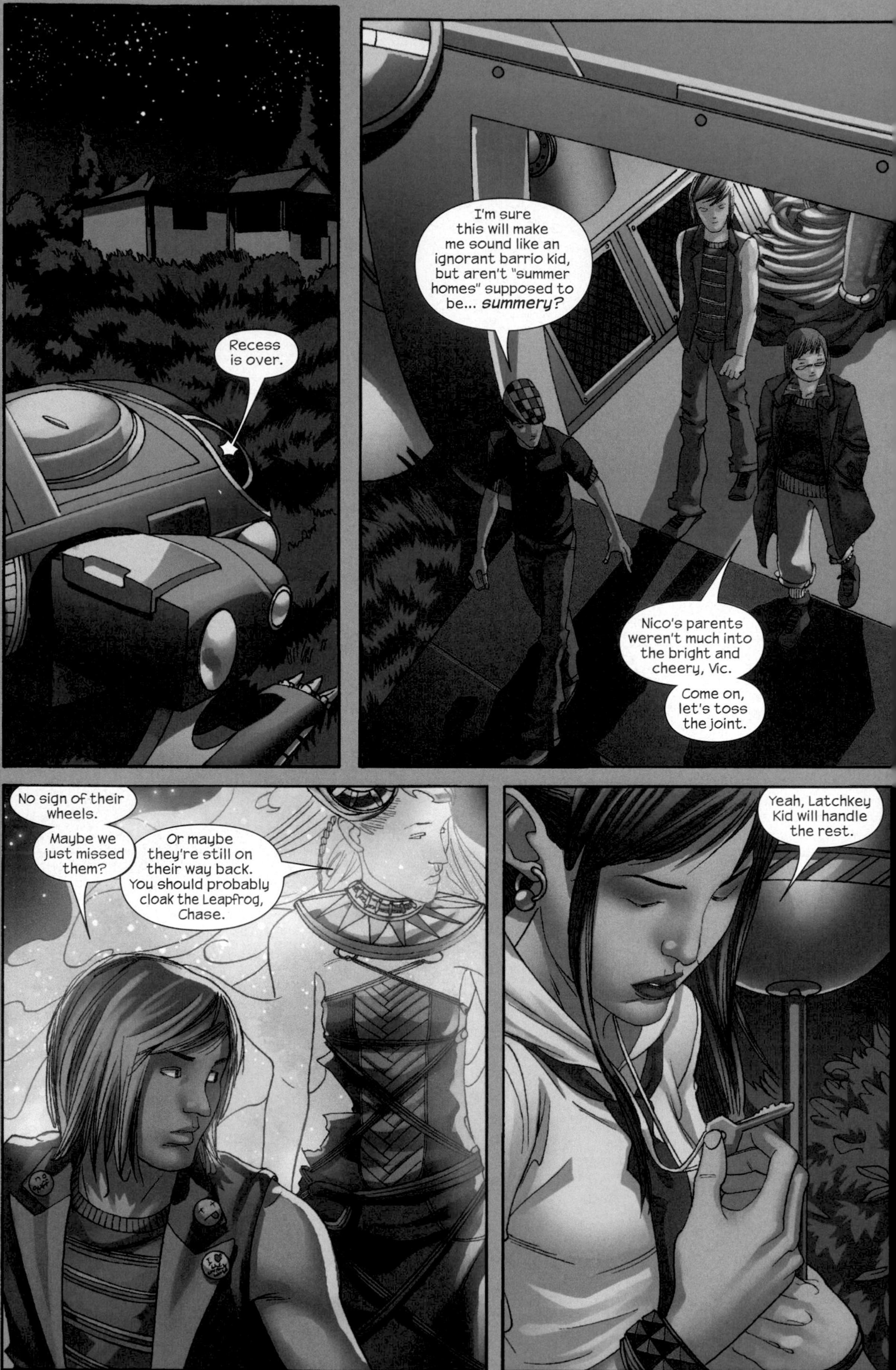
Recess is over.
I'm sure this will make me sound like an ignorant barrio kid, but aren't "summer homes" supposed to be... *summery?*
Nico's parents weren't much into the bright and cheery, Vic.
Come on, let's toss the joint.
No sign of their wheels.
Maybe we just missed them?
Or maybe they're still on their way back. You should probably cloak the Leapfrog, Chase.
Yeah, Latchkey Kid will handle the rest.

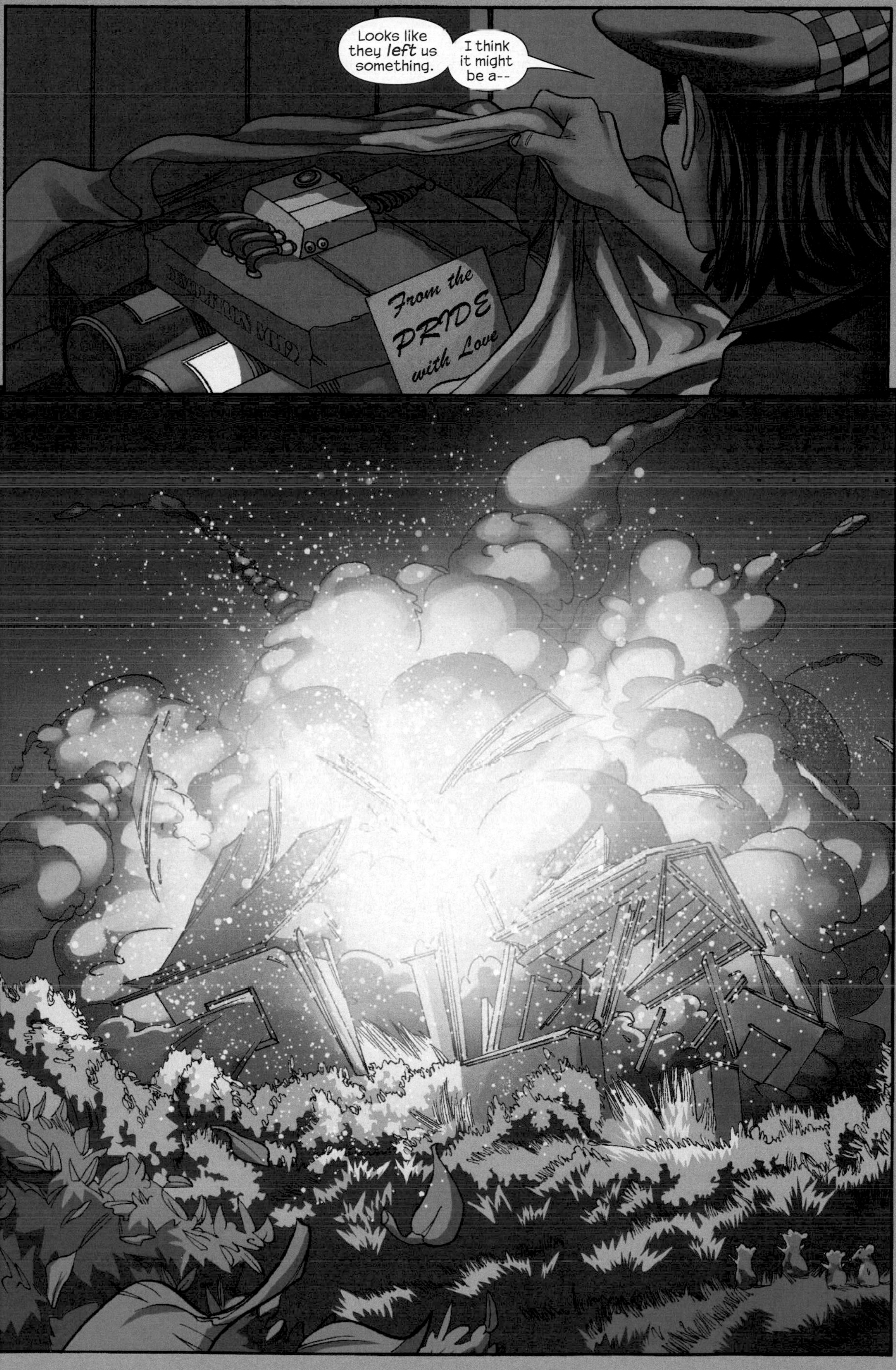
Looks like they *left* us something.
I think it might be a--
From the PRIDE with Love

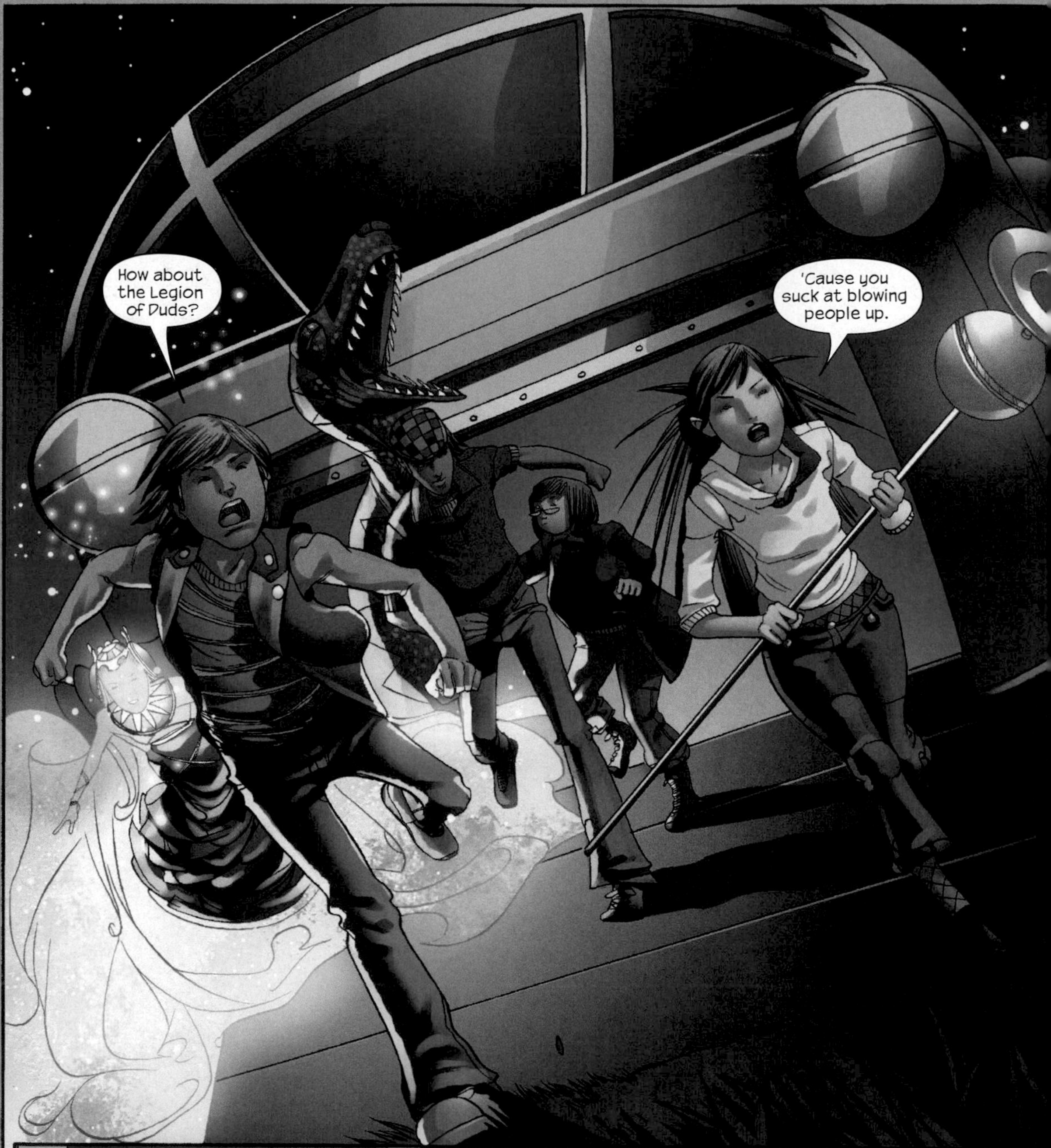
How about the Legion of Duds?
'Cause you suck at blowing people up.
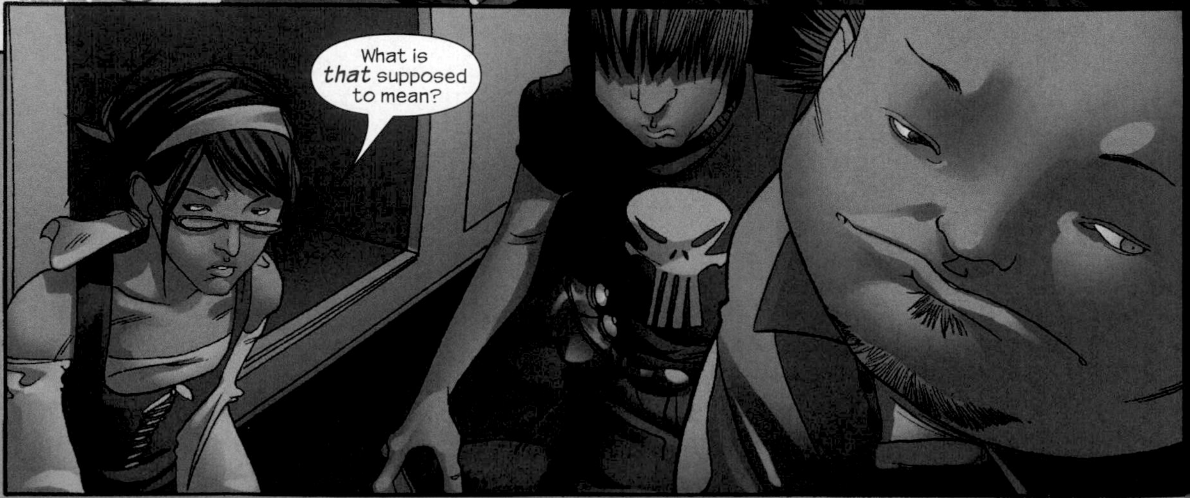
What is *that* supposed to mean?

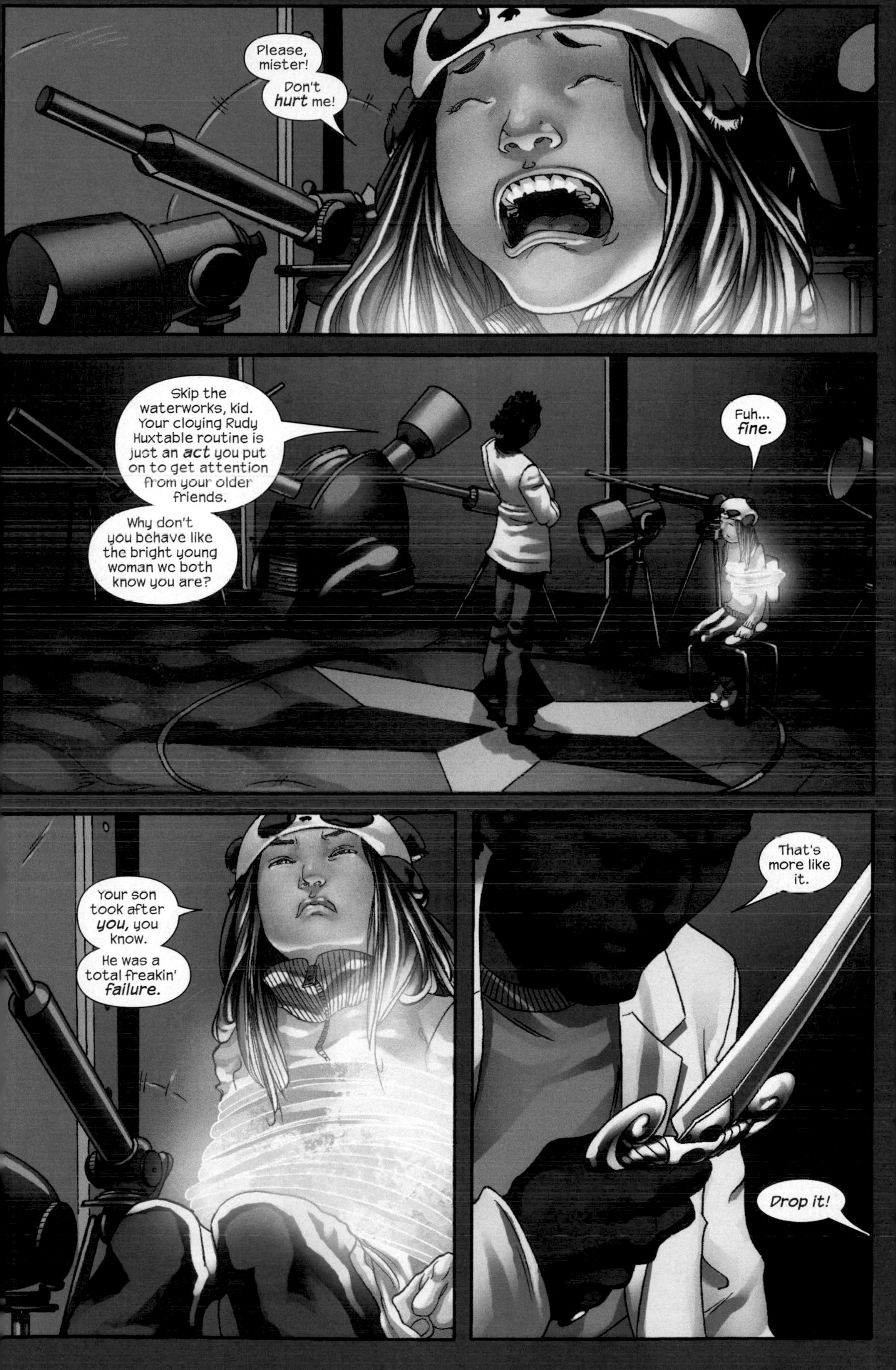
Please, mister!
Don't *hurt* me!
Skip the waterworks, kid. Your cloying Rudy Huxtable routine is just an *act* you put on to get attention from your older friends.
Why don't you behave like the bright young woman we both know you are?
Fuh... *fine.*
Your son took after *you,* you know.
He was a total freakin' *failure.*
That's more like it.
Drop it!

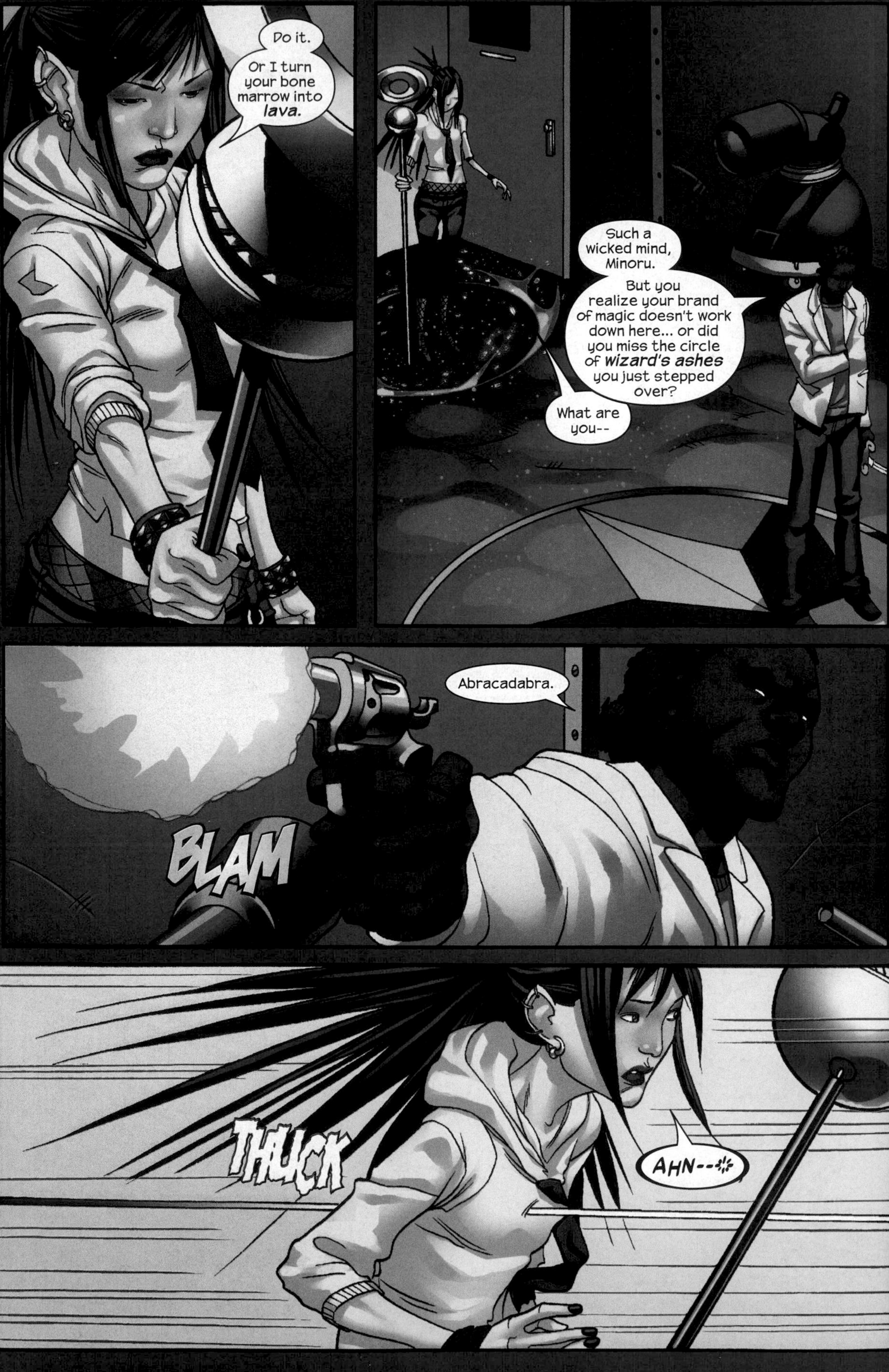
Do it.
Or I turn your bone marrow into *lava.*
Such a wicked mind, Minoru.
But you realize your brand of magic doesn't work down here... or did you miss the circle of *wizard's ashes* you just stepped over?
What are you--
Abracadabra.
BLAM
THUCK
AHN--

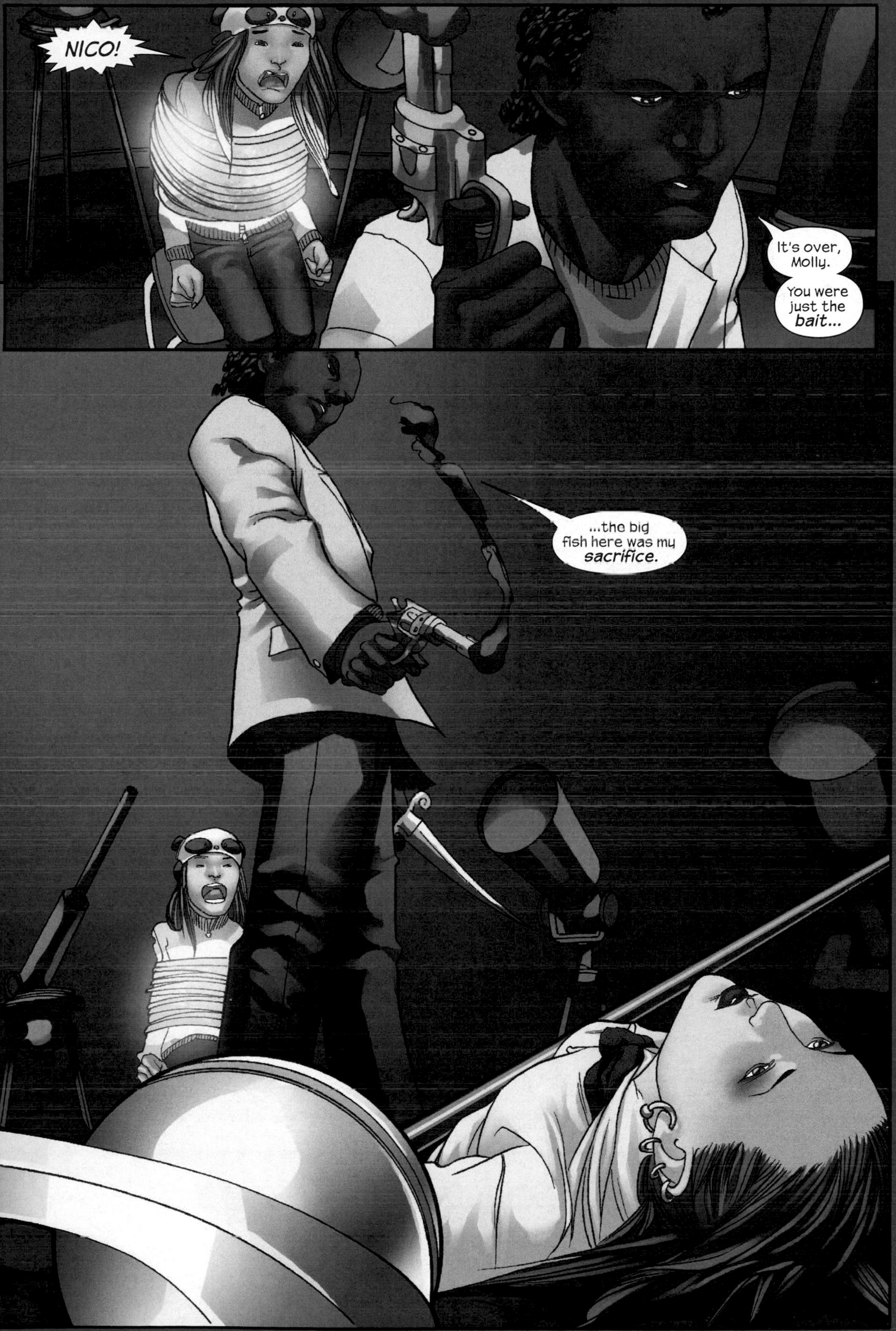
NICO!
It's over, Molly.
You were just the *bait*...
...the big fish here was my *sacrifice*.

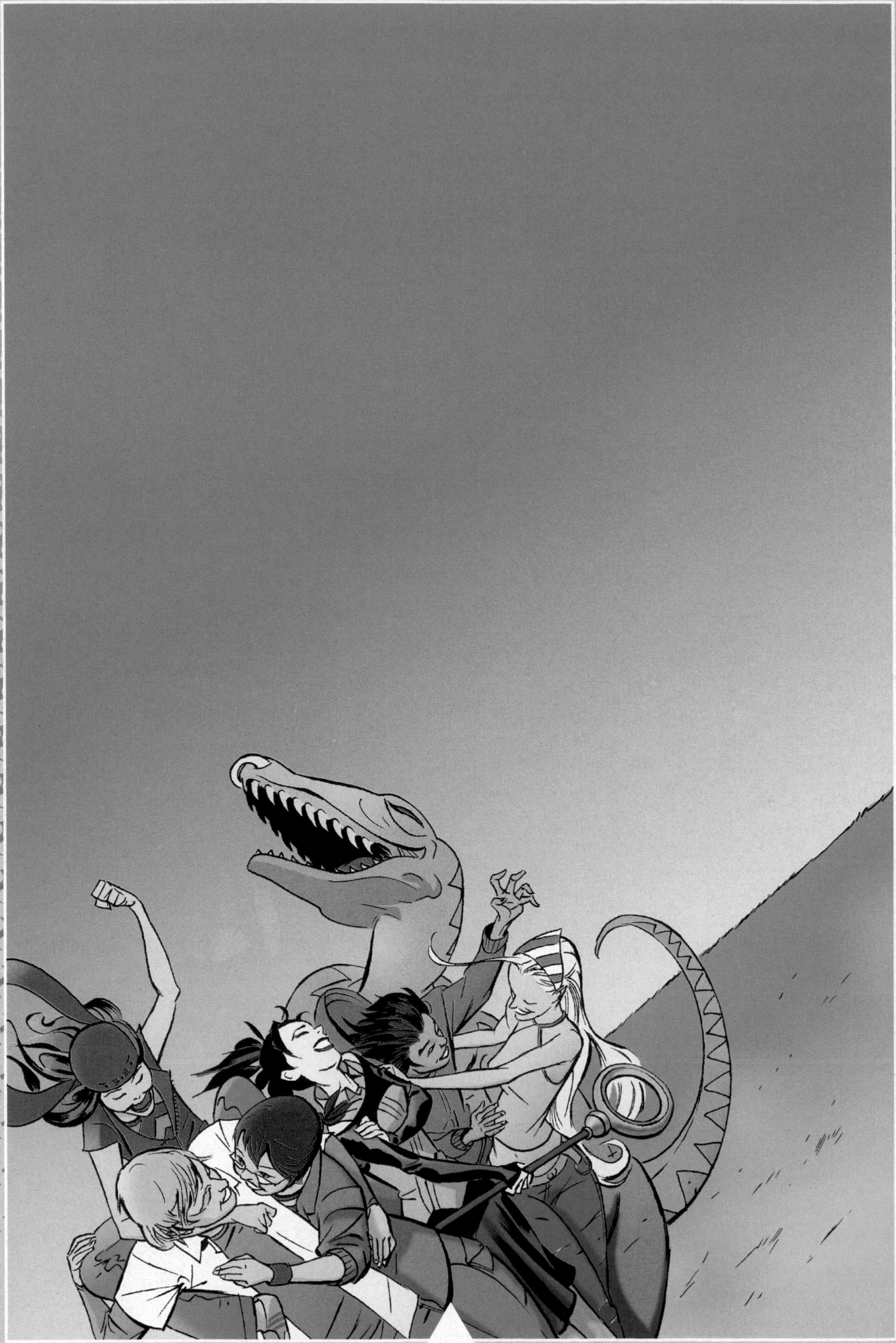

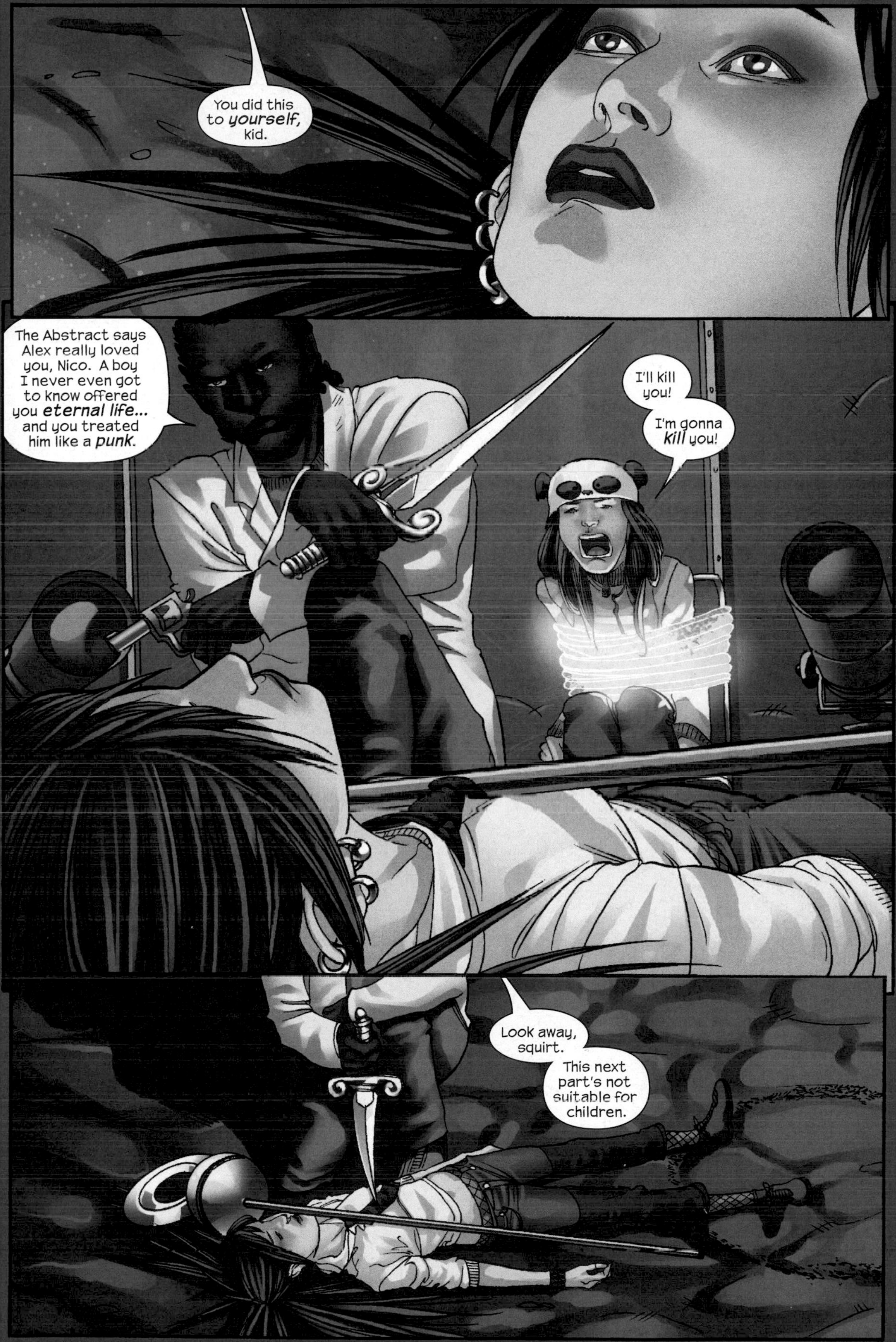
You did this to *yourself,* kid.
The Abstract says Alex really loved you, Nico. A boy I never even got to know offered you *eternal life...* and you treated him like a *punk.*
I'll kill you!
I'm gonna *kill* you!
Look away, squirt.
This next part's not suitable for children.

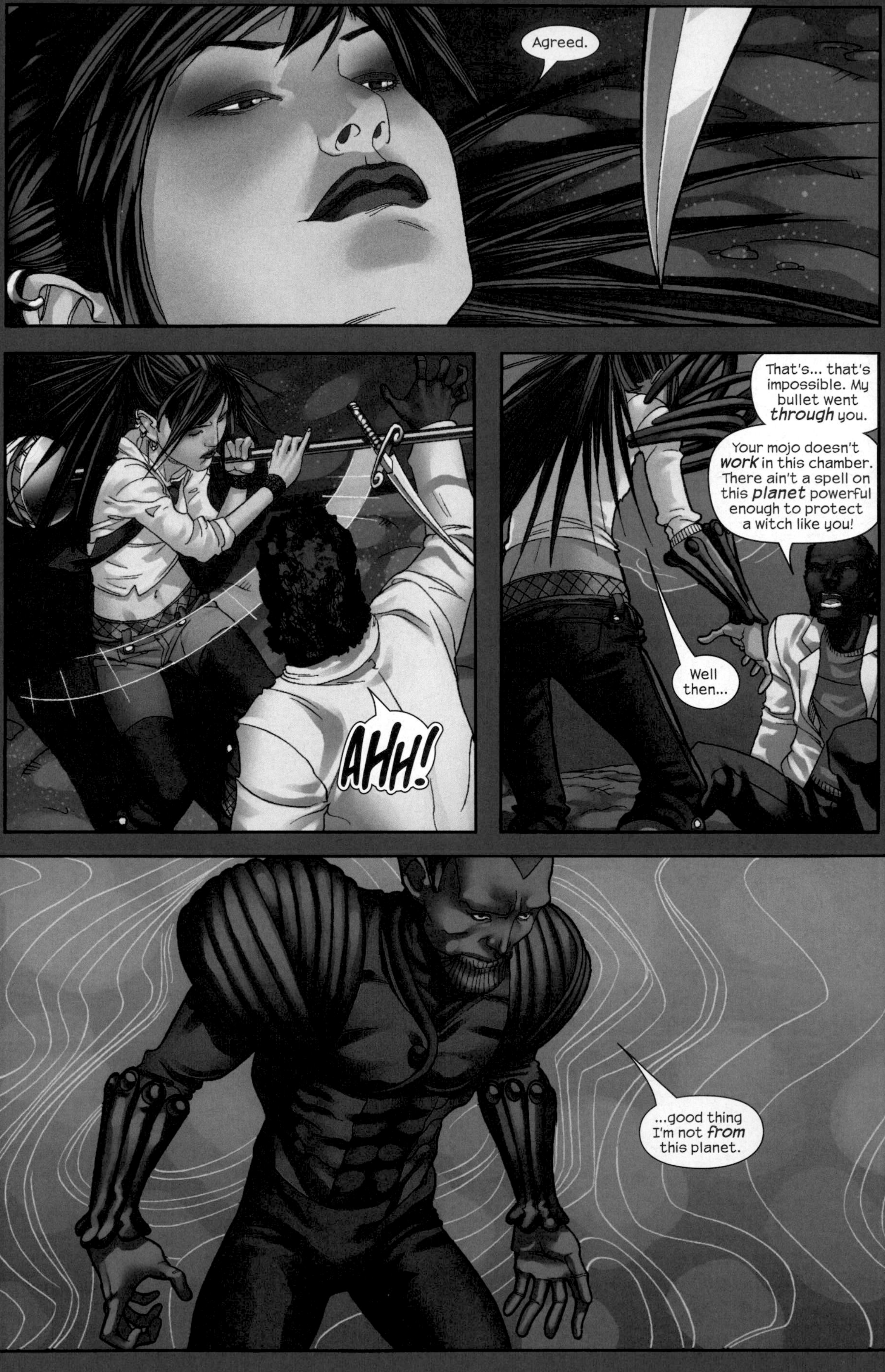

Agreed.
AHH!
That's... that's impossible. My bullet went *through* you.
Your mojo doesn't *work* in this chamber. There ain't a spell on this *planet* powerful enough to protect a witch like you!
Well then...
...good thing I'm not *from* this planet.

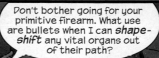

Don't bother going for your primitive firearm. What use are bullets when I can *shape-shift* any vital organs out of their path?

What *are* you?

My name is *Xavin*, Super-Skrull-in-training. I was forced to abandon my outpost world to protect my mate from murderous thugs like *you.*

I'm a runaway.

The Minoru girl and I came up with this plan in *secret*, in case you and your soldiers were still *spying* like the cowards you are.

Get back, or I... I cut the mutant.

Your threats against the hatchling are meaningless, human...

...seeing how the *real* Nico has already rescued her.

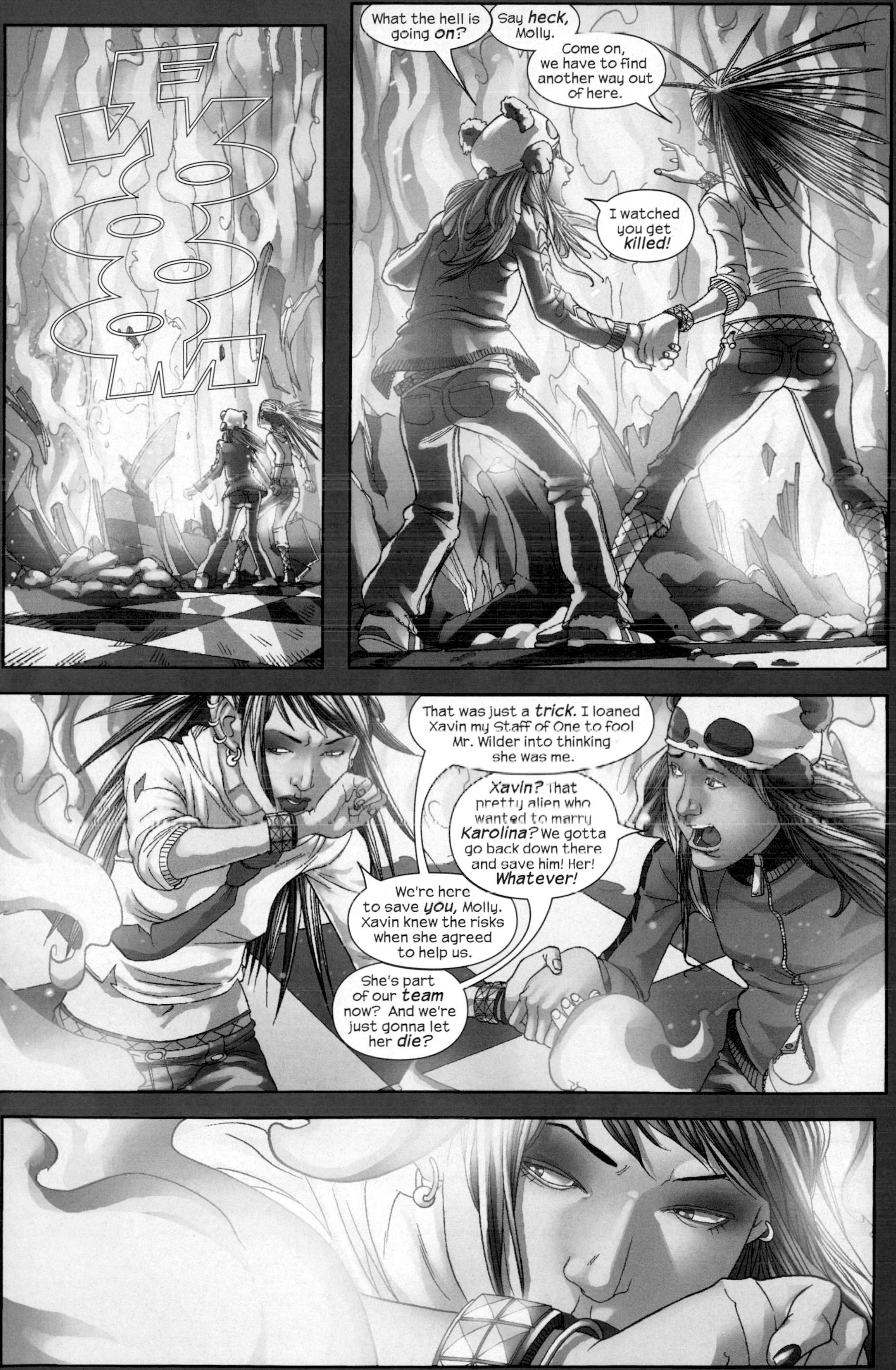

What the hell is going on?
Say heck, Molly.
Come on, we have to find another way out of here.
I watched you get killed!
That was just a trick. I loaned Xavin my Staff of One to fool Mr. Wilder into thinking she was me.
Xavin? That pretty alien who wanted to marry Karolina? We gotta go back down there and save him! Her! Whatever!
We're here to save you, Molly. Xavin knew the risks when she agreed to help us.
She's part of our team now? And we're just gonna let her die?

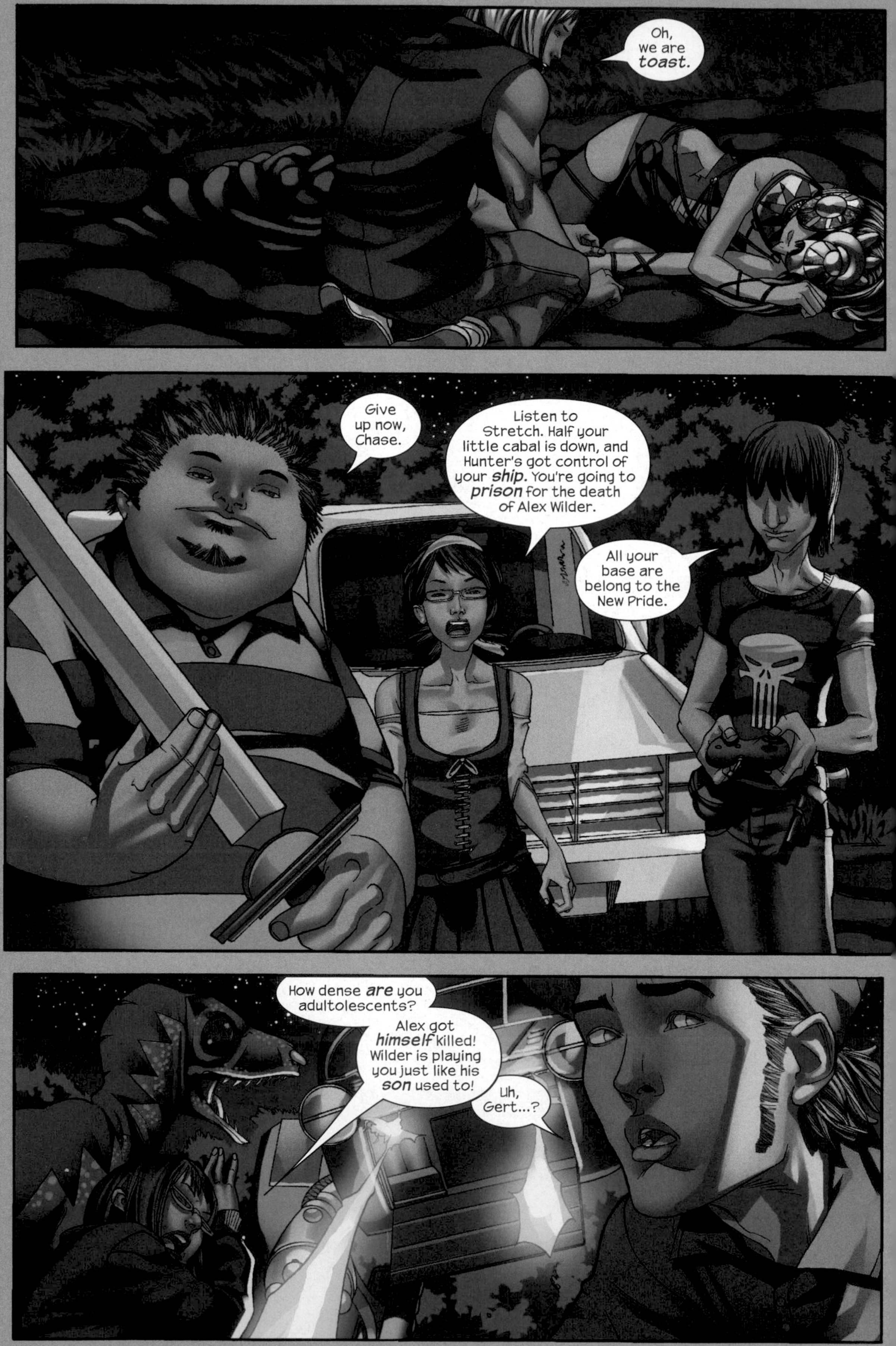

Oh, we are toast.
Give up now, Chase.
Listen to Stretch. Half your little cabal is down, and Hunter's got control of your ship. You're going to prison for the death of Alex Wilder.
All your base are belong to the New Pride.
How dense are you adultolescents?
Alex got himself killed! Wilder is playing you just like his son used to!
Uh, Gert...?

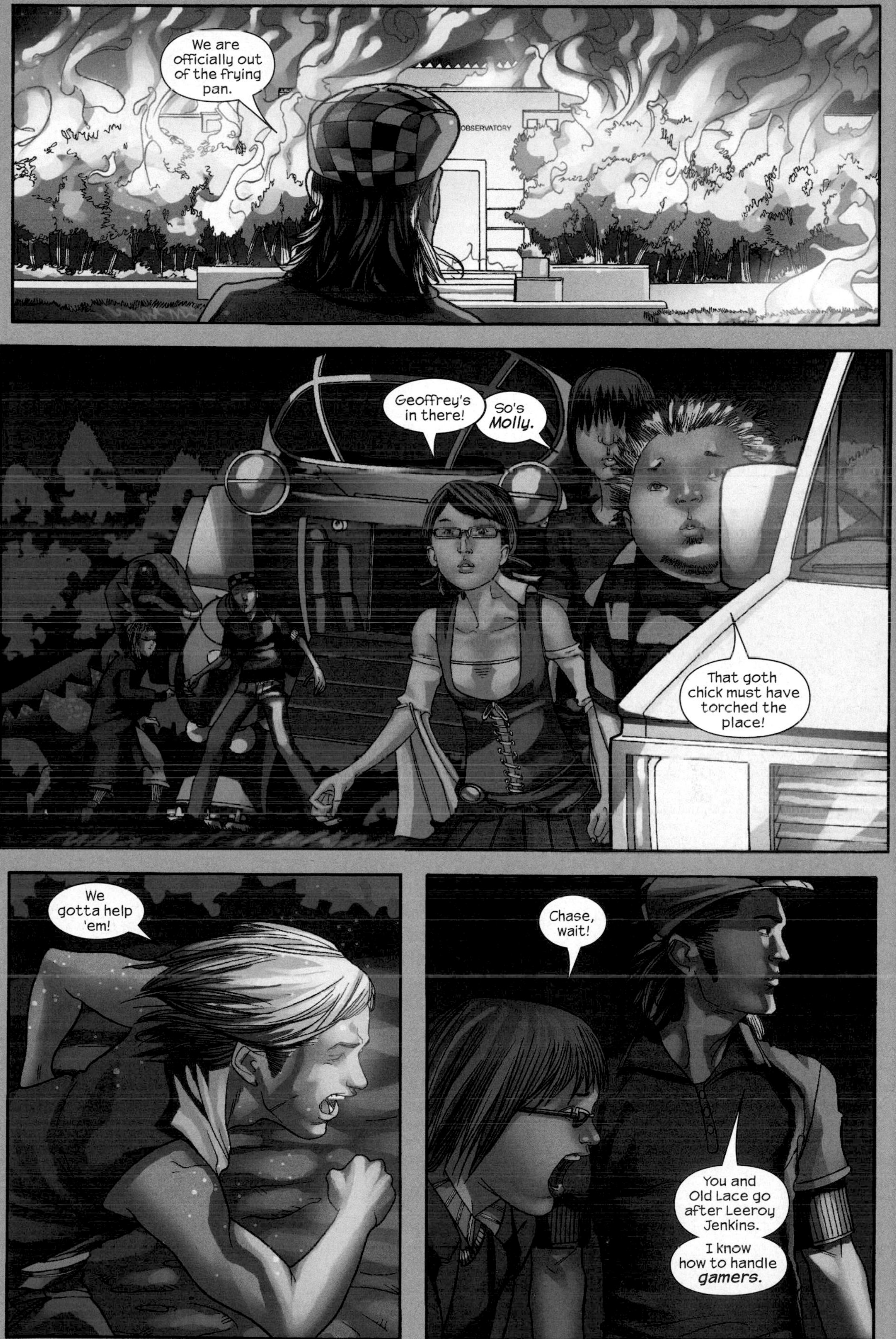

We are officially out of the frying pan.
OBSERVATORY
Geoffrey's in there!
So's Molly.
That goth chick must have torched the place!
We gotta help 'em!
Chase, wait!
You and Old Lace go after Leeroy Jenkins.
I know how to handle gamers.

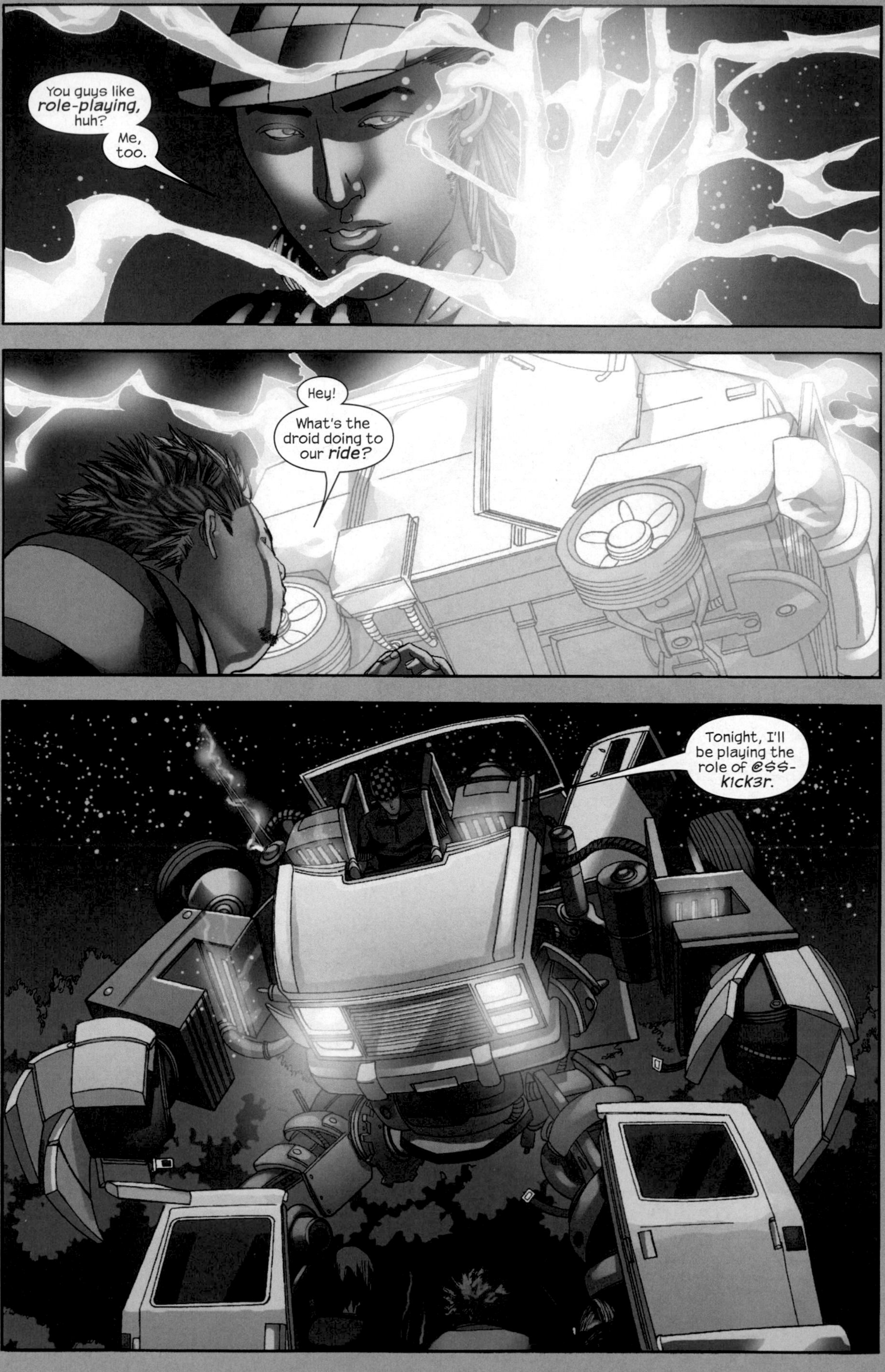
You guys like *role-playing,* huh?
Me, too.
Hey!
What's the droid doing to our *ride?*
Tonight, I'll be playing the role of @$$-K1CK3r.

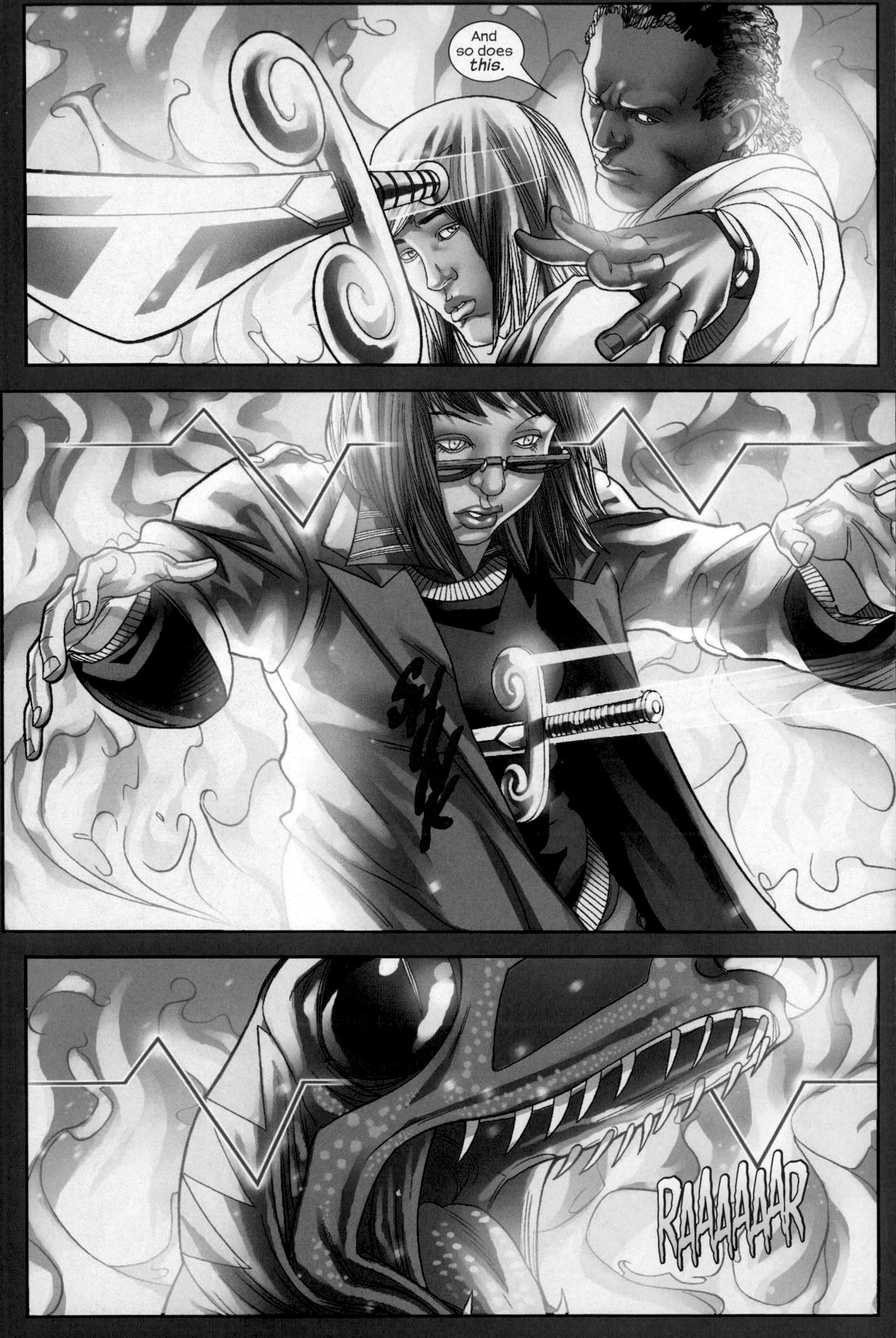
And so does *this*.
RAAAAAAR

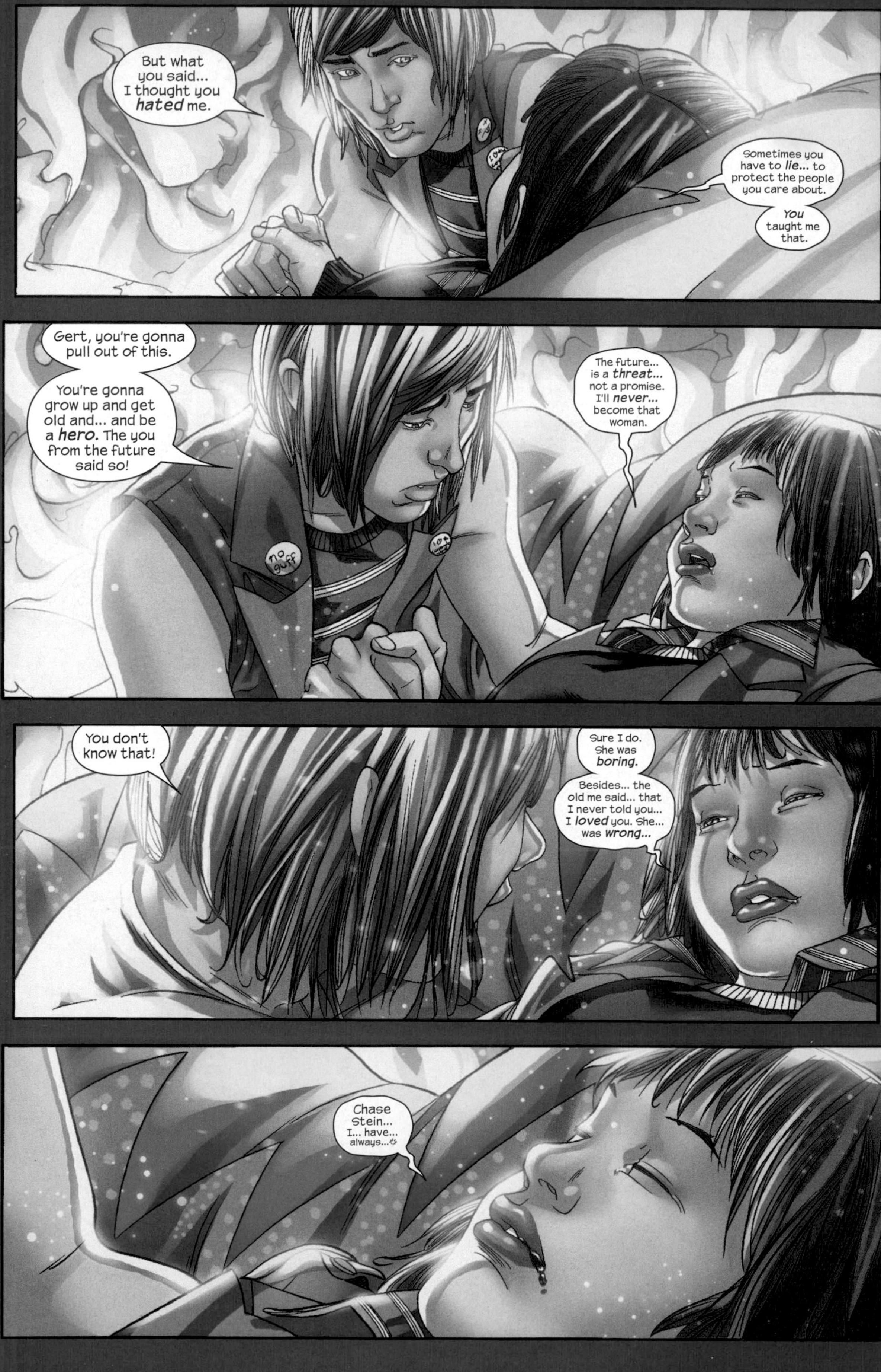
But what you said... I thought you hated me.
Sometimes you have to lie... to protect the people you care about.
You taught me that.
Gert, you're gonna pull out of this.
You're gonna grow up and get old and... and be a hero. The you from the future said so!
The future... is a threat... not a promise. I'll never... become that woman.
You don't know that!
Sure I do. She was boring.
Besides... the old me said... that I never told you... I loved you. She... was wrong...
Chase Stein... I... have... always...

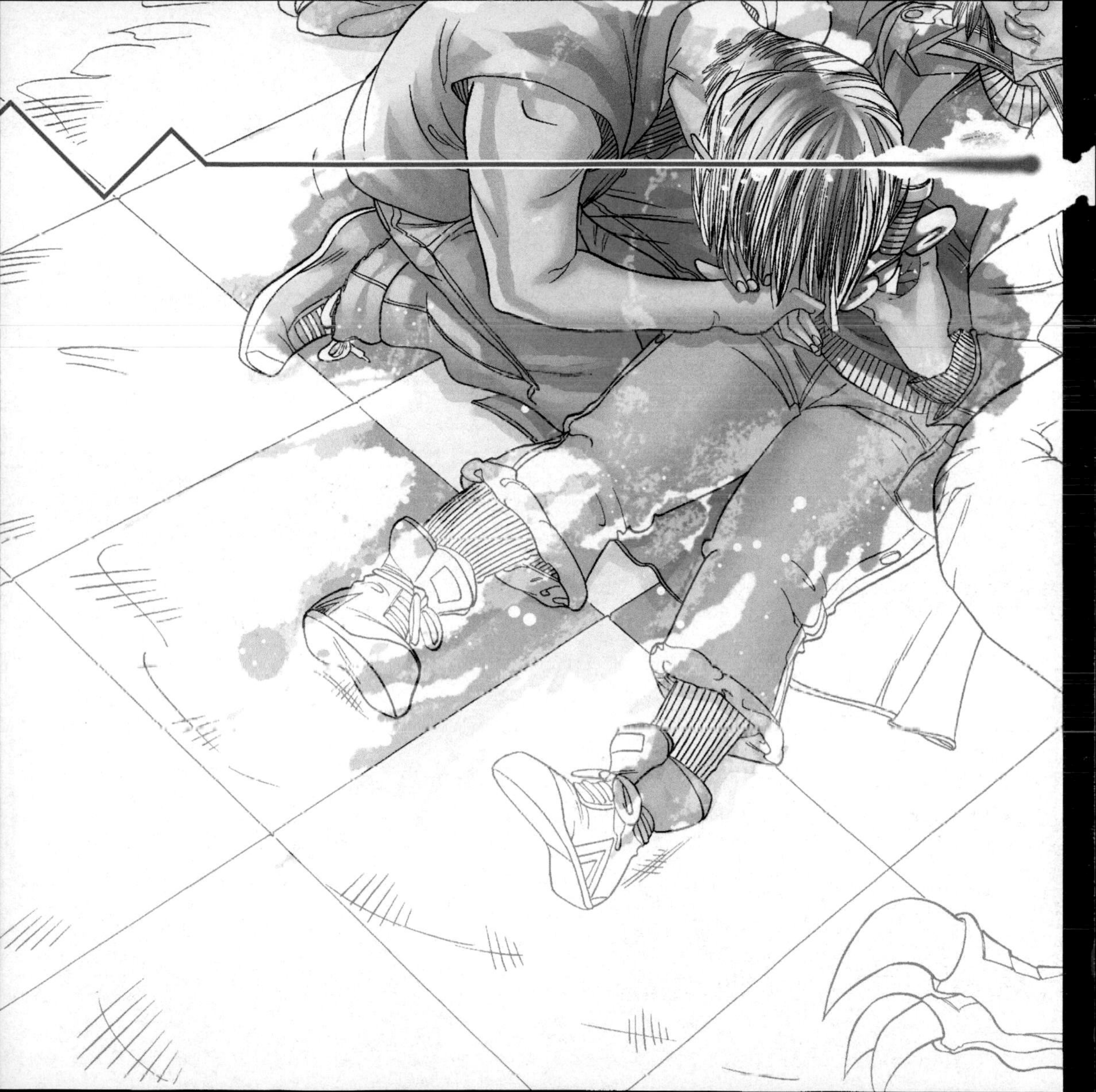

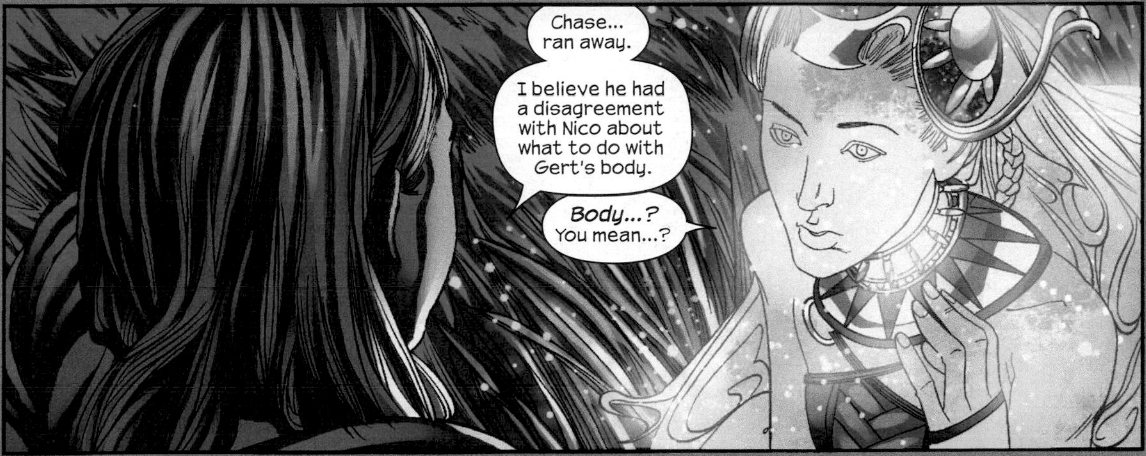
Chase... ran away.
I believe he had a disagreement with Nico about what to do with Gert's body.
Body...? You mean...?

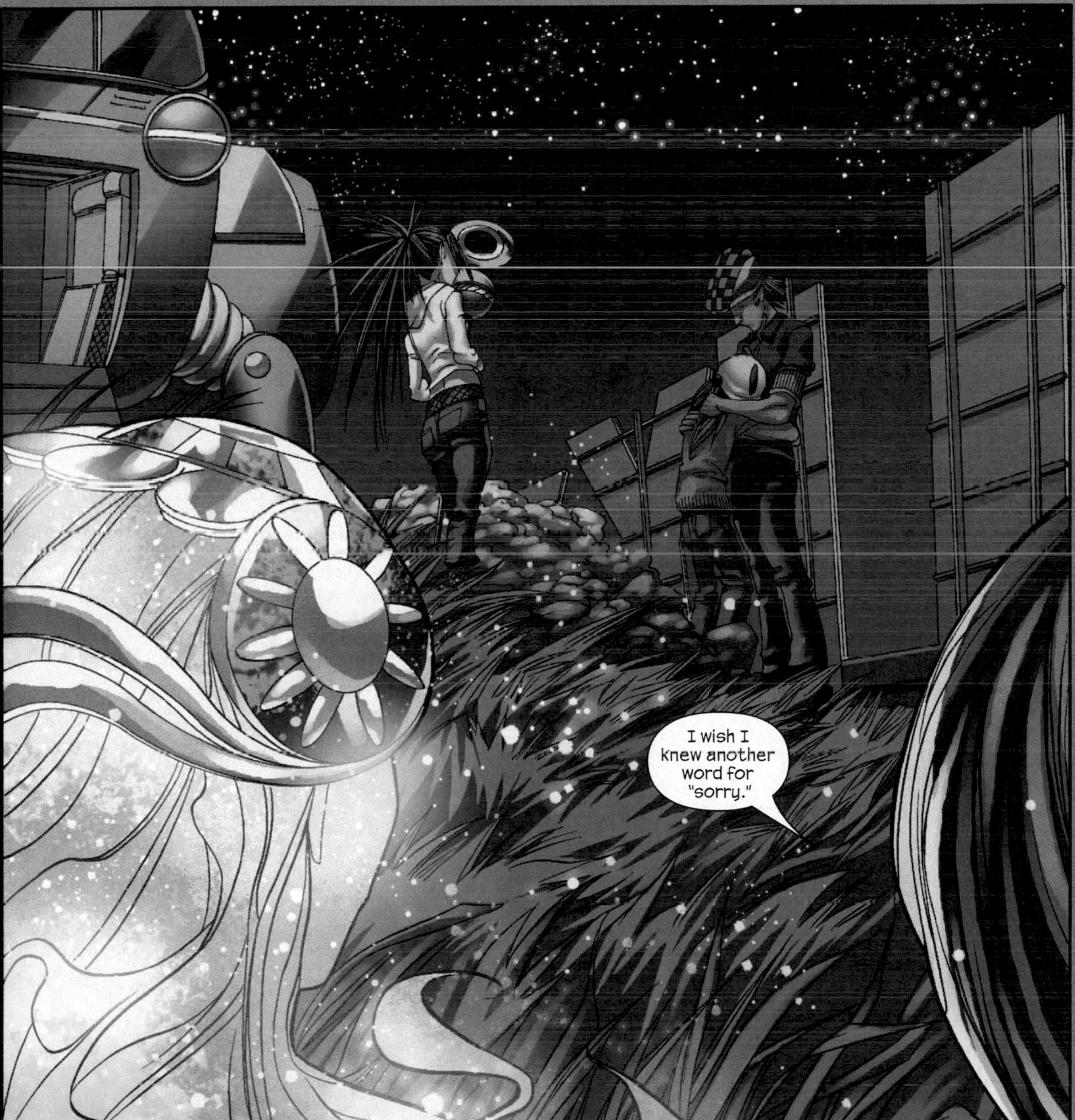
I wish I knew another word for "sorry."

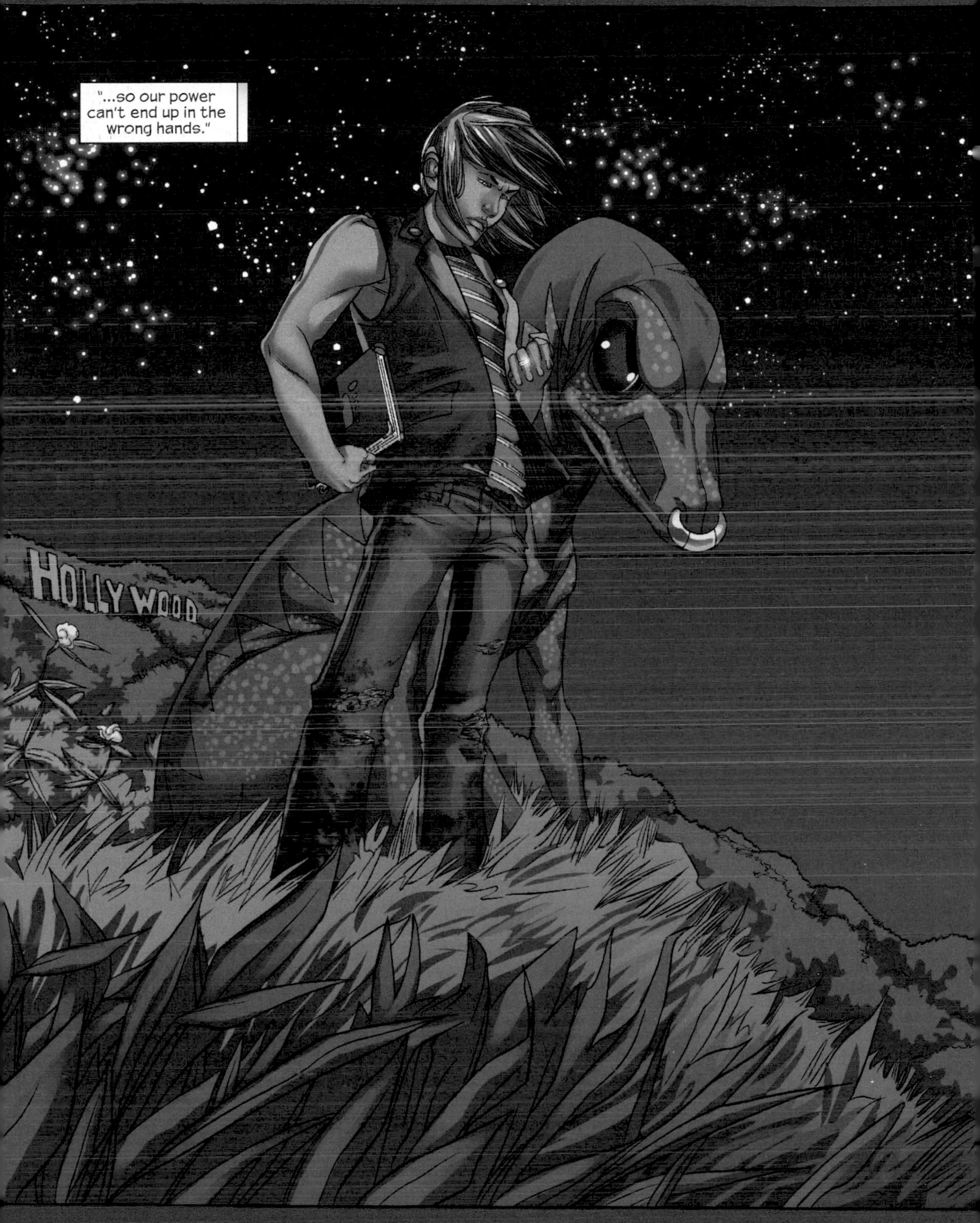
"...so our power
can't end up in the
wrong hands."
HOLLYWOOD

ADRIAN ALPHONA SKETCHBOOK

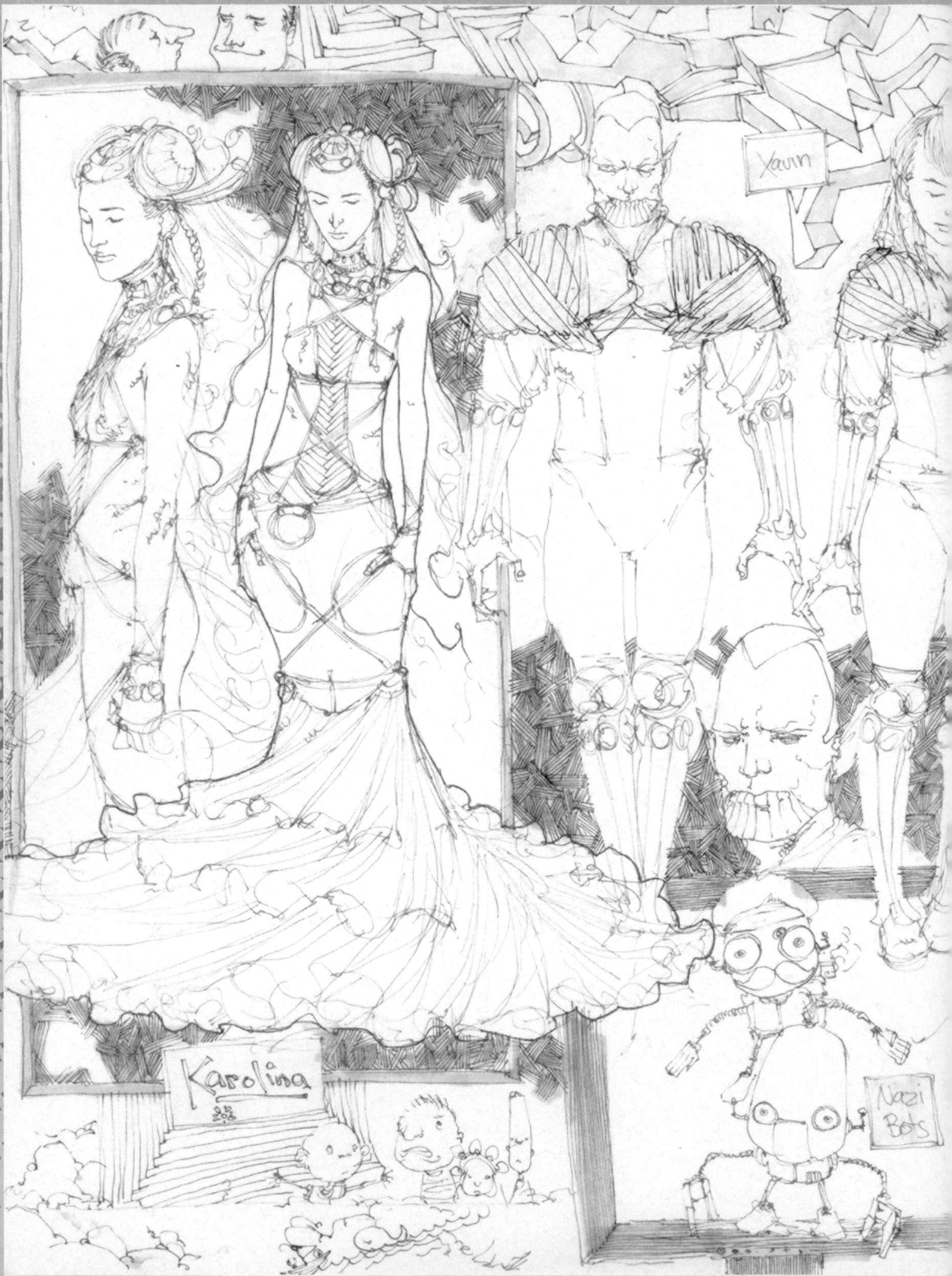
Xavin
Karolina
Nazi Bots

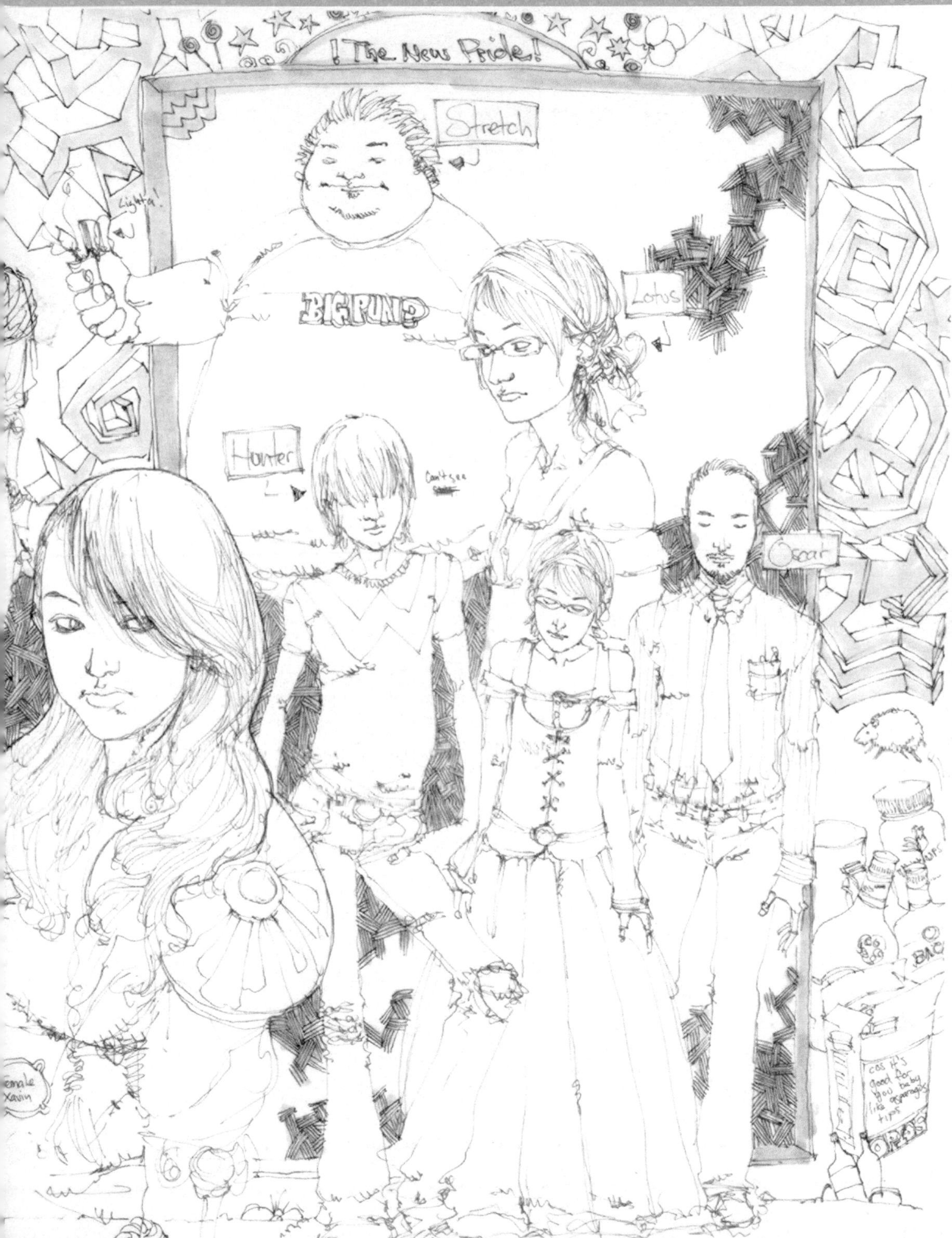

! The New Pride !
Stretch
Lighter!
BIGPUN
Lotus
Hunter
Can't see
Oscar
Female Xavin
cos it's good for you baby like asparagus tips
Runaways #14 Designs Jan06

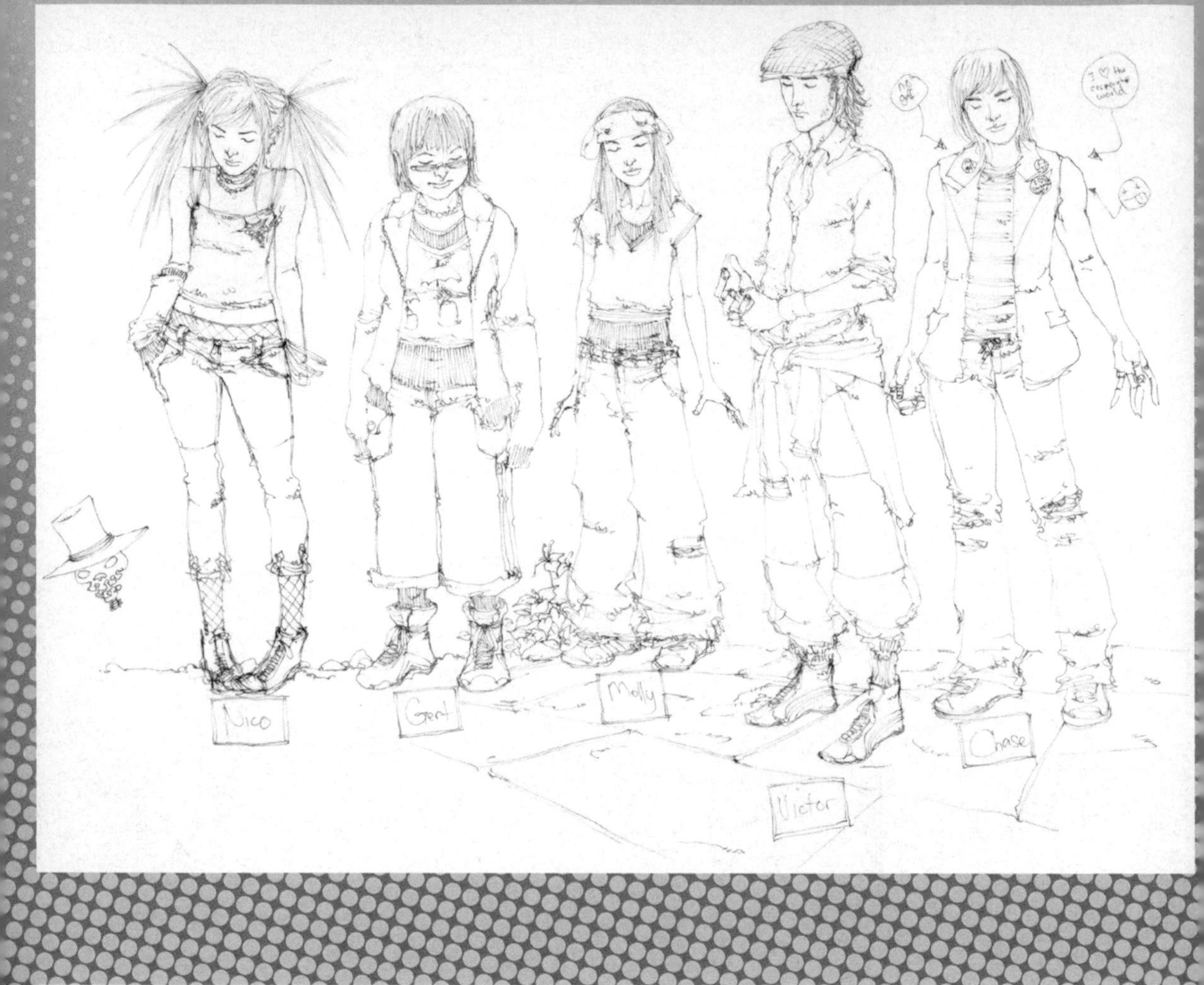
Nico
Gert
Molly
Victor
Chase

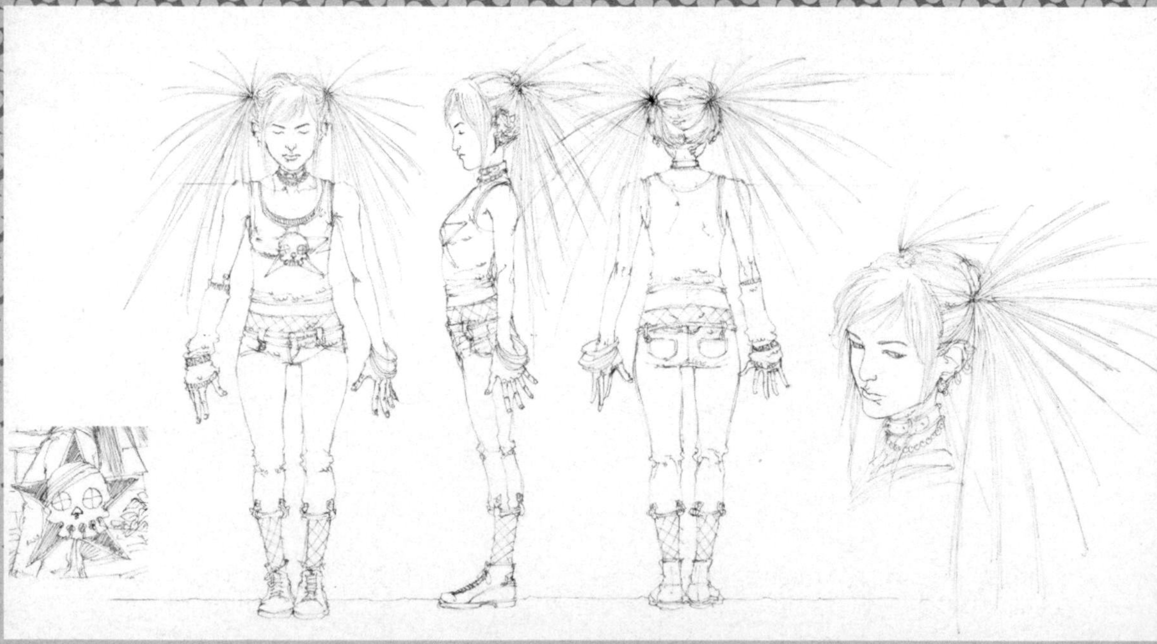

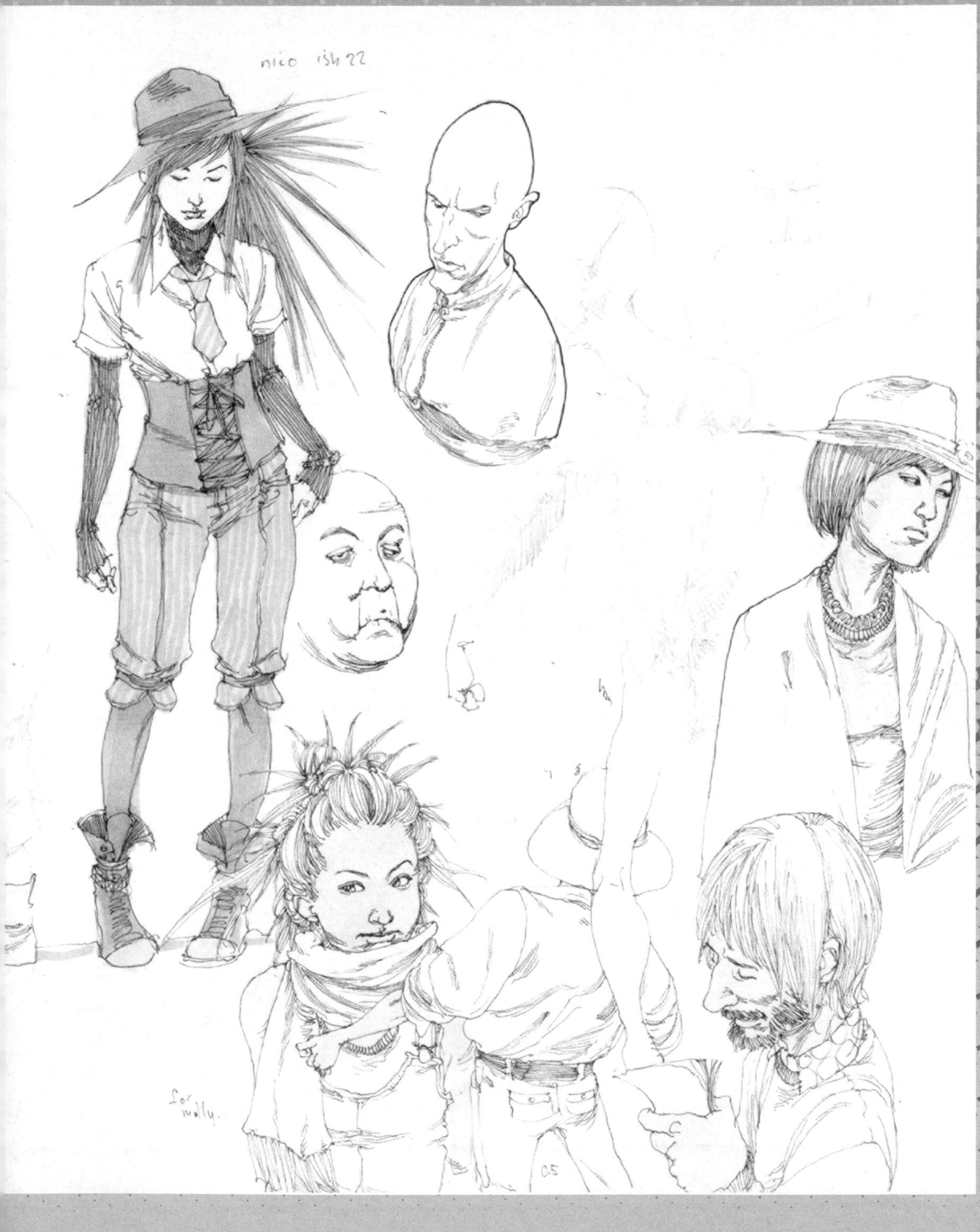
nico ish 22
for molly.
05

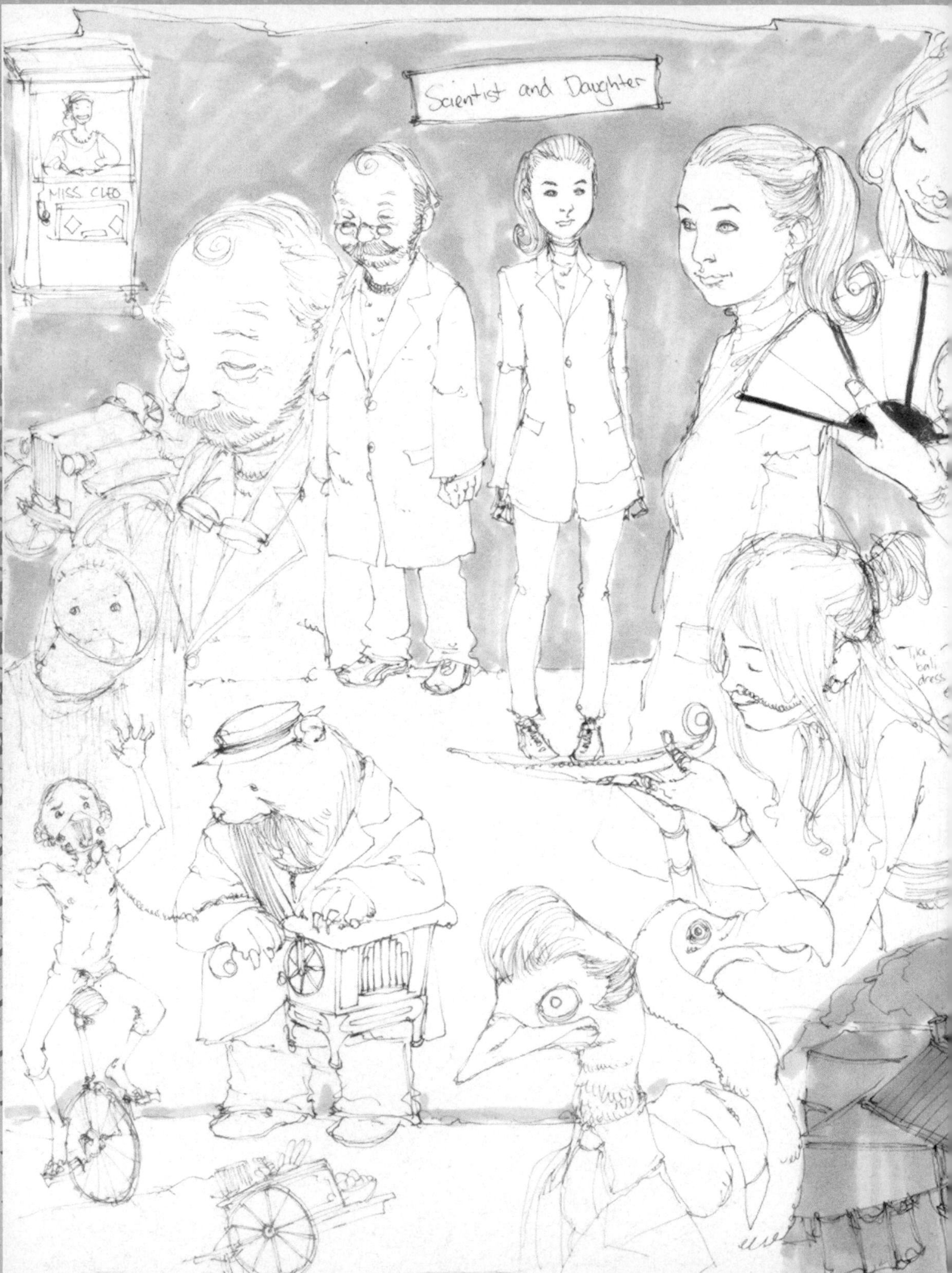
Scientist and Daughter
MISS. CLEO
Like bali dress

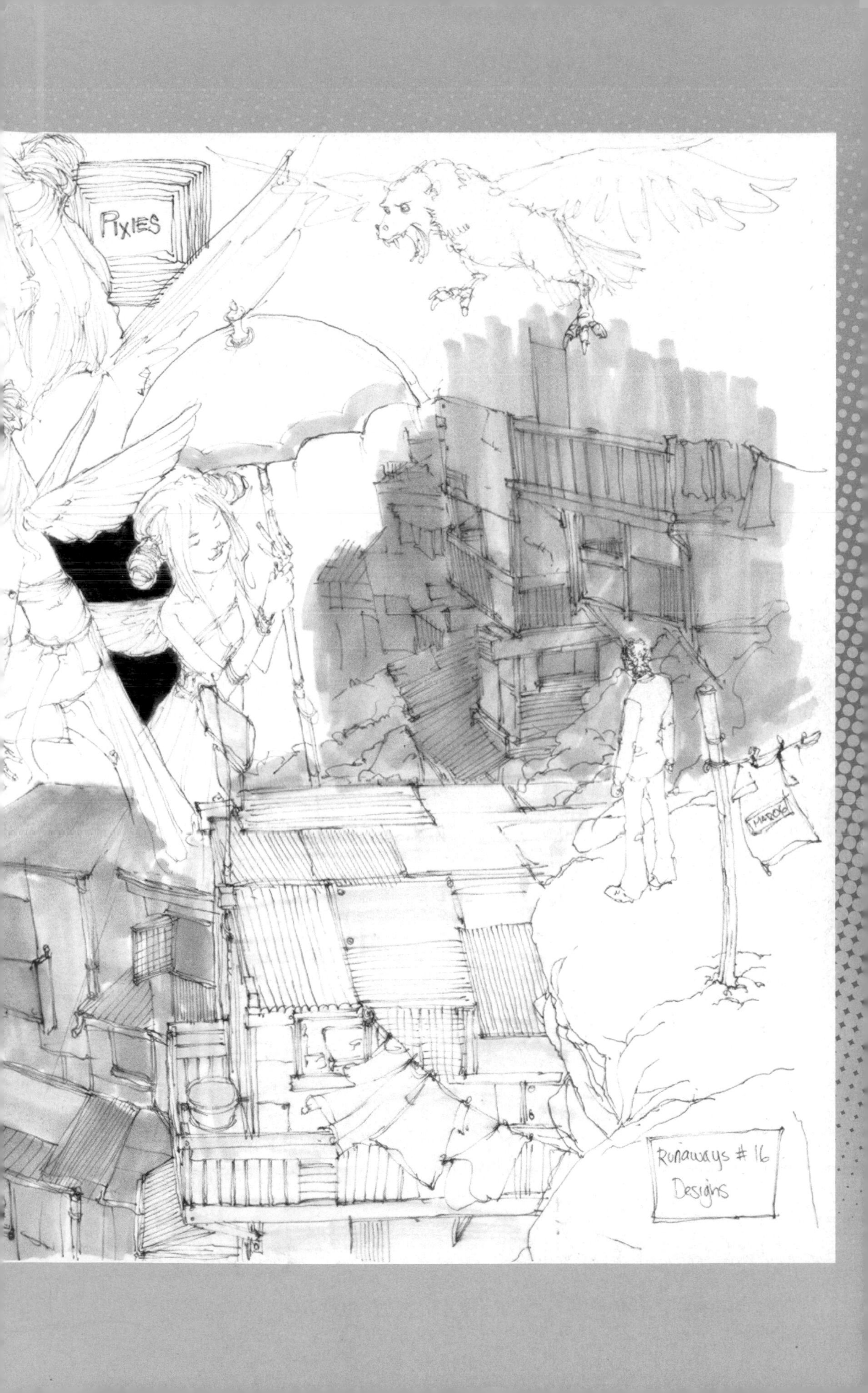
PIXIES
Runaways # 16
Designs

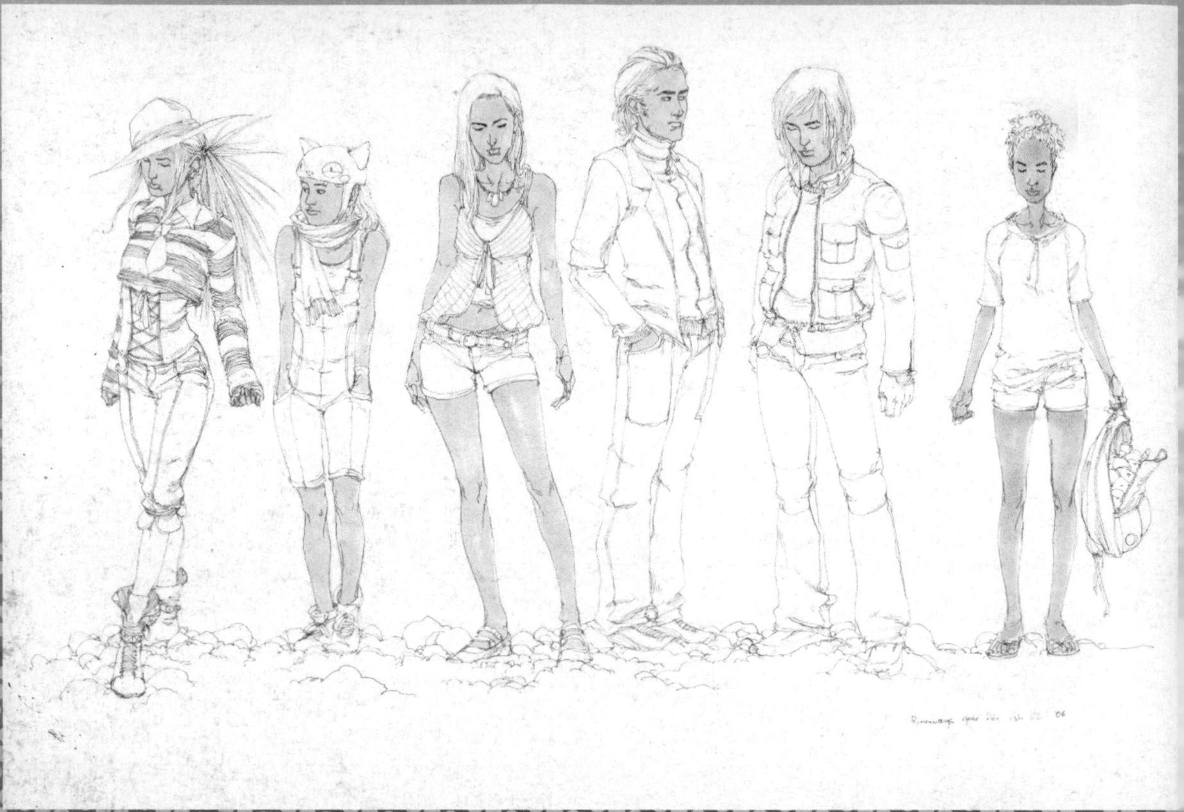
Runaways '06

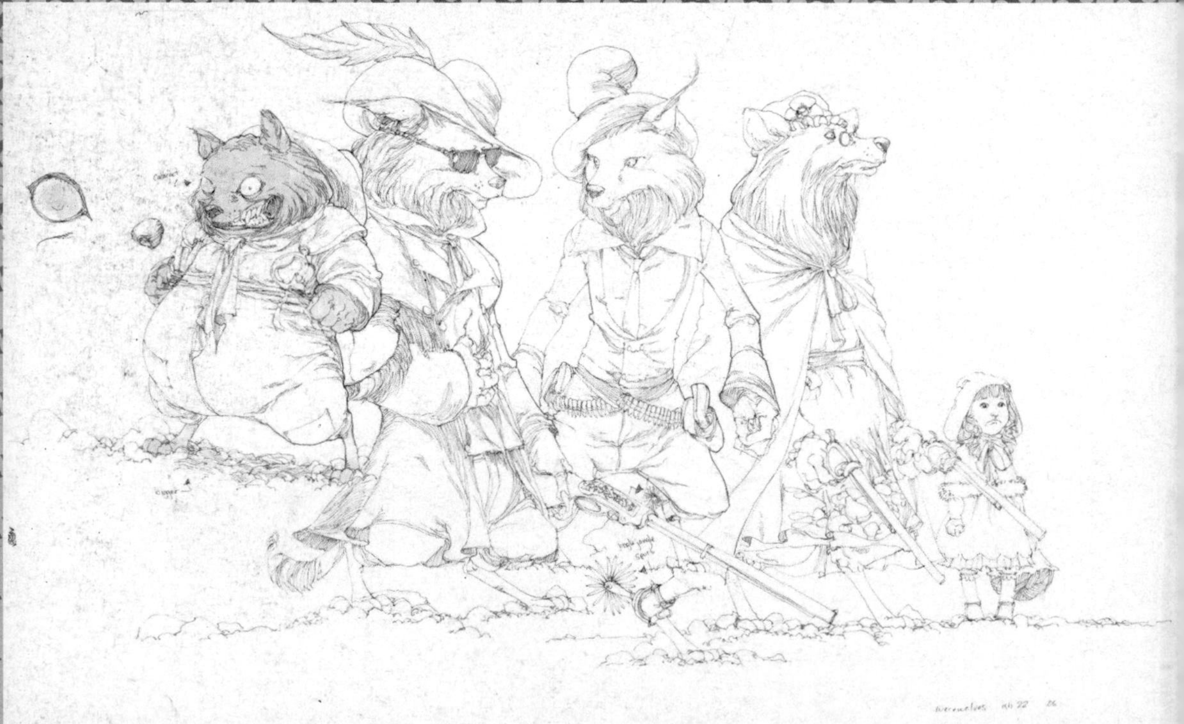
Werewolves 22 06